Who Are You?

The Encyclopedia of Personal Identification

By scott french

Published by:
Intelligence Here Inc.
Mt. Shasta, CA 96067

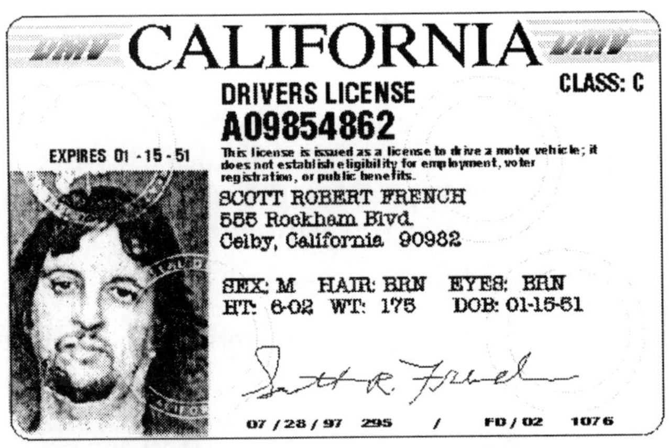
DMV
CALIFORNIA
DMV
DRIVERS LICENSE
CLASS: C
A09854862
EXPIRES 01-15-51
This license is issued as a license to drive a motor vehicle; it does not establish eligibility for employment, voter registration, or public benefits.
SCOTT ROBERT FRENCH
555 Rockham Blvd.
Celby, California 90982
SEX: M HAIR: BRN EYES: BRN
HT: 6-02 WT: 175 DOB: 01-15-51
07/28/97 295 / FD/02 1076

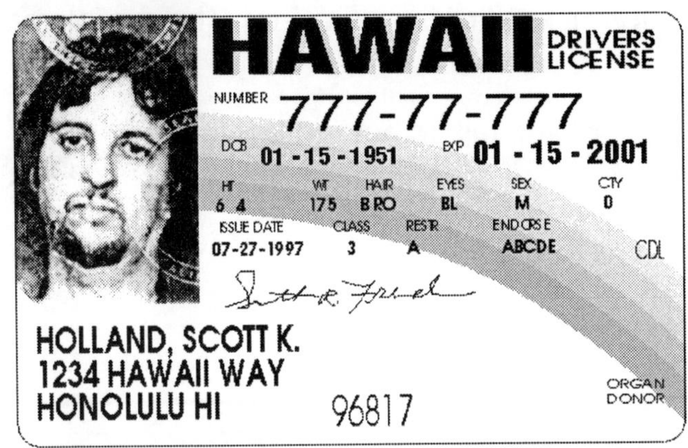
HAWAII
DRIVERS LICENSE
NUMBER 777-77-777
DOB 01-15-1951
EXP 01-15-2001
HT 6 4
WT 175
HAIR BRO
EYES BL
SEX M
CTY 0
ISSUE DATE 07-27-1997
CLASS 3
RESTR A
ENDORSE ABCDE
CDL
HOLLAND, SCOTT K.
1234 HAWAII WAY
HONOLULU HI 96817
ORGAN DONOR

NEW GRANADA
NG-296427
SCOTT ENGLISH
21-07-1945
M
BLUE
1.83M
25-07-1996
24-07-2006
* * * * *
<<NG-427-ENGL>>
DRIVERS LICENSE

Disclaimer

Every effort has been made to ensure that this publication contains the most current information available. However, Intelligence Incorporated does not guarantee the accuracy of the information contained herein. Inclusion in **Who Are You** does not imply an endorsement of any kind.

Some concepts and techniques covered in this book would be illegal if preformed.

Neither Intelligence Here nor Scott French accepts any responsibility or liability incurred from the use of materials in this book.

Laws change, please talk to a good lawyer.

Intelligence Here
404 N. Mt. Shasta Blvd # 134
Mt. Shasta, CA 96067-2232
www.intelligencehere.com

Special thanks to:

Maxie Harper Graphics
The FBI
Arthur of The ID Shop
Mike A
Chris Hibbert
Don Ray
Arnold Cornez, J.D.
Gail Cooper
J.Wolf
J.H-D
Steve Mc Grew: New Light Industries
AAMVA
The Treasury Department
Several criminals
And others who do not wish to see their name in print

Publisher's Cataloging in Publication

French, Scott
Who Are You/Scott French – Mt. Shasta, CA:
Intelligence Here, c2000

Includes bibliographical references and index.
ISBN 1-88-0231-18-2

1. Identification–United States–Drivers license, Social Security, IRS. 2. False Identification. 3. Identity theft. 4. Banking–Doucuments, laws, etc.

Intelligence Here publishes cutting edge books and video tapes on surveillance, investigations, security and generally interesting stuff.

Our materials are utilized by many government and law enforcement agencies, 10,000 private detectives, investigative reporters, researchers and other nosy people.

For the latest in surveillance and privacy oriented materials, please visit and bookmark our web site:

www.intelligencehere.com

CONTENTS

Introduction

This book is the culmination of several years of research on my part as well as input from many experts in the areas of identification, forgery, ID theft, state-of-the-art counterfeiting, security and ancillary fields.

I have tried to present an unbiased look at both sides of the ID/privacy dilemma; i.e., how the government tracks its citizens from birth to death, as well as how people manipulate government procedures, the internet and other sources in order to take advantage, or escape from these very same procedures.

I have not differentiated from showing how criminals, privacy seekers, and nefarious individuals steal ID's, counterfeit various forms of ID (as well as credit cards and checks) or how law enforcement and private citizens can prevent and/or prosecute these crimes.

I sincerely feel one should see all sides of the situation – I also sincerely suggest one does not commit any illegal act, with or without the use of the information presented herein unless one is willing to accept the possible consequences.

Don't do the crime unless you can do the time.

At any rate, **Who Are You?** is designed to be the most complete work on Identification, from government sponsored ID implants, to fake ID's, ever published.

While I have given individual credit for certain chapters, or parts thereof, I should point out that this work includes not only my efforts (along with my researchers) but a number of moderately famous (infamous?) criminals, the FBI, various other government agencies, top notch graphic artists, engineers, reporters and private agencies that specialize in privacy and violations thereof.

From the bottom of my heart I thank you all.

Remember this is just information – I'm not teaching how to bomb the World Trade Center, nor even suggesting one steals someone else's ID.

What I am attempting to accomplish is to present the most comprehensive look at the ID game ever published. Some readers will be appalled at various sections that detail exactly how to "borrow" personalities, make holograms, procure fake ID's – others will be equally as horrified realizing the government is selling your drivers license photos to private companies, keeping a database on virtually everything you do including your banking habits, travel arrangements, traffic violations and selling (or sharing) this information with people that, to my way of thinking, have no legal right of access.

I believe most people, even some in the investigative field, have no real concept of what is going on now, much less what is being proposed.

By the same token I believe most people have no concept of legal avenues that allow a second passport, offshore bank account (or ATM card), or other methods of protecting one's legal activities from GS-11 government bureaucrats that live only to over trample their job restrictions.

The government, your government, has been proposing such freedom preserving ideas as a national ID card (which was defeated by a few senate votes – or was it?. read on), finally has passed laws restricting the sale of drivers license information to most private parties, restrained a very obnoxious law or two, but is still on the relentless hunt to know where every citizen is, has been, and should be, at all times.

How bad is this situation? Well take the new currency, yes it is much harder to counterfeit, I guess it lasts longer, and the imbedded bar code could easily track each bill, and each transaction throughout the bills life.

They contain enough magnetic ink that if too many of the new bills are carried on one's person they will set off airport metal detectors. One senator has just suggested a program in which every bank transaction be recorded, a tax on the money if it has not been through a reader in a certain time period.

He also suggests that the bills "run out of value" after a certain date.

This book is designed to point out various options, most legal, some not that still exists for persons desiring a modicum of privacy.

Okay, not going to jump on the constitution train here, not going to run down the IRS (if you are affiliated with that particular agency please note I have finally gotten my tax info up to date, haven't claimed trips to the Bahamas as a write-off and have become a citizen – especially after our last little get-together).

But hey, that shouldn't concern my readers, right?

This information is real and as up to date as I can make it. Wherever possible I have included sites or sources one can access in order to stay informed on an up-to-the minute basis.

Please bookmark and check Intelligence Here's web site on a regular basis for more information.

www.intelligencehere.com

Thank you for your help in this matter.

sf

The Ultimate Tracking Device

Okay, the idea of a national ID card was bad, most of us agree, correct? Then came the legal squabbles about selling drivers license info (including photos), releasing Social Security numbers, etc.

Some of you, well, not my audience; of course, but some of you may know of the friend of a friend who has been electronically chained to a certain area via an ankle bracelet.

Lee Lapin covers (in B3 How To Get Anything On Anybody) GPS (satellite based tracking) in many of its manifestations including cell phones that can be silently called and will report the users exact location as well as allow the person monitoring the call to eavesdrop on all local audio.

Scary.

Well welcome to the future. The following is, as far as I can tell, a real project which dwarfs all other forms of people tracking.

A Palm Beach, Florida-based telecommunications company has developed a miniature digital monitoring device that can be implanted directly into a person's body.

Applied Digital Solutions recently announced it had acquired patent rights to develop a unique transceiver, which would be powered by muscle movements of implants and will be able to be tracked anywhere on earth via the GPS system.

The company plans to complete a device by the end of this year.

Once installed just under the subject's skin, the transceiver sends and receives data and can be continuously tracked by GPS technology.

As one might expect ADS stresses the ideas that such a unit will be used to help track medical patients, Alzheimer patients and other politically correct subjects. They do mention in passing that the unit could also be employed by law enforcement and for other "security" purposes.

They imply the unit is going to be tiny enough to be inserted “inconspicuously” – I would read this as maybe you shouldn’t let your dentist use nitrous oxide, never let a doctor knock you out, don’t take any suspicious pills, etc.

ADS also suggests the unit could track “abducted children and military, diplomatic and other essential government personnel."

I would bet it could track democrats, socialists, political undesirables and lawyers just as easily.

Actually the last application might not be so bad.

Think of all money Germany could have saved on those little yellow Stars of David that Jews were required to wear.

"We believe its potential for improving individual and e-business security and enhancing the quality of life for millions of people is virtually limitless," said ADS Chairman and CEO Richard Sullivan in a recent statement.

Patent documents refer to the device as a "personal tracking and recovery system." But, ADS said the device, named the Digital Angel, could also have non-human applications. For example, it could be secretly hidden on or in valuable personal belongings and works of art.

Or illegal immigrants.

Or people who have visited the Bahamas recently.

Birth Certificate

This is one of the most important, if not the single most important chapter in this book, given that each U.S. citizen has up to four forms of ID verifying birth: the report of birth form and hospital birth certificate, both issued at the hospital of birth; a county birth certificate; and information held at the state vital statistics bureau.

REPORT OF BIRTH FORM AT A GLANCE	
Type	▪ Not a form of ID in and of itself
Method of Issuance	▪ Issued by hospital of birth at the time of birth
Information Contained	▪ Child's name ▪ Mother's maiden name ▪ Father's name ▪ Sex of child ▪ Race of child ▪ Age of mother ▪ Race of mother ▪ Age of father ▪ Race of father ▪ Mother's Social Security Number ▪ Father's Social Security Number ▪ Date of birth ▪ Time of birth ▪ Place of birth ▪ Medical information
Use	▪ Used to create hospital birth certificate ▪ Submitted to city or county recorder or registrar for creation of county birth certificate ▪ No other use in creating ID documents
Security Issues +/-	▪ +: Fraudulent form has very little value

HOSPITAL BIRTH CERTIFICATE AT A GLANCE	
Type	▪ Not a form of ID in and of itself
Method of Issuance	▪ Issued upon birth by hospital of birth
Information Contained	▪ Child's name ▪ Mother's maiden name ▪ Father's name ▪ Name and signature of attending physician ▪ Date of birth ▪ Time of birth ▪ Seal of hospital ▪ Stamp of hospital, including name and address
Use	▪ Serves as legal proof of birth of the child until county birth certificate is issued ▪ Valid as a legal birth document even after county birth certificate has been issued ▪ Proof of U.S. citizenship ▪ Limited acceptance as a means to obtaining other primary ID's ▪ Limited acceptance for school enrollment
Method of Fraud	▪ Generic hospital birth certificate forms available from false document wholesalers
Security Issues +/-	▪ +: Generally issued only once by hospital; later copies are rarely given out ▪ +: Hospital birth certificate of an adult should look appropriately aged; new-looking documents for adults are a sign of fraud ▪ +: Must contain all of the info listed in "Information Contained" to be valid, including name and address of hospital facility, hospital seal, and signature of physician; should be printed on customized hospital form ▪ -: Difficult to verify authenticity of hospital birth certificate ▪ -: Hospital birth certificates come in many different styles

Type

These two "sister documents" are where the journey of creating an identity begins – whether for legitimate or fraudulent purposes. Although neither has any value as an ID in and of itself, together they provide that key that opens the door to every type of ID that is available to a U.S. citizen. See *Use,* below.

Method of Issuance

The report of birth form comes first. This form, containing the information listed in the above table, is issued immediately upon the birth of a child by the hospital where the birth happens. In those rare cases where a baby is not born in a hospital, the physician who is attending to the mother at home fills out a similar form. (In some *exceedingly* rare cases, no physician is present at all, and no report of birth form is created. See "Baptismal Certificates.)

The hospital birth certificate is completed soon after. This form is necessary because of the gap of time between a child's birth and when the county actually issues and mails its "official" birth certificate. As its name implies, this certificate is issued by the hospital of birth at the time of birth.

Use

The report of birth form serves two purposes exactly: the information it contains will create the hospital birth certificate, and it is sent to the applicable county official for creation of the official county birth certificate. The report of birth form has no value in and of itself, and is not considered valid proof of birth.

The hospital birth certificate, on the other hand, *does* in this country serve as legal proof of birth. Until the county birth certificate is issued, the hospital birth certificate is the *only* document that serves as valid proof of the child's birth.

However, the hospital birth certificate does not lose its validity once the county has issued its certificate, as might seem to be the case. Because the U.S. has never developed a standardized system for registering or recording births, the different documents that are issued over time have had to serve these purposes. For example, in many rural areas, common practice has been that a person's hospital birth certificate was the only birth document they obtained; unless an individual needed a county birth certificate for a particular reason, one was simply never created.

Because of irregularities such as these in the birth registry system, the hospital birth certificate continues to serve as a valid proof of birth.

Therefore, the hospital birth certificate, whether legitimate or forged, has great value in two areas. First, as proof of U.S. birth, the hospital birth certificate provides proof of U.S. citizenship – since, currently, all persons born on U.S. soil are automatically granted U.S. citizenship. This leads to two forms of fraud: on the one hand, adults from other countries will often obtain or manufacture fraudulent hospital birth certificates to gain the privileges of U.S. citizenship; on the other, pregnant women from other countries will often attempt to give birth in the United States, thus, guaranteeing citizenship for their child.

The second area of value of a hospital birth certificate is its use to obtain other forms of primary and secondary ID. As mentioned, the birth certificate provides the gateway to obtaining the full array of ID's available to the U.S. citizen. Compared to county and state documents, the hospital birth certificate has limited value in this area; many agencies – including the U.S. State Department, which issues passports, and most state departments of motor vehicles (DMV's) – will not accept these documents as proof of birth for creating an ID. However, the list of IDs that one might indeed obtain with a hospital birth certificate includes Social Security cards, voter registration cards, and, in a few states, driver's licenses and state identity cards. These certificates are also accepted in some states for parents to enroll their children in school.

Method of Fraud

The report of birth form is rarely counterfeited or obtained falsely. Given its extremely limited purpose and its one-time use, it is of little value to counterfeiters.

Hospital birth certificates, however, are valid for a much wider variety of uses, and thus have a greater value for fraud. The most common method of creating a fraudulent hospital birth certificate is to obtain a generic hospital birth certificate form, available from false document wholesalers. If the forger is being extremely careful, he or she will then age the certificate by either leaving it in bright sun or washing in a solution of tea. The aging process is covered in more detail in the following discussion of county and state birth certificates.

Security Issues

Again, since it has such limited value, the report of birth form has little to offer as a fraudulent document, and security concerns are negligible.

The primary security issue regarding the hospital birth certificate is that, given its non-standardized nature, a wide variety of forms and styles are existing, which makes them very attractive to counterfeiters. Adding to this is the fact that hospital birth certificates are difficult to verify: if a certificate is presented and the holder claims that the hospital in question has been shut down for many years, there is little one can do to substantiate or disprove that claim – especially if said hospital was supposedly located in another state.

On the other hand, some factors do exist to help safeguard against fraudulent hospital birth certificates. The key is to examine carefully the document itself. Hospital birth certificates are issued only once, upon birth; if a person needs a later copy, they will be directed to go to the applicable county office. As a result, a hospital birth certificate for an adult should be appropriately aged and worn – a step that many would-be forgers never consider. Also, an authentic hospital birth certificate should contain all the information listed in "Information Contained" in the table above, especially the name, address, and seal of the hospital and the attending doctor's signature. Also, authentic hospital birth certificates are almost always printed on forms customized for the hospital in question, not on generic blank forms.

COUNTY BIRTH CERTIFICATE AT A GLANCE	
Type	• Not a form of ID in and of itself
Method of Issuance	▪ Issued by county registrar ▪ Information from hospital report of birth is entered onto county birth rolls for that year and month, from which certified copies of birth certificate are made ▪ In some cases, information is now entered on computer as well, which is used to generate certificate ▪ Generally issued on a state-prescribed form; in the absence of such a form, safety paper, parchment, or even regular paper may be used
Information Contained	▪ Varies; contains some, but generally not all , of the information contained on the report of birth form: ▪ Child's name ▪ Mother's maiden name ▪ Father's name ▪ Sex of child ▪ Race of child ▪ Age of mother ▪ Race of mother ▪ Age of father ▪ Race of father ▪ Mother's Social Security Number ▪ Father's Social Security Number ▪ Date of birth ▪ Time of birth ▪ Place of birth ▪ Signature of county registrar, recorder, or clerk ▪ Date issued ▪ Medical information
Use	▪ "Key" document used for obtaining all other forms of ID ▪ Proof of U.S. citizenship ▪ Supporting document to show

	eligibility for employment in U.S. ▪ Used by those in need to obtain government assistance
Method of Fraud	▪ The "infant death" method (described in detail below) ▪ Obtaining birth certificate via birth notices ▪ Creation of authentic-looking certificate (described below)
Security Issues +/-	▪ +: Certificate must contain appropriate identifying features for authenticity (described in detail below) ▪ +: Difficulty in obtaining mother's maiden name ▪ +: Many agencies accept only certified copies of birth certificate as proof of birth ▪ +: Cross referencing (described in detail below) ▪ -: As with hospital BC's, wide variety of designs and styles exists ▪ -: Notarized—as opposed to certified copies of birth certificate accepted by many state and local agencies, including motor vehicle departments and voter registration offices

STATE BIRTH CERTIFICATE AT A GLANCE	
Type	▪ Not a form of ID in and of itself
Method of Issuance	▪ Issued by state bureau of vital statistics ▪ Information either the county birth record or an abstract forwarded by county registrar's offices ▪ Always issued on an official state form, carrying state seal and special numbering
Information Contained	▪ Similar to the county birth certificate, contains some but generally not all of the following: ▪ Child's name ▪ Mother's maiden name ▪ Father's name ▪ Sex of child ▪ Race of child ▪ Age of mother ▪ Race of mother ▪ Age of father ▪ Race of father ▪ Mother's Social Security Number ▪ Father's Social Security Number ▪ Date of birth ▪ Time of birth ▪ Place of birth ▪ Medical information ▪ Signature of state registrar ▪ Date issued ▪ Date filed ▪ State birth number (described below)
Use	▪ "Key" document used for obtaining all other forms of ID ▪ Proof of U.S. citizenship ▪ Supporting document to show eligibility for employment in U.S. ▪ Used by those in need to obtain government assistance
Method of Fraud	▪ The "infant death" method (described in detail below) ▪ Obtaining birth certificate via birth notices ▪ Creation of authentic-looking certificate (described below)
Security Issues +/-	▪ +: Certificate must contain appropriate

	identifying features for authenticity (described in detail below) ▪ +: Difficulty in obtaining mother's maiden name ▪ +: Many agencies accept only certified copies of birth certificate as proof of birth ▪ +: Cross referencing (described in detail below) ▪ -: Standard form makes it easier to create official-looking documents ▪ -: Notarized – as opposed to certified copies of birth certificate accepted by many state and local agencies, including motor vehicle departments and voter registration offices

County Birth Certificate At A Glance

Type

As with hospital birth certificates, neither county nor state birth certificates are themselves accepted as forms of ID.

Method of Issuance

The biggest difference between these two documents is the place and method of issue. As its name suggests, the county birth certificate is issued by the county recorder, registrar, or clerk's office (we will use these three terms interchangeably for the rest of this book). Note that some very large cities, for example, New York City, have their own city registry that issues city birth certificates. These are identical in stature to county birth certificates, and the discussion to follow applies equally to them.

The county birth certificate is created directly from information sent by the hospital on its report of birth form, which it forwards to the applicable county office at regular intervals. The county registrar or clerk enters the hospital report information onto the county birth rolls; in some cases today, this information is also entered onto computer.

The issuance of the county birth certificate depends upon the method by which the information was entered. In those counties using computers, the computer simply generates a birth certificate when requested. In the former, pre-computer case, the information on the birth roll is imprinted onto a larger sheet of paper, which is then certified and becomes an official copy of the birth certificate.

In either case, the county birth certificate is generally issued on a state-prescribed form, which in turn is modeled after a standard national form whose use if being promoted by the federal government. However, many counties do not make use of any such standard; in its absence, the county birth certificate may be issued on safety paper, parchment, or even standard bond paper.

It is generally standard procedure for the county office to send a certified copy of the birth certificate to the parents of the issue a few weeks after birth.

At regular intervals throughout the year, the county registrar's office sends the information on its birth rolls – as a birth report or abstract – to the State Bureau of Vital Statistics. The bureau creates a file from all records received for the year in question, creating a state birth certificate for each person born in that state in that year.

State birth certificates are visually quite distinct from their county or hospital counterparts. Whereas the former two types allow a range of styles and designs, state certificates are almost always issued on an official state form, modeled after the U.S. standard form. They always carry the state seal, and, most important, they are distinguished by special numbering.

Information Contained

The county and state birth certificates vary from place to place in terms of the information they contain. It is standard for both to contain the name of the child, its sex, and the date and place of birth. Beyond that, different certificates may contain any of the other items listed on the hospital report of birth form. The county birth certificate also contains the signature of the county registrar, recorder, or clerk, as well as the date of issue; the state certificate has the signature of the state registrar, the date issued, and the date filed.

The state birth certificate contains one additional piece of information that makes it unique among these forms: the state birth number. This is a unique number assigned to each statistic bureau file that allows the state to catalog and count all births, deaths, and marriages that take place during a given year. Currently, all state birth numbers take the form:

123-45-67890X

Where "1" is always the actual number "1," signifying that the birth took place in the United States. "23" is a two-digit number that shows the state in which the birth happened; determined alphabetically for the 48 contiguous states and the District of Columbia, this number ranges from "01" for Alabama to "49" for Wyoming, with Alaska and Hawaii receiving the designations "50" and "51," respectively. A listing of all birth certificate numbers follows later in this chapter.

Use

The value of these two documents cannot be underestimated. Unlike hospital birth certificates, which have only limited acceptance, county and state birth certificates have virtually universal acceptance as the "keys" to obtaining all other forms of ID in the U.S. A county or state birth certificate can be presented to obtain a driver's license, social security card, voter registration card, passport, library card, and so on.

In addition, as legal proof of U.S. birth, these documents serve as proof of U.S. citizenship, entitling the bearer to all the rights and privileges such citizenship provides. As described above, pregnant women from other countries will often enter the U.S. to deliver their babies here, in order to obtain a valid U.S. birth certificate and it's inherent right for their children. County and state birth certificates are also used by those in need to obtain government assistance, and, since the passage of the Immigration Reform and Control Act of 1986, they have been required by potential employers as supporting documents to prove the applicant's right to work in the United States.

Given all of this, the value of fraudulent county or state birth certificates is clearly *extremely high.*

Method of Fraud

There are two key methods for obtaining a fraudulent county or state birth certificate. The first involves gaining possession of an actual birth certificate, then doctoring it with new information. (Note that although both are discussed here, county certificates are generally preferred by counterfeiters, since they are easier and faster to obtain than state certificates). The first step in this process is to find the birth certificate of some one of the same race, sex, and approximate age. This can be done directly by visiting the county registrar's office (for county certificates) or state bureau of vital statistics (for state certificates) and checking the certificates in and around the year of the forger's birth to find an appropriate match.

If this is not feasible, old newspapers, available on microfiche or microfilm at most libraries, can be consulted. The counterfeiter checks the "birth notices" section of the local paper for the time period around his or her desired birth date. Though these notices do not contain the race or sex of the child, they do contain the child's name as well as both father's and mother's name, which should provide enough information.

Once an appropriate person has been selected, the next step is to obtain a copy of that person's birth certificate. Depending on the age of the person named on the certificate in question, the counterfeiter can either pose as the person's parent or as the person him or herself.

The second method is commonly known as the "infant death" method. This is similar to the above, except, instead of applying for the birth certificate of a living person and doctoring it once obtained; the person seeking a fraudulent identity obtains the birth certificate of someone who has *died.* Again, the key here is to find some one of the same race whose birth date was within a few-year range of the person seeking the certificate. Places to find potential candidates include the obituary section of the newspaper or the local cemetery.

Because requesting the birth certificate of someone who is known to be dead would obviously raise questions, there are two things to keep in mind when pursuing this method. One, it is best to avoid persons who died in high-profile ways, such as airplane accidents or natural disasters. The names of these people are often publicized, making it easier for a county or state official to recognize that one is requesting the birth certificate of a dead individual. Also, these names are easy targets for would-be counterfeiters, so that it is very possible that more than one person would be applying for the same individual's birth certificate – a situation that is sure to raise questions among the county or state official handling the request.

The best-case scenario is to find someone who was born in one state and died in another. The closer a target has died to his county of birth, the more likely that the county or state registrar's office will have word of this death and will have stamped "deceased" on the birth certificate. Obviously, claiming to be the person named on such a certificate would raise a few questions of its own. These odds are decreased greatly when one poses as an individual born in say, Arkansas, when that individual has died on a ranch in Montana. This is not a foolproof system, however, as we shall soon see.

Once the certificate has been obtained, the doctoring process begins. To create an authentic-looking certificate, be sure to follow ALL of these steps:

- Copy the certificate. Care should be taken here to produce a duplicate of high quality, since it will need to be copied one more time

- Using this copy, delete all the information contained on the certificate with correction fluid. Be careful to use the fluid sparingly, as using too much will create a sloppy original and will be a dead giveaway that the certificate is a fake. The only information to leave on the form is the attending physician's signature, and, if it is a state certificate, the first three numbers of the preprinted birth number

- If you have access to computer scanning equipment, this step can be changed. Scan the certificate onto a computer, then clean it up onscreen. Print out the cleaned-up certificate, then continue as follows

- Copy the clean copy onto a heavy-grade paper, such as parchment or card stock. You are now ready to work to create a false document

- You will now need to obtain an embossing tool that can be used to create an official-looking seal. Again, it is easier to do this on a county certificate, because the odds are anyone viewing the certificate will not know exactly what that county's official seal looks like; on a state certificate, which is stamped with the state seal, counterfeiting is somewhat more difficult

  These tools are available from most shops selling office or legal supplies. They are fairly inexpensive – around $40. One way to obtain such a tool with the right marking is to claim it is being used as a prop in a production. The seal should have the words "(pick a name) County Health Department" or "(pick a name) County Registrar's Office" printed around its border; be sure to use the name of a county that actually exists! Use the tool to stamp your blank certificate, and you're ready to get to work.

- Complete the form with the new information desired. Be sure to take into account the age of the person named on the certificate, so that the certificate will reflect the time period in which it was supposed to have been created accurately. Particularly, watch out for the following:

1. Older birth certificates were created using electric, or manual typewriters – or even, in the case of some county certificates, were hand written – not today's word processors. If you don't have access to an older typewriter, rent one.

2. Terminology has changed. Where today's forms simply use "Black" and "White" as racial designations, in times past these were usually "Negro" and "Caucasian."

3. Zip codes were rarely used with addresses until the mid-1970's.

It does no good to have a certificate that is "culturally accurate" if the paper itself looks crisp and new. If you are creating a certificate for an adult, be sure to follow one of these two methods:

1. Place the document in direct sunlight for two or three days.

2. Bring water to a boil, and add tea. Continue boiling for a few minutes, then add the document. (Weight the document to keep it fully submerged if necessary.) Turn off the heat, allow the certificate to sit in the solution for a few hours. Dry the certificate using either a heater or an air conditioner until fully dry.

Whichever method you use, two steps in the aging process remain:

- First, fold and re-fold the certificate to give it an appropriately worn look
- Then, place it underneath a heavy, flat object such as a large book for up to twelve hours

Security Issues

As the above discussion makes clear, obtaining and creating a valid-looking birth certificate is a time-consuming and detailed process. Certain safety issues are in effect that makes the successful use of a forged certificate even more difficult. Among these is the amount of detailed information that each county and state birth certificate contains; a successful fake must contain each and every element. For example, the use of the U.S. standard certificate body has become increasingly common in recent years. As more state and counties adopt this standard – which is updated every ten years – as their model, the ability for counterfeiters to produce official-looking fakes with standard blank documents decreases.

Other features used to detect fraud for county birth certificates include:

- The document's heading, at the top of the document, which should clearly state the name of the county, words such as "Issued by" with the name of the county health department or court clerk, and the corresponding address of the health department or court
- The city of birth, which should, obviously, be located in the above-named county
- The registrar's file number, which is the certificate's reference number for locating it in the county birth rolls
- The filing date, which, as the date that the birth was entered onto the county's birth roll, should (again obviously) be *after* the birth date
- The certificate issue date, which, being the date that this date that this copy of the certificate was issued, should be consistent with the appearance of the document (a more recent issue date should equal a newer-looking document, and vice versa)
- The seal of the registrar or health department, which will be found on each and every county document

Other important features include:

- The signatures of the physician and informant. These theoretically were placed on the certificate at the time of birth, and they should be age-suitable to the age of the holder, regardless of when this copy of the certificate was issued
- The signature of the county official. This, by contrast, should be consistent with the issue date of the certificate itself
- Whether the certificate is handwritten, typewritten, or word processed
- The use of racial designations
- The form of the addresses; these last three items should reflect the time period in which the certificate was created, as described in "Method of Fraud," above

For State Certificates, Four Features Stand Out As Safeguards Against Fraud

- The certificate will almost always be printed on a standardized form

- The name of the issuing body – the State Bureau of Vital Statistics, or the State Health Department – will appear on the header of the certificate

- The certificate will ALWAYS contain a state birth number, formatted according to the description in "Information Contained," above. It will, in addition, almost always contain a registrar's file number

- The certificate will be embossed with the seal of the state bureau of vital statistics, and will be signed by the state registrar

Other security features exist to protect against the creation of fraudulent birth certificates, whether state or county. For one, most counties now ask for the mother's maiden name of the issuee when one is requesting a birth certificate.

The maiden name of an individual's mother (see that section) is the most powerful security tool currently in use in the U.S., without it, obtaining a birth certificate of a person either still living or deceased becomes highly problematic.

Also, in a case that applies specifically to those attempting the "infant death" method, most counties and now some states make use of a system known as "cross-referencing."

Cross referencing is matching the death certificate of a person with his or her birth certificate. This is easily accomplished when one is born and dies in the same county: a person dies, and the attending physician fills out a report of death form, similar to the hospital report of birth form in the information it contains. This form is forwarded to the county registrar, who creates a death certificate. The official then pulls the birth certificate of the individual from the birth rolls, marks it "deceased," and sends the information on to the State Bureau of Vital Statistics.

Some states now attempt to use this information to perform a cross reference check similar to that which happens on the county level; that is, to take all the individuals who have died in that state, determine which ones were born in that state, and mark the applicable birth certificates "deceased." There is even talk of creating a national cross-referencing system, so that all deceased U.S. citizens will appropriately have their birth certificates marked.

However, the problems with attempting both state and national cross-referencing systems are many. They include the following:

- Many people die in such a condition that it is difficult if not impossible to determine their place of birth. This includes anyone who dies alone without any surviving relatives, street people with no identification, and so on

- The only way to guarantee accurate cross-referencing would be to send the death notices of every individual in the country to the registrar's office of every county in the country – which, given that there are over 5,000 such offices in the U.S., is clearly prohibitive in terms of time and expense

- With larger populations to deal with, both state and national cross-referencing registries would be in danger of "killing off" living persons; that is, anyone whose name and birth information were close enough to the deceased person could find that their birth certificate has been erroneously marked as "deceased"

- In states that have attempted cross-referencing, a cutoff date – generally around 1960 – has been used. Anyone born before this cutoff date has a fair chance of finding a clear birth certificate for some one of approximately his or her age

- Because birth records exist at so many levels – hospital, county, state – even cross-referencing that led to the correct marking of one set of birth and death certificates would not necessarily filter up or down to the others. The possibility of finding a clean birth certificate always exists

Other security issues unrelated to the question of cross-referencing exist with relation to fraudulent birth certificates. For example, though the U.S. standard certificate is coming into more widespread use, on the county level in particular a wide variety of designs and styles are still prevalent in the creation of birth certificates. This makes it easier to create authentic-looking forgeries with the proper tools. On the other hand, the fact that most states now use a single standardized form means that, if a counterfeiter can obtain this form or a reasonable copy, he or she has a potent weapon with which to create any number of official-looking forms.

A separate issue concerns the question of certification versus notarization. Most agencies, especially at the federal level, will only accept a certified copy of a birth certificate as proof of birth and/or citizenship. The certified copy must be signed by the person who is responsible for the certificate; their signature attests not only that the certificate in question is a true copy of the original, but also that the information contained on this copy is correct. For birth certificates, the "caretaker" is considered to be *only* the county registrar, recorder, or clerk for the county in which the birth happened. Certification provides some measure of security against fraud, since the signature of the "caretaker" in question can be easily verified.

On the other hand, many state and local agencies such as motor vehicle departments and voter registration offices will accept certificates that have been notarized instead of certified. A notarized document that is, one that has been reviewed, signed, and stamped with the seal of a notary public, verifies only that the certificate in question is a true copy of the original; the accuracy of the information contained within is not addressed.

Because many officials are unfamiliar with the difference between certification and notarization, it is possible to use the seal of a notary public as a way of "officializing" one's fraudulent birth certificate, and obtain valid forms of ID with it.

STATE BIRTH CERTIFICATE NUMBERS

Number	State	Number	State
01	Alabama	26	Nebraska
02	Arizona	27	Nevada
03	Arkansas	28	New Hampshire
04	California	29	New Jersey
05	Colorado	30	New Mexico
06	Connecticut	31	New York
07	Delaware	32	North Carolina
08	District of Columbia	33	North Dakota
09	Florida	34	Ohio
10	Georgia	35	Oklahoma
11	Idaho	36	Oregon
12	Illinois	37	Pennsylvania
13	Indiana	38	Rhode Island
14	Iowa	39	South Carolina
15	Kansas	40	South Dakota
16	Kentucky	41	Tennessee
17	Louisiana	42	Texas
18	Maine	43	Utah
19	Maryland	44	Vermont
20	Massachusetts	45	Virginia
21	Michigan	46	Washington
22	Minnesota	47	West Virginia
23	Mississippi	48	Wisconsin
24	Missouri	49	Wyoming
25	Montana	50	Alaska
		51	Hawaii

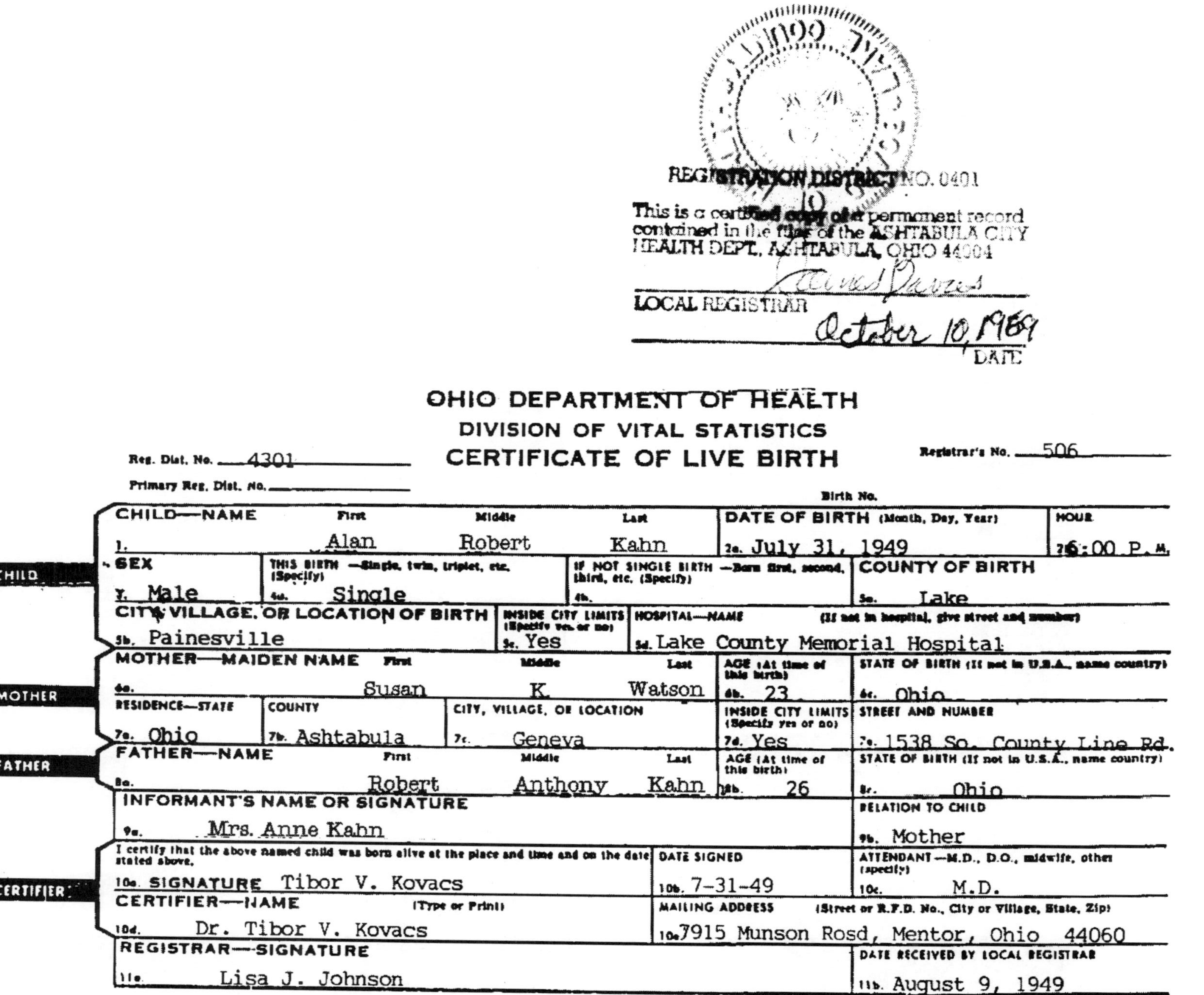

REGISTRATION DISTRICT NO. 0401
This is a certified copy of a permanent record contained in the files of the ASHTABULA CITY HEALTH DEPT, ASHTABULA, OHIO 44004

LOCAL REGISTRAR

October 10, 1989
DATE

OHIO DEPARTMENT OF HEALTH
DIVISION OF VITAL STATISTICS
CERTIFICATE OF LIVE BIRTH

Reg. Dist. No. 4301
Primary Reg. Dist. No.
Registrar's No. 506
Birth No.

CHILD	CHILD—NAME First Middle Last: 1. Alan Robert Kahn	DATE OF BIRTH (Month, Day, Year) 2a. July 31, 1949	HOUR 2b. 6:00 P.M.
	SEX 3. Male	THIS BIRTH—Single, twin, triplet, etc. (Specify) 4a. Single; IF NOT SINGLE BIRTH—Born first, second, third, etc. (Specify) 4b.	COUNTY OF BIRTH 5a. Lake
	CITY, VILLAGE, OR LOCATION OF BIRTH 5b. Painesville	INSIDE CITY LIMITS (Specify yes or no) 5c. Yes	HOSPITAL—NAME (If not in hospital, give street and number) 5d. Lake County Memorial Hospital
MOTHER	MOTHER—MAIDEN NAME First Middle Last: 6a. Susan K. Watson	AGE (At time of this birth) 6b. 23	STATE OF BIRTH (If not in U.S.A., name country) 6c. Ohio
	RESIDENCE—STATE 7a. Ohio; COUNTY 7b. Ashtabula	CITY, VILLAGE, OR LOCATION 7c. Geneva; INSIDE CITY LIMITS (Specify yes or no) 7d. Yes	STREET AND NUMBER 7e. 1538 So. County Line Rd.
FATHER	FATHER—NAME First Middle Last: 8a. Robert Anthony Kahn	AGE (At time of this birth) 8b. 26	STATE OF BIRTH (If not in U.S.A., name country) 8c. Ohio
	INFORMANT'S NAME OR SIGNATURE 9a. Mrs. Anne Kahn		RELATION TO CHILD 9b. Mother
CERTIFIER	I certify that the above named child was born alive at the place and time and on the date stated above. 10a. SIGNATURE Tibor V. Kovacs	DATE SIGNED 10b. 7-31-49	ATTENDANT—M.D., D.O., midwife, other (specify) 10c. M.D.
	CERTIFIER—NAME (Type or Print) 10d. Dr. Tibor V. Kovacs	MAILING ADDRESS (Street or R.F.D. No., City or Village, State, Zip) 10e. 7915 Munson Rosd, Mentor, Ohio 44060	
	REGISTRAR—SIGNATURE 11a. Lisa J. Johnson		DATE RECEIVED BY LOCAL REGISTRAR 11b. August 9, 1949

OR PRINT IN PERMANENT INK

CERTIFIED COPY OF A BIRTH RECORD

FILL IN THIS FORM WITH TYPEWRITER OR LEGIBLE PRINT IN PERMANENT BLACK INK

STATE OF ______
Department of Health Services
VITAL STATISTICS

BIRTH NO. ______

REGISTRAR'S NO.

CHILD

CHILD - NAME First Middle Last	DATE OF BIRTH (Month, Day, Year)	HOUR
1.	2a.	2b.

SEX	THIS BIRTH -- Single, Twin, Triple, etc.	IF NOT SINGLE BIRTH -- Born First, Second, Third, etc. (Specify)	COUNTY OF BIRTH
3.	4a.	4b.	

CITY, TOWN, OR LOCATION OF BIRTH	INSIDE CITY LIMITS	HOSPITAL --- NAME (Specify Yes or No) (If not in hospital, give street and number)
5b.	5c.	5a.

MOTHER

MOTHER -- MAIDEN NAME First Middle Last	AGE (at time of this birth)	STATE OF BIRTH (if not in U.S.A., name country)
6a.	6b.	6c.

RESIDENCE - STATE	COUNTY	City, TOWN, OR LOCATION	ZIP CODE	INSIDE CITY LIMITS (Specify Yes or No)	STREET AND NUMBER
7a.	7b.	7c.	7d.	7e.	7f.

FATHER

FATHER -- NAME First Middle Last	AGE (at time of this birth)	STATE OF BIRTH (if not in U.S.A., name country)
	8b.	8c.

INFORMANT	RELATION TO CHILD
9a.	9b.

CERTIFIED

I certify that the above named child was born alive at the place time and on the date stated above.	DATE SIGNED (month, day, year)	ATTENDANT -- M.D., D.O., Midwife, Other (Specify)
10a.	10b.	10c.

CERTIFIER - NAME (Type or Print)	MAILING ADDRESS (Street, or R.F.D. No., City or Town, State, Zip)
10d.	10e.

DEATH UNDER ONE YEAR OF AGE

REGISTRAR - SIGNATURE	DATE RECEIVED BY LOCAL REGISTRAR Month Day Year
11a.	11b.

I do hereby certify that the above is a true copy of the essential facts recorded on the birth record on file at this office for the individual named hereon.

Witness my hand and offical seal this the ____ By ______________________
Register of Deeds

day of __________ 19 ____

© GOES 346

How to Get a Real Fake Birth Certificate

There are a few reputable suppliers that will supply authentic birth certificates and other "real" paperwork already filled out and stamped with the applicable documentation. The following is a letter from a Canadian firm – a sample of one of their BC's follows.

Inside Address
123 Happy Go Lucky Lane
Ilove, HI 12345

Dear Mr. French:

In order for us to complete your birth certificate, please answer the following questions with the information you would like put into your certificate. We do not give you just some useless information about how to go about getting a real birth certificate, we create 2 for you. For an additional charge, we can send you a camouflage passport, identification card, and drivers license from a nonexistent country. The birth certificates will be from a State of our choice with the **authentic seal** and **rubber stamp** to make it appear genuine.

We have heard that some people are using the birth certificates to obtain driver's licenses and social security cards. We do not support or sanction this act and will not be held liable for any misuse of our products. The first birth certificate will allow you to appear to be a minor. It is great for women who want to be younger than they are in real life.

The second birth certificate will be closer to your real age. Again, we have heard some people use the first birth certificate to apply for a Social Security card, as they appear to be minors just getting a card for the first time. This allows them to avoid the interrogation process, at the bureaucratic Social Security Administration office. Being a minor allows you to mail in your information. Once you have the birth certificate and SSN everything else is easily acquired through the regular channels. After all, the government issued you the SSN themselves.

A new birth certificate is a good start, but without supporting documents, it will not help you start you life over. That is why we can create other products for you as well. The best piece of support documentation you can get would be a high school diploma and a college degree. These two items will increase your earning power and give yourself more credibility as a new person. If you are interested in either of these items, the price is **$XX.xx** for either the diploma or college degree. You can **save 50%** and get both for **$XXX.xx!** We can do just about any school you would like.

If you have a special or specific layout in mind, send a copy of the diploma or degree you have and we can redo it with any name you like.

We also have **Certificates of Baptism** which can be useful for back up identification, and for getting a Social Security card, and Driver's License. These products are top quality as well and can be filled out with any Church name that you would like to have showing on it. The fee for this product is **$XXX.xx**
Many people inquire why we do not have brochures of our products. The reason is simple: Our products are so genuine looking that our competition would get ideas for free. In addition, the government and universities would probably harass us even more if they say our products for sale. Be advised, our products will get you the results that you want and need. We are more expensive that the nickel and dime carbon copy stuff you see in magazines and booklets, but the quality is far better.

When you return you cashier's check, money order, or cash in the amount of **$XXX.xx** U.S. funds with the requested information, we will prepare **2 genuine U.S. birth certificates** for you. You may also charge your order to your VISA or Master Card. Sorry, no COD's will be accepted. Personal checks will no be accepted. Allow 3 to 4 weeks for delivery.

Send to **Creative Solutions** RR1 Box 63-8114 Eldorado Ontario, Canada K0K1Y0.

Sincerely,

John W. Doe
Creative Solutions

Baptismal Certificate

BAPTISMAL CERTIFICATE AT A GLANCE	
Type	Not a form of ID in and of itself
Method of Issuance	▪ Issued by church that performs the baptism
Information Contained	▪ Child's name ▪ Mother's maiden name ▪ Father's name ▪ Date of birth ▪ Place of birth ▪ Date of baptism ▪ Place of baptism ▪ Signature of presiding minister ▪ Seal of presiding minister
Use	▪ Used in limited cases in lieu of a birth certificate to obtain various ID documents ▪ In some cases, used to obtain a birth certificate itself
Method of Fraud	▪ Varies; no standard for baptismal certificates exist, so generic counterfeit forms are available
Security Issues +/-	▪ +: Authentic certificate will contain specific features ▪ +: Possible to verify through church named on document ▪ -: Wide variety of styles and designs makes forgery difficult to detect

Type

As with birth certificates, a baptismal certificate is not accepted in this country as a form of ID in and of itself.

Method of Issuance

The baptismal certificate is simply filled out by the church of baptism at the time the baptism happens. No other records are necessary for the completion of the baptismal certificate.

Use

Other than for the obvious purposes of church records, the baptismal certificate has two important uses in the world of identification:

- Some government agencies accept baptismal certificates in lieu of birth certificates for obtaining select IDs. For example, the Social Security administration accepts baptismal certificates for issuing a social security card, as long as the certificate was created within five years of the holder's birth. In another example, many DMV's will accept baptismal certificates for issuing a driver's license to the holder – generally, they require that the certificate be created no more than two years after the holder's birth

- In rare cases, the baptismal certificate may actually be used to obtain a county birth certificate. This is most often the case when a child was born at home or otherwise outside a hospital. Without any hospital records to rely on, most country registrar's offices will accept a baptismal certificate as proof of birth for the issuing of an official county birth certificate

Method of Fraud

Because no standard form exists for the baptismal certificate, the issue of fraud becomes complex. Blank baptismal certificates are available through the mail from a great number of identification companies, and these, when properly aged are most commonly used when someone is attempting to create a fraudulent document.

Security Issues

As just stated, the lack of a uniform style in the baptismal document form makes detection of a forgery difficult. However, two tools are at one's disposal when attempting to determine a certificate's authenticity.

One is the feature of the certificate itself. Specifically, one should pay careful attention to the name and seal of the church, which should be *pre-printed* on the paper of the certificate. Most churches use customized forms; if the form shows a blank where the church name should go, or the church name is missing entirely; it is probably a fake. An authentic certificate will also contain the signature of the minister who performed the baptismal rite. Finally, a baptismal certificate issued when the holder was an infant should look appropriately worn.

The other tool comes via the church named on the certificate itself. One common error in fraudulent baptismal certificates is that the forger forgets that many churches do not practice a baptism on infants, waiting until childhood or even adulthood to perform the ritual. If the church named on the certificate follows this practice, but the birth date and baptism date indicate that the baptism happened on an infant, the document is most likely a fake. Also, many churches can provide a resource in that they may keep a baptismal register. This list, which provides the names and dates of everyone baptized within the church in a given year, can provide an accurate cross-check to determine the validity of a baptismal certificate.

Please note the addresses, phone numbers and document prices for the State Bureau of Vital Statistics to follow are accurate at the time of this writing. I would suggest you double check with one or more of the sources I've listed before actually placing an order.

Certificate of Baptism

Church of

____

____

This is to Certify

That ______________________________

Child of ______________________________

and ______________________________

born in ______________________________
(CITY) (STATE)

on the ________ day of ______________ 19____

was **Baptized**

on the ________ day of ______________ 19____

According to the Rite of the Roman Catholic Church

by the Rev. ______________________________

the Sponsors being { ______________________________
____

as appears from the Baptismal Register of this Church.

Dated ______________

____
Pastor

NO. 314 F. J REMEY CO. INC. N.Y

STATE BUREAUS OF VITAL STATISTICS

State	Address	Phone Number	Cost of Birth Certificate
Alabama	Center for Health Statistics State Department of Public Health 434 Monroe Street Room 215 Montgomery, AL 36130-1701	205-261- 5033	$5.00
Alaska	Department of Health and Social Services Bureau of Vital Statistics P.O. Box H-02G Juneau, AK 99811-0675	907-465- 3392	$7.00
American Samoa	Registrar of Vital Statistics Vital Statistics Section Government of American Samoa Pago Pago, AS 96799	684-633- 1222	$2.00
Arizona	Vital Records Section Arizona Department of Health Services P.O. Box 3887 Phoenix, AZ 85030	602-258- 6381	$8.00
Arkansas	Division of Vital Records Arkansas Department of Health 4815 West Markham Street Little Rock, AR 72201	501-661- 2134	$5.00
California	Vital Statistics Section Department of Health Services 410 N Street Sacramento, CA 95814	916-445- 2684	$11.00
Canal Zone	Panama Canal Commission Vital Statistics Clerk APO Miami, FL 34011	NA	$2.00
Colorado	Vital Records Section Colorado Department of Health 4210 East 11th Avenue Denver, CO 80220	303-320- 8474	$6.00
Connecticut	Vital Records Department of Health Services 150 Washington Street Hartford, CT 06106	203-566- 1124	$5.00
Delaware	Office of Vital Statistics Division of Public Health P.O. Box 637 Dover, DE 19903	302-739- 4721	$5.00
District of	Vital Records Branch	202-727-	$8.00

Columbia	Room 3009 425 I Street, NW Washington, DC 20001	5314	
Florida	Department of Health and Rehabilitation Services Office of Vital Statistics P.O. Box 210 Jacksonville, FL 32331-0042	904-359-6000	$8.00
Georgia	Georgia Department of Human Resources Vital Records Unit Room 217-H 47 Trinity Avenue, SW Atlanta, GA 30334	404-656-7456	$3.00
Guam	Office of Vital Statistics Department of Public Health and Social Services Government of Guam P.O. Box 2816 Agan, GU, M.I. 96910	671-734-7292	$5.00
Hawaii	Vital Records State Department of Health P.O. Box 3378 Honolulu, HI 96801	808-586-4533	$2.00
Idaho	Vital Statistics Unit Idaho Department of Health and Welfare 450 West State Street Statehouse Mall Boise, ID 83720-9990	208-334-5988	$8.00
Illinois	Division of Vital Records Illinois Department of Public Health 605 West Jefferson Street Springfield, IL 62702-5079	217-782-6533	$15.00
Indiana	Division of Vital Records State Department of Health 1330 West Michigan Street P.O. Box 1964 Indianapolis, IN 46206-1964	317-633-0276	$6.00
Iowa	Iowa Department of Public Health Vital Records Section Lucas Office Building 321 East 12th Street Des Moines, IA 50319	515-281-4944	$6.00
Kansas	Office of Vital Statistics Kansas State Department of Health and Environment Landon State Office Building 900 Southwest Jackson Street Topeka, KS 66612-1290	913-296-1400	$6.00

Kentucky	Office of Vital Statistics Department for Health Services 275 East Main Street Frankfort, KY 40621	502-564-4212	$5.00
Louisiana	Vital Records Registry Office of Public Health P.O. Box 60630 New Orleans, LA 70160	504-568-2561	$8.00
Maine	Office of Vital Records Human Services Building Station 11 State House Augusta, ME 04333	207-289-3184	$5.00
Maryland	Division of Vital Records Department of Health and Mental Hygiene Metro Executive Building 4201 Patterson Avenue P.O. Box 68760 Baltimore, MD 21215-0020	410-225-5988	$4.00
Massachusetts	Registry of Vital Records and Statistics 150 Tremont Street Room B-3 Boston, MA 02111	617-727-0110	$6.00
Michigan	Office of the State Registrar and Center for Health Statistics Michigan Department of Public Health 3423 North Logan Street Lansing, MI 48909	517-335-8656	$10.00
Minnesota	Minnesota Department of Health Section of Vital Statistics 717 Delaware Street, SE P.O. Box 9441 Minneapolis, MN 55440	612-623-5120	$11.00
Mississippi	Vital Records State Department of Health P.O. Box 1700 Jackson, MS 39215-1700	601-960-7981	$11.00
Missouri	Department of Health Bureau of Vital Records 1730 East Elm Street P.O. Box 570 Jefferson City, MO 65102	314-751-6400	$4.00
Montana	Bureau of Records and Statistics State Department of Health and Environmental Sciences Helena, MT 59620	406-444-2614	$5.00
Nebraska	Bureau of Vital Statistics State Department of Health	402-471-2871	$6.00

	301 Centennial Mall South P.O. Box 95007 Lincoln, NE 68509-5007		
Nevada	Division of Health – Vital Statistics Capitol Complex 505 East King Street Room 102 Carson City, NV 89710	702-885-4480	$7.00
New Hampshire	Bureau of Vital Records Health and Human Services Building 6 Hazen Drive Concord, NH 03301	603-271-4654	$3.00
New Jersey	State Department of Health Bureau of Vital Statistics South Warren and Market Streets CN-370, Trenton, NJ 08625	609-292-4087	$4.00
New Mexico	Vital Statistics Bureau New Mexico Health Services Division 1190 Saint Francis Drive Santa Fe, NM 87504-0968	505-827-0121	$10.00
New York (excluding New York City)	Vital Records Section State Department of Health Empire State Plaza Tower Building Albany, NY 12237-0023	518-474-3075	$15.00
New York City	Bureau of Vital Records Department of Health of New York City 125 Worth Street Room 133 New York, NY 10013	212-619-4530	$5.00
North Carolina	Department of Human Resources Vital Records Section P.O. Box 27867 Raleigh, NC 27611	919-733-3526	$5.00
North Dakota	Division of Vital Records State Department of Health Office of Statistical Services Bismarck, ND 58505	701-224-2360	$7.00
Northern Mariana Islands	Office of Vital Statistics Superior Court Commonwealth of the Northern Mariana Islands Saipan, MP 96950	670-234-6401	$3.00
Ohio	Division of Vital Statistics Ohio Department of Health 246 North High Street Columbus, OH 43215-0098	614-466-2531	$7.00
Oklahoma	Vital Records Section	405-271-	$5.00

	State Department of Health 1000 Northeast 10th Street P.O. Box 53551 Oklahoma City, OK 73152	4040	
Oregon	Oregon State Health Division Vital Statistics Section P.O. Box 14050 Portland, OR 97214-0050	503-731- 4108	$8.00
Pennsylvania	Division of Vital Statistics State Department of Health Central Building 101 South Mercer Street P.O. Box 1528 New Castle, PA 16103	412-656- 3100	$4.00
Puerto Rico	Department of Health Demographic Registry P.O. Box 11854 Fernandez Juncos Station San Juan, PR 00910	809-728- 7980	$2.00
Rhode Island	Division of Vital Statistics Rhode Island Department of Health Room 101 Cannon Building 3 Capitol Hill Providence, RI 02908-5097	401-277- 2811	$5.00
South Carolina	Office of Vital Records and Public Health Statistics South Carolina Department of Health and Environmental Control 2600 Bull Street Columbia, SC 29201	803-734- 4830	$6.00
South Dakota	South Dakota Department of Public Health Vital Records Program 523 East Capitol Street Pierre, SD 57501	605-773- 4961	$5.00
Tennessee	Tennessee Vital Records Department of Health and Environment C3-324 Cordell Hull Building Nashville, TN 37247-0350	615-741- 1763	$10.00
Texas	Bureau of Vital Statistics Texas Department of Health 1100 West 49th Street Austin, TX 78756-3191	512-458- 7364	$8.00
Utah	Bureau of Vital Records Utah Department of Health 288 North 1460 West P.O. Box 16700	801-538- 6380	$11.00

	Salt Lake City, UT 84116-0700		
Vermont	Vermont Department of Health Vital Records Section Box 70 60 Main Street Burlington, VT 05402	802-863-7275, $5.00	
Virgin Islands – St. Croix	Registrar of Vital Statistics Charles Harwood Memorial Hospital St. Croix, VI 00820	NA	$10.00
Virgin Islands – St. Thomas and St. John	Registrar of Vital Statistics Knud Hansen Complex Hospital Ground Charlotte Amalie St. Thomas, VI 00802	809-774-9000	$10.00
Virginia	Bureau of Vital Records State Department of Health P.O. Box 1000 Richmond, VA 23208-1000	804-786-6228	$5.00
Washington	Department of Health Center of Health Statistics 1112 South Quince Street P.O. Box 9709 ET-11 Olympia, WA 98504-9709	206-753-5936	$11.00
West Virginia	Vital Registration Office Division of Public Health State Capitol Complex Building 3 Room 516 Charleston, WV 25305	304-558-2931	$5.00
Wisconsin	Vital Records 1 West Wilson Street P.O. Box 309 Madison, WI 53701	608-266-1371	$8.00
Wyoming	Vital Records Services Division of Health and Medical Services Hathaway Building Cheyenne, WY 82002	307-777-7591	$5.00

Notary Nonsense

When one deals with almost any form of "verified" ID paper, such as a birth certificate, one runs into the concept of notarization. A notary public is a kin of licensed witness.

He, or she, is authorized to declare a copy of a document matches the original in all respects as well as verifying signature(s) on any document.

The latter operation is based on viewing a legal photo ID (they normally ask for a drivers license), and comparing the signatures. The signee is also required to sign in the notary's log book, and in many states leave a thumbprint behind.

Notaries are licensed by the state, normally after passing a simple test and swearing to uphold truth, justice and the American way of life.

All notary stamps used to employ a embossed seal – now many states simply use a rubber stamp as the verification mark.

It is a crime for an NP to endorse anything that is not exactly as it should be.

How do some people get around this minor stumbling block?

- Anyone (within reason) can become a notary. There are cheat books as well as day-long seminars that teach one to pass the test and register as a notary public. Of course becoming one's own NP is a pretty much a self defeating concept

But if one's *friend* became a…

- The next concept is, in my opinion, a much better option – a number of companies (let your fingers do the walking) sell notary supplies including the log book and stamp. As far as I am aware *none* check to make certain the buyer is really a notary public

So, hypothetically speaking one could simply call a company and order one's stamp, etc. over the phone and pick it up, or have it shipped to the correct address without any government intervention.

Just a thought.

Your Mother

This special section looks at whether one of the single most important security factors involved with IDs, real or fraudulent: the issue of a mother's maiden name (MMN).

We will look at this topic from three angles: the importance of the MMN as a security issue; how to obtain a person's MMN; and how to protect one's own MMN.

Everyone knows what their mother's maiden name is: her last name when she was born, in other words, the last name of her parents. But what many people do not know is how important this one name can be in either securing or protecting against use of a fraudulent identity.

Banks, credit card companies, and other financial institutions use the MMN as a safety feature of their client's accounts; when someone calls or visits the institution for account information, they will be asked to supply the MMN before the records will be released.

By the same token, many agencies such as state bureaus of vital statistics and the Social Security Administration require a MMN before they will issue new copies of any other document to an applicant.

After obtaining a MMN, an IA can gain access to almost all of another person's financial and personal records, and can use the information (or money or credit or whatever) as his or her own.

Securing a MMN is also the first step to applying for a fraudulently obtained birth certificate, the base upon which many new identities are constructed.

Why has the MMN become such an important security password? Three reasons:

- Everybody has one. If you have a mother, you have a MMN
- Everybody knows his. As opposed to say, an arbitrary password or numeric code, most everyone remembers his MMN

- It's hard for anyone else to obtain. Other than birth certificates, no form of common/carry ID contains the MMN. Thus, if one were to lose one's wallet, anyone who fourd it up would not have access to this important code word

Also, because it is so personal and family-centered, a MMN is not something that can be easily found in general records.

How To Obtain A Mother's Maiden Name

As the preceding point indicates, obtaining a person's MMN is not easy. However, a surprisingly large number of sources does exist that offer the potential for finding this information.

Keep in mind that none of these are foolproof; but, with a little trial-and-error, one may very well obtain the information one seeks. The sources in question include the following: The person him – or herself.

Clearly, the most direct way to find a person's MMN is to ask him or her directly. Why would one divulge this information to a perfect stranger?

Pretext

Or, as some people prefer to call it, lying. If one can become a person that the targets wants to give out information to, the information will be made available.

If done carefully and casually, say in the course of an unrelated conversation, a person can often be prompted to talk about family, including divulging his MMN. On the other hand, if someone gets the sense that they are being pumped for this information, they will often feel suspicious and refuse to reveal the name.

One way around this is to construct some ruse in which obtaining the MMN would be required. For example, one could call as a representative from a credit card company utilized by the target.

The pretext person is calling to verify that the target wishes to cancel his or her service. When they (of course) say they do not, the caller claims that someone had previously called asking for termination of this account.

The caller then asks for certain information to verify that the person is indeed who he or she says he is, and that the account should not be closed. This information would, of course, include the person's MMN.

Other fairly common pretexts include pretending to be the target, calling the local phone company and explaining your check book isn't balancing and you don't see a payment on your phone bill.

"I really can't afford to have this phone turned off can you see if I paid you guys?"

"Yes, sir/madam, we show a payment of $67.98 on July 17th, you are paid up until August 21."

"Did you happen to record the check number I paid with?"

The answer to this will probably be negative, but no mind.

Move on.

Now one directly calls the target claiming to be an employee of the collection department for their telephone company informing them that you are about to cut off their phone service due to a non-payment of $67.98.

Target will protest; it was, after all, paid. "Collection agent" than asks for check and account number to "verify" the payment.

Okay, still ain't got the MMN, but it now it may be possible to call the bank and explain you have had several unauthorized inquiries into your credit recently and you feel that you are about to become the victim of identity theft – you wish to change the identifiers on your account.

You would prefer to substitute a different MMN, replacing the one they have on file.

Right?

You're not sure but when you opened the account you probably gave it out, what do they have on file?

Maybe yes, maybe no...

If you are going to pull a credit report, or have one pulled, it will probably not contain the MMN directly.

A good pretext person will call a creditor listed on the report and pretend to be another creditor.

The game here is convincing the creditor that you are brothers-in-the Lord's fight against deadbeats.

You are trying to track down a skip, one the target agency has an inquiry on. Ask the cover questions, hell, any information is useful; do they have a recent address, phone, business phone, etc.

Great, this all helps but you still get the feeling something is amiss here could they pull the original application and check his references?

Of course, you will return the favor if something funny is happening.

Many people list their mother as a reference, or at least other family members. Jury duty is one of my favorite lies – "Hello Mr. X, this is John Smith from the County Commissioner's office. We are attempting to select a jury pool and the computer pulled up your name as never having been contacted, much less served on a jury."

Can you explain these please? It is a felony to provide false information in order to avoid one's civic duty.

You did serve/never contact/just moved here? Perhaps I have the wrong John X, we file our records by your mother's maiden name, yours, is, I believe Cooper. Is this correct?"

"No, no sir, its XXXX"

In some cases, it is possible to obtain the MMN from a person without even needing to contact them. If a woman does not change her name upon marriage – increasingly common these days – then her current last name is her MMN. And if an unmarried woman has a baby, that child's last name is the MMN.

Often, an unusual child's middle name may be the same as the MMN.

Go To The Family

Families are a gold mine in terms of determining a person's MMN. Remember that a MMN is the same as the last name of the mother's parents; thus, if one can determine the parent family name that is the MMN. This is also true of any of the mother's brothers: their last name will be the same as the MMN.

If one can determine if the mother has unmarried sisters, their last name will be the MMN as well.

Finding these relatives and their names can take some work. One option is to look in old newspapers (available at most libraries on microfilm or microfiche) in the person's hometown to see if he or she has ever been mentioned in the paper.

This will most commonly take place for weddings, funerals, and so on. If a wedding announcement, for example, can be found, the guests will often be mentioned, including the family of both the bride and the groom. If grandparents of either party are named, and if the last name of the grandparents is different from that of the party in question, that name is the MMN.

A shortcut is to go through a newspaper archive service – best is Dialog (Palo Alto California, not cheap, but quite complete), try NL Search, doesn't cover as many papers, or go back as far, but far less expensive.

Third net based alternative is www.concentric.net/~Stevewt/ A number of links from newspapers across the country.

One can also try contacting relatives directly, first simply by looking them up by the person in question's last name in the phone book, or better yet, on one of the many net based servers such as WHOIS, which allow the addition of search limits (such as geographical location).

A couple of pretexts work on relatives – one can become a genealogy researcher, offering to do a family tree. A good idea here is to explain you are a grad student doing this for a thesis, and you will deliver the results free of charge.

By asking for a little bit of information on that person's siblings, parents, and grandparents, the MMN can easily be obtained.

Family Tree Researcher

A more professional version of the preceding is to pose as a family member and contact a genealogical researcher to construct a family tree. It is best if using this approach to have some information on the names of members of the family in question; it would look strange to a researcher if one did not know anything about one's own family!

A good way to pretext this area is to access the Mormon Church genealogical information files.

They actually have the largest and most concentrated files on American family roots available.

The files can be accessed by non-Mormons, either by visiting lovely Salt Lake City, Utah or not quite so-lovely South San Francisco, California and dig through the files.

Ah, but the good news is most of these files are now on-line...

www.familysearch.org

A little research here and one is now more equipped with more family background tools than most FBI agents have at their disposal.

The CIA has a theory I subscribe to called the Christmas Tree Concept. Find a few facts, hang 'em on a simple premise (or tree, if one wishes to be specific) and next thing you know you are in possession of a believable story.

Or a very nice tree.

If family information is not known, one possible approach is to tell the researcher that the family member in question is a possible heir apparent to some ancestral bequest, and you are trying to make positive verification that he or she is indeed the true heir. In this case, you do not want to give out any family information, since you do not want to influence the researcher's results.

In the latter case, you will be asked to provide the date and place of birth of the person in question. If you do not have this information, it can be easily and legally obtained through an information brokerage. An information broker may provide only the date of birth and SSN; however, using the numbering scheme described in the chapter on social security cards, the state of birth can be obtained from the SSN, and a little more research can narrow down the actual city.

If you choose to use a broker rather than doing the leg work on your own, beware it may take a great deal of time and money; and some unscrupulous researchers will simply generate a false family tree just to get paid.

Be sure to verify any information obtained by posing as the individual in question at a bank or other institution and using the information to see if it is accepted. Also, if you choose to go by this method, remember to have the researcher go back at least two generations, the information and the request appear to be valid.

Financial Institutions

A person's bank or other financial institution may itself provide a source of the MMN, if it is approached correctly. Because these institutions use the MMN as a security password, obtaining it from them necessarily involves pretexting.

A thin, but workable approach is to use an invented MMN; when it does not match the one on the account application, claim that a spouse filled out the original application, and must have used his or her MMN on it instead. In some cases, the institution will then add the invented MMN as valid password.

Another scheme is more involved. It requires obtaining the target individual's account number (following him or her into the bank and "accidentally" seeing a deposit slip is one method for this), then calling the bank as the individual and asking a question about the account. When the account is pulled up, one must have access via a window and binoculars or a telescope to see the screen itself; if one can accomplish this, the MMN will be visible from the screen.

A third option is to attack the target's account number by posing as a worker from one branch of the bank, and calls the individual's home branch to request information on the account. By claiming the individual has no ID on him or her and you need some way to verify that he or she is the account holder, you may be able to obtain the MMN from the worker at the home branch.

Social Security Administration

Governmental agencies are other possible sources for obtaining an individual's MMN. The following is a scheme that is possible if one is able to obtain the individual in question's SSN.

This bit is not only illegal, but also dangerous, so consider the risk factor before indulging. In this scheme one calls the Social Security Administration posing as an employee for another agency, such as the DMV. One claims the individual has presented his or her Social Security card to apply for a drivers license, but the card does not look authentic.

Verify the SSN, then tell the Social Security Administration you wish to verify the MMN on the Social Security card application to prove the applicant's identity. The employee may/or may not then provide this information this information.

Department of Motor Vehicles

The DMV itself is another resource in obtaining a MMN. An applicant for a drivers license includes the MMN on his or her original application form.

Obtaining this application provides access to an individual's MMN.

The ease of this process varies from state to state. In some states, the original drivers license application is part of the public record, along with the driving record itself.

If this is so, the application will be sent on request (with the proper fee) simply by supplying the name and date of birth for the individual in question.

Keep in mind that in order to obtain this application you must know in what state the individual's current drivers license were obtained.

In some cases, this is the state of birth, which can be determined directly from birth records or indirectly from the SSN or the voter registration office.

If the person has moved, he or she will have filled out an application for a drivers license in his or her new state of residence.

One can also utilize an information broker or determine the target's current and last locations from the credit header, limiting the search to an acceptable level.

Hint – Look at the tag on their car...

State Bureau of Vital Statistics

If one knows the state in which the individual in question was born, one can contact the state vital statistics bureau to obtain a copy of the target's birth certificate, which contains the MMN.

The simplest approach is to pose as the individual and claims that the original birth certificate has been lost however, many states now require the MMN *before* issuing a birth certificate, making this method a bit less that reliable.

There are other approaches are variations on the same basic scam. One can call the vital statistics bureau posing as an employee of another official agency suggesting that one needs verification of a birth certificate.

Other options include "working for the Mexican Immigration Removal Center", and needing to positively identify a candidate for deportation. The MMN will be used as proof positive of identification; or posing as a State Department employee at a passport office or a DMV investigator. In these cases, one needs the vital statistics bureau to verify an applicant's birth certificate information – including the MMN, which only the *real* applicant would know – before issuing the passport or drivers license.

Also, one should check the SSN death record file to see whether any viable clues appear.

Marriage Records

Another potent source of a MMN is the individual's marriage record application. The information from this application – including, in some cases, the applicant's MMN – becomes part of the state's permanent and *public* records (in most states).

California has begun a new "un-public" recording system, which, if the happy couple is willing to pay a bit extra, will not list this information in an easily accessible public record.

Most people do not bother with this added expense.

If one knows the year and county of the marriage (obtainable from old newspapers, available on microfilm or microfiche at the public library), one can view this record at the county clerk's office by looking under either the bride's or the groom's last name (it is filed under both).

The listing for the bride is will be under her maiden name.

If you are not located physically near the library, recorder or courthouse in question, some very good alternatives exist. See the section on obtaining public records.

If the groom is the target, the next step depends on the record itself. Some states include the original application as part of the marriage record, on which both applicant's MMN's can be found. If not, it may be necessary to go to the groom's *parents* marriage record, which will contain the MMN.

The process is the same: the county and year of the marriage must be determined, then the record looked up at the county clerk's office. The further back the marriage took place, the more difficult this process will be especially if the parents were married in a different city or county from that in which they are currently living.

This might be a good time for a pretext call – besides the actual participants, the licenses will have other names, such as those of the witnesses, who may be quite happy to talk to an old school mate of their good friends.

Obituaries

A potentially simple source of obtaining a MMN is the obituary section of the newspaper. The key here is locating the story of a sibling or other close relative of the person in question; in some cases, the MMN of the surviving parent will be printed.

The downside to this approach is that it requires checking the obituary column to see whether an individual's family member has died.

Who's Who

Once again we're back at one of my favorite money making schemes Who's Who.

What if you could print a book that sold for, say $100. and you knew everyone involved would buy at *least one copy*, if not many more in order to impress their friends.

And, and, you didn't have to write a damn thing. The customers provided you with all the relevant information.

Free.

Who's Who publications are put out by Marcus Publishing. These books, which include Who's Who in America, Who's Who in the East *(West, South, North)*, Who's Who in Medicine, Who's Who in Science, and so on, list the names of notable Americans either generally, by region, or by discipline. Each listing contains information on the person in question including, somewhat surprisingly, the MMN. If the person one is researching has prominence in any field whatsoever, the Who's Who series might be a good place to look.

These books can be ordered directly from Marcus, though they are expensive. They are also carried by most libraries, and can be accessed online via CompuServe.

A Who's Who – related scam that one might use to obtain a MMN is to contact Marcus Publishing for an application, send it to the individual in question, and put as the return address POB that one has rented.

The application asks for the MMN, and, if the individual responds, one would obtain that piece of information with ease.

Yearbooks

If one knows or can determine where the individual's mother went to high school, obtaining a copy of her high school yearbook will provide the MMN. This approach is most successful if one can estimate the year in which mom graduated.

It's hardly even a pretext to call the school librarian in Hell's Bluff, Wyoming and explain you, after inventing Nutra Sweet, have become bored with those damn millionaire yacht club members and wondered what ever happened to your old lover…

You'll get it.

How To Protect Your Mother's Maiden Name

Given all of the above, it might seem that trying to prevent someone from gaining your MMN and using it access your accounts would be an impossible task. But, there is actually one simple step you can take to safeguard your MMN against such abuses: wherever possible, invent one.

Remember that there is a difference between the two types of agencies that use one's MMN. On the one hand, government agencies such as the State Bureau of Vital Statistics and the Social Security Administration will use the MMN as part of your official "governmental identity package," and thus will cross-check to verify the accuracy of a MMN that is included in an application for documents.

On the other hand, banks and other financial institutions use the MMN as a security password only. If your real MMN is "Smith," but you use "Jones" on a bank account application, the bank will not check this for accuracy; every time you try to access the account, they will expect you to use "Jones" as your MMN.

This provides a great deal of leverage in keeping accounts safe from fraudulent use. Even if someone manages to obtain your actual MMN through one of the methods described above, it will be of no use to him or her if your accounts bear an invented MMN as their password. To take this step even further, you can use a different MMN for each account. The trick here is to use the last name of a friend or two; something you can remember. It's really embarrassing to stutter when the nice bank clerk asks you for your mom's name.

Comments like, "I didn't know her that well before she got married," just don't cut it.

Social Security – The Inside Story

SOCIAL SECURITY CARD AT A GLANCE	
Type	3. Secondary ID
Method of Issuance	▪ Issued by the Social Security Administration, a branch of the federal government ▪ Possible to apply for oneself or one's child at any time ▪ Required document: primary ID (adult); birth or baptismal certificate (child)
Information Contained	▪ Issue's name (printed) ▪ Issue's signature ▪ Issue's Social Security Number (SSN)
Use	▪ Proof of eligibility to gain employment in the U.S. ▪ Indirect proof of U.S. citizenship or naturalized immigration status ▪ Serves as tax/banking document for certain foreigners (special cards only) ▪ In some states, SSN is used as drivers license/state ID number ▪ SSN also commonly used as ID number by the IRS, schools, and other financial institutions
Method of Fraud	▪ Creation of counterfeit cards using older valid cards ▪ Valid Social Security cards are easily obtained with a fraudulent birth certificate and ID; or with birth certificate only in some cases

Security Issues	▪ +: Complex numbering system ▪ +: Cross-checking of names and Social Security numbers on income tax forms ▪ +: Changes in card itself to make forgery more difficult ▪ -: Older cards extremely easy to counterfeit ▪ -: Obtaining cards with a falsified birth certificate/ primary ID almost foolproof ▪ -: Persons under the age of 18 can ▪ apply for Social Security cards by mail

Type

The Social Security card is considered to be a secondary ID that is, a document that can support a claim to identification, but must be used in conjunction with other forms or cards to verify the holder's identity. This document cannot stand alone as a proof of ID.

Method of Issuance

Since their debut in the 1930s, Social Security cards have been issued by the Social Security Administration, a branch of the federal government, as proof of employment eligibility and as a quasi-federal ID. A Social Security card may be obtained at any point in one's life, and parents may apply for one for their children. The Social Security Administration requires "forms of evidence" of identity before issuing a card to an applicant; these "forms of evidence" include a drivers license for adults and a birth or baptismal certificate for children.

Social Security cards are one of the least descriptive of all forms of ID. They contain only two pieces of information about the holder: his or her name (shown twice, once printed and once in signature) and the Social Security number (SSN) that he or she has been assigned. This stems from the history of the card, which, when it was introduced in the 1930s, created fears of a national ID that the federal government could use to track individuals at any time and any place. To allay these concerns, the cards contain only minimal information; early cards even bore the legend, "not for identification purposes."

The Social Security card numbering system contains information on the issue in and of itself.

Use

The Social Security card serves three major purposes:

- It is the key document that verifies that the bearer is eligible to work in the U.S. Since the passage of the Immigration Control and Reform Act of 1986, Social Security cards have played an even more important role as a tool that employers use to determine if job applicants have a legal right to work in this country. Of course, this act has also led to a subsequent rise in the value of Social Security cards as forgeries

- Because "forms of evidence" that prove U.S. citizenship (or at least not naturalized immigrant status) are necessary to receive a Social Security card, the card itself has become viewed as indirect proof of citizenship or naturalized status. This has also boosted the card's value among counterfeiters, since it can be useful to those who are attempting to obtain the rights and privileges of citizenship in this country

- Finally, special cards are often issued to foreigners who need them for tax or banking purposes. These forms do not confer eligibility for employment, and in fact, the words "Not valid for employment purposes" are printed on them. However, the numbers on these cards are identical in form to those of regular Social Security cards, making them easily available for fraudulent use

The SSN itself also serves some important functions in the world of ID. In some 23 states, (at the moment) a person's SSN is also used as their drivers license or state ID number. This number is also commonly used as the bearer's ID number by the IRS, schools, and financial institutions such as banks and credit bureaus.

Does The United States Already Have A National ID Card?

Well, yes and no.

In 1935, your government realized that many low-end workers, reaching middle age, were concerned about their employer's lack of retirement benefits. After all, no one wanted to work his entire life only to spend the golden years on the street selling pencils. The government decided to take matter in hand and passed the Social Security Act of 1935. This act gave each employee in the United States the right to enroll in the Social Security system which would hold paid-in benefits for the subscribers retirement years. In essence, the Social Security Administration created a forced savings program that gave the government a large influx of dollars with a vague promise to pay them out to those who lived longed enough to collect.

The Social Security Numbers or SSN's was intended for use only by the Social Security program. In 1943, Franklin Delano Roosevelt, signed into effect Executive Order #9397 which required all federal agencies to use the SSN when creating a new recording keeping system, thereby enhancing the usefulness of the number.

In 1961, your friends, the IRS decided to use SSN as a tax payer ID number. In 1974 a bill called the Privacy Act required authorization for government agencies to use SSN in their data bases and mandated some disclosures when some agencies requested the number. The exceptions to this rule were agencies which were already using the SSN as an identifier before 1975, they were allowed to continue using it as is. In 1976 The Tax Reform Act was passed providing authority to all state and local tax folks, welfare, drivers licenses, or motor vehicle registration to use the number in order to establish identity.

One should remember; this is in direct contradiction to the reasons behind the issuance of the SSN in the first place. The Social Security Number was to be used strictly to hold benefits for individual subscribers and then pay them back at the appropriate time. When the IRS adapted the SSN as a primary identifier, the concept of employing this nine digits to track an individual's income and earnings became somewhat paramount.

Bear in mind that when the administration issued the first Social Security cards, they specifically utilized the wording "not to be used for purposes of identification."

By 1977, enough American citizens were becoming nervous about the creeping infestations of the SSN's that The Privacy Protection Study Commission was formed. One of their recommendations was that the bill signed by President Roosevelt (EO 9397) be revoked because a number of agencies were using that Executive Order as an authorization to demand SSN's. The order was actually never revoked, but it did have the effect of over-zealous "clerk–types" quoting EO 9397, as their authority, to demand a citizen's Social Security Number.

Even today, the law limits the authority to collect one's SSN strictly to income or revenue producing entities, which must report said income or revenue to the IRS. This means that one's employer has a right to the SSN as do stock brokers, money lenders, and in some cases banks.

Notice I said in some cases – said, *some* banks. If one opens an interest bearing checking account, savings account or invests in an instrument of revenue such as a Certificate of Deposit, one is obligated to provide the required SSN so the IRS can keep track of your lifestyle and tax the hell out of it. On the other hand, if one deals with a bank *without* utilizing an income bearing account, the bank has no right to demand a Social Security number (see the section on opening a bank account without a SSN).

So why does everyone from the DMV to your local video rental store demand your SSN?

Because they can.

The SSN makes for a unique identifier that works in almost all data banks and allows other data bases to exchange information based almost strictly this nine digit identifier. While it is possible to get a credit report on someone using their name and address, or name and date of birth, all credit agencies, mortgage agencies, etc., far and away prefer to work with a valid Social Security Number. The Social Security Number has become one of the main privacy invasion tools in America.

An example of the SSN's power is the fact a number is now issued to every US citizen at birth and the Social Security Administration has publicly stated they will no longer issue new cards to anyone but infants after the year 2000 (with some minor exceptions which will entail in-depth interviews).
Off hand, the only more invasive suggestion I can think of is the possibility of a true national ID card (covered elsewhere), having one's SSN's tattooed upon themselves at birth, or the inclusion of a micro chip under each individuals skin which carry identifying information which can be read from a distance.

The Social Security Number Itself

By now, most people are aware that a certain amount of information can be derived strictly from ones SSN. Many books have popularized the concept that the first three digits tell where the card was issued, while this is true, the numbers actually supply quite a bit more information on the applicant as well as to the legitimacy of the number.

A number of features and practices also exist to help detect and protect against use of falsified Social Security cards. These include the following:

- The system by which SSN's are assigned is quite complex. The SSN takes the form of:

  123-45-6789 where "123" is a three-digit number that shows the state or area in which the card was issued; "45" is a two-digit number that shows which group this card belongs to, and where that group falls in the sequence of all groups; and "6789" is a four-digit serial number, ranging from 0001 to 9999 that is unique to the particular card.

The first two parts of this number are the ones to check that can be giveaways to fraud. For example, the "123" number can only fall within one of the following ranges: 001-595, 600-649, or 700-728; if the first three digits fall anywhere outside of this range, for example, "850," the card is almost certainly a fake. Note that the 700-728 range does not designate a particular area or state; rather, these numbers have been reserved for special groups of people, including members of the railroad retirement system and certain Vietnam refugees. A person presenting a card with a number in this range should appear to be either the correct age or nationality.

Group numbers, the "45" section of the SSN, are assigned sequentially according to a certain pattern. For each three-digit area number, a group number is assigned according to the following scheme:

first groups: 01, 03, 05, 07, 09
second groups: 10, 12, 14, 16, 18, 20 (up to 98)
third groups: 00, 02, 04, 06, 08
fourth groups: 11, 13, 15, 17, 19 (up to 99)

Each group is used until the 9,999 possible numbers assigned to it are used up. For example, in the 01 group, the first serial number would be 01-0001, and the last would be 01-9999; when that number is reached, the next number assigned is 03-0001, and so on.

For each three-digit area or state number, group numbers are assigned in the above sequence until the full population of card bearers has been reached, For example, a state such as California, with a huge population, issues cards with area numbers ranging from 545-573, then continues with 602-626. The first number issued is 545-01-0001; this continues through 545-99-9999, at which point the next number issued is 546-01-0001, and so on through 573-99-9999; the numbering then picks up with 602-01-0001, continuing on through the 626s. The fact that California's numbering currently ends with 626 means that the number 626-99-9999 has not yet been reached.

A less populated state, such as Wyoming, has only one three-digit number for its SSN's: 520. The first card such issued was 520-01-0001, and the number 520-99-9999 has not yet been reached.

Knowing how the numbering system of SSN's works is a great help in detecting fraud. Armed with a list of area numbers, anyone examining a card has an effective tool to determining the card's validity. For example, if someone presents a card that begins with area number "523" but claims to have been born in Wyoming, the examiner will have some indication of possible fraud, since the area number and the state does not match.

Also, lists of group numbers currently in use are available, so that if, for example, Wyoming's group numbers end with 33, a card numbered 520-37-4564 would be indicative of fraud.

Finally, because the numbers are issued sequentially according to the somewhat complex pattern described above, the person looking at a Social Security card has some guide to gauging whether a card seems appropriately aged. An 18-year-old presenting a California card numbered 547-33-9747 is an indicator of potential fraud; since California's numbering system begins with range 543-573 and continues with 602-626, a young person is much more likely to have a higher numbered card.

Area Numbers For Social Security Cards

STATE	NUMBER(S) ASSIGNED	STATE	NUMBER(S) ASSIGNED
Alabama	416-424	Montana	516-517
Alaska	574	Nebraska	505-508
American Samoa	581-586	Nevada	530
Arizona	526-527; 600-601	New Hampshire	001-003
Arkansas	429-432	New Jersey	135-158
California	545-573; 602-626	New Mexico	525; 585; 648-649
Colorado	521-524	New York	050-134
Connecticut	040-049	North Carolina	237-246
Delaware	221-222	North Dakota	501-502
District of Columbia	577-579	Ohio	268-302
Florida	261-267; 589-595	Oklahoma	440-448
Georgia	252-260	Oregon	540-544
Guam	581-586	Pennsylvania	159-211
Hawaii	575-576	Philippine Islands	581-585
Idaho	518-519	Puerto Rico	581-585; 596-599
Illinois	318-361	Rhode Island	035-039
Indiana	303-317	South Carolina	247-251
Iowa	478-485	South Dakota	503-504
Kansas	509-515	Tennessee	408-415
Kentucky	400-407	Texas	449-467; 627-645
Louisiana	433-439	Utah	528-529; 646-647
Maine	004-007	Vermont	008-009
Mariana Island	586	Virgin Islands	580
Maryland	212-220	Virginia	223-231
Massachusetts	010-034	Washington	531-539
Michigan	362-386	West Virginia	232-236
Minnesota	468-477	Wisconsin	387-399
Mississippi	425-428; 588	Wyoming	520
Missouri	486-500		

SOCIAL SECURITY
000-00-0000
THIS NUMBER HAS BEEN ESTABLISHED FOR
NAME
SIGNATURE

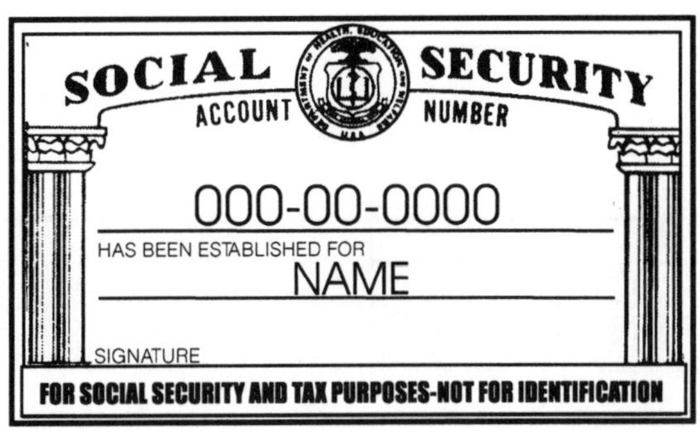
SOCIAL SECURITY
ACCOUNT NUMBER
000-00-0000
HAS BEEN ESTABLISHED FOR
NAME
SIGNATURE
FOR SOCIAL SECURITY AND TAX PURPOSES-NOT FOR IDENTIFICATION

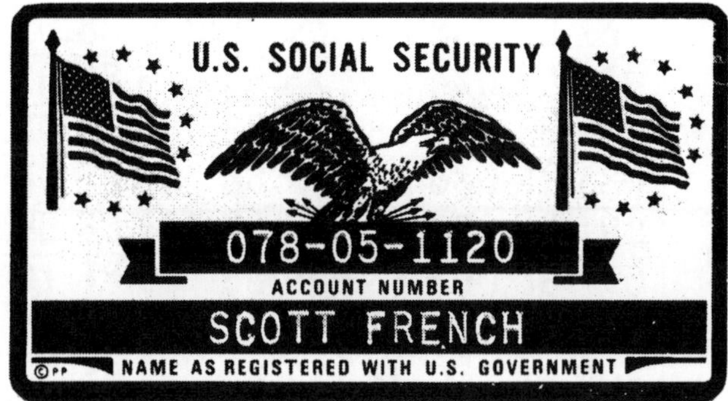
U.S. SOCIAL SECURITY
078-05-1120
ACCOUNT NUMBER
SCOTT FRENCH
NAME AS REGISTERED WITH U.S. GOVERNMENT

Social Security Group Numbers

Anything with an asterisk is a change affective of this printing. This list shows the SSN area and group numbers that are in the process of being issued as of this printing.

001 94 002 92 003 92 004 02 005 98 006 98
007 98 008 84 009 82 010 84* 011 82 012 82
013 82 014 82 015 82 016 82 017 82 018 82
019 82 020 82 021 82 022 82 023 82 024 82
025 82 026 82 027 82 028 82 029 82 030 82
031 82 032 82 033 82 034 82 035 66 036 66
037 66 038 66 039 66 040 02 041 02 042 02*
043 98 044 98 045 98 046 98 047 98 048 98
049 98 050 88 051 88 052 88 053 88 054 88
055 88 056 88 057 88 058 88 059 88 060 88
061 88 062 88 063 88 064 88 065 88 066 88
067 88 068 88 069 88 070 88 071 88 072 88
073 88 074 88 075 88 076 88 077 88 078 88
079 88 080 88 081 88 082 88 083 88 084 88
085 88 086 88 087 88 088 88 089 88 090 88
091 88 092 88 093 88 094 88 095 88 096 88
097 88 098 88 099 88 100 88 101 88 102 88
103 88 104 88 105 88 106 88 107 88 108 88
109 88 110 88 111 88 112 88 113 88 114 88
115 88 116 88 117 88 118 88 119 88 120 88
121 88 122 88 123 88 124 88 125 88 126 88
127 88 128 88 129 88 130 88* 131 88* 132 88*
133 86 134 86 135 06 136 06 137 06 138 06
139 06 140 06 141 06 142 06 143 06 144 06
145 06 146 06 147 06 148 06* 149 06* 150 04
151 04 152 04 153 04 154 04 155 04 156 04
157 04 158 04 159 78 160 78 161 78 162 78
163 78 164 78 165 78 166 78 167 78 168 78
169 78 170 78 171 78 172 78 173 78 174 78
175 78 176 78 177 78 178 78 179 78 180 78
181 78 182 78 183 78 184 78 185 78 186 78
187 78 188 78 189 78 190 78 191 78 192 78
193 78 194 78 195 78 196 78 197 78 198 78
199 78 200 78 201 78 202 78* 203 76 204 76
205 76 206 76 207 76 208 76 209 76 210 76

211 76 212 57 213 57 214 57* 215 57* 216 55
217 55 218 55 219 55 220 55 221 92 222 92*
223 85 224 85 225 85 226 85 227 85 228 85
229 85 230 85 231 85* 232 47 233 47 234 47
235 45 236 45 237 93 238 93* 239 93* 240 91
241 91 242 91 243 91 244 91 245 91 246 91
247 99 248 99 249 99 250 99 251 99 252 99
253 99 254 99 255 99 256 99 257 99 258 99
259 99 260 99 261 99 262 99 263 99 264 99
265 99 266 99 267 99 268 04 269 04 270 04
271 04 272 04 273 04 274 04 275 04 276 04
277 04 278 04 279 04 280 04 281 04 282 04
283 04 284 04 285 04 286 04 287 04 288 04
289 04 290 04 291 04 292 04 293 04* 294 02
295 02 296 02 297 02 298 02 299 02 300 02
301 02 302 02 303 23* 304 21 305 21 306 21
307 21 308 21 309 21 310 21 311 21 312 21
313 21 314 21 315 21 316 21 317 21 318 96
319 96 320 96 321 96 322 96 323 96 324 96
325 96 326 96 327 96 328 96 329 96 330 96
331 96 332 96 333 96 334 96 335 96 336 96
337 96 338 96 339 96 340 96 341 96 342 96
343 96 344 96 345 96* 346 96* 347 94 348 94
349 94 350 94 351 94 352 94 353 94 354 94
355 94 356 94 357 94 358 94 359 94 360 94
361 94 362 25 363 25 364 25 365 25 366 25
367 25 368 25* 369 25* 370 23 371 23 372 23
373 23 374 23 375 23 376 23 377 23 378 23
379 23 380 23 381 23 382 23 383 23 384 23
385 23 386 23 387 19 388 19 389 19 390 19
391 19 392 19 393 19 394 19 395 19 396 19
397 17 398 17 399 17 400 55 401 55 402 55
403 55 404 55 405 55* 406 53 407 53 408 87
409 87 410 87 411 87 412 87 413 87 414 87
415 87* 416 51 417 51 418 51 419 49 420 49
421 49 422 49 423 49 424 49 425 87 426 87
427 87 428 85 429 97 430 97 431 97 432 97
433 99 434 99 435 99 436 99 437 99 438 99
439 99 440 13 441 13 442 13 443 13 444 13
445 13 446 13 447 13* 448 11 449 99 450 99
451 99 452 99 453 99 454 99 455 99 456 99

457 99 458 99 459 99 460 99 461 99 462 99
463 99 464 99 465 99 466 99 467 99 468 37
469 37 470 37 471 37 472 37 473 37* 474 35
475 35 476 35 477 35 478 29 479 29 480 29
481 29 482 29 483 29* 484 27 485 27 486 17
487 17 488 17* 489 15 490 15 491 15 492 15
493 15 494 15 495 15 496 15 497 15 498 15
499 15 500 15 501 25 502 25 503 31 504 29
505 41 506 41 507 39 508 39 509 17 510 17
511 17 512 17 513 17 514 17 515 17* 516 35
517 33 518 59* 519 57 520 41 521 99 522 99
523 99 524 99 525 99 526 99 527 99 528 99
529 99 530 99 531 43 532 43 533 43 534 43
535 43 536 43 537 43 538 43 539 43 540 57
541 57 542 57* 543 55 544 55 545 99 546 99
547 99 548 99 549 99 550 99 551 99 552 99
553 99 554 99 555 99 556 99 557 99 558 99
559 99 560 99 561 99 562 99 563 99 564 99
565 99 566 99 567 99 568 99 569 99 570 99
571 99 572 99 573 99 574 29 575 87* 576 85
577 31 578 31 579 29 580 33 581 99 582 99
583 99 584 99 585 99 586 41 587 85 589 89
590 89 591 89 592 89 593 89 594 89 595 89*
596 62 597 62 598 62 599 62* 600 95 601 95
602 17 603 17 604 17 605 17 606 17 607 17
608 17 609 17 610 17 611 17 612 17 613 17
614 17 615 17* 616 17* 617 17* 618 17* 619 17*
620 17* 621 17* 622 17* 623 15 624 15 625 15
626 15 627 70 628 70 629 70 630 70 631 70*
632 70* 633 70* 634 70* 635 68 636 68 637 68
638 68 639 68 640 68 641 68 642 68 643 68
644 68 645 68 646 50 647 50 648 20 649 20*
650 12 651 12 652 12 653 12* 654 07 655 07
656 07 657 07 658 07* 659 01 660 01 661 01*
667 07 668 07 669 07 670 07 671 07 672 07
673 07* 674 07* 675 07* 680 20 700 18 701 18
702 18 703 18 704 18 705 18 706 18 707 18
708 18 709 18 710 18 711 18 712 18 713 18
714 18 715 18 716 18 717 18 718 18 719 18
720 18 721 18 722 18 723 18 724 28 725 18

726 18 727 10 728 14

This data becomes of particular import if one has the artistic urge to makeup a brand new SSN for one reason or another. Although most private individuals, store clerks and the like, will not recognize the verification factors inherent in the Social Security Number, many government clerks, including DMV types, may well follow some simple guidelines to establish that the number at least fits the valid issue format. The Social Security Administration has for years perfected the art of negative information providing, i.e., they will tell whether a particular number has been issued and is in use, but under normal circumstances they will not reveal who (or many cases "who's") actually using it.

Just as with a name, it is possible for one to legally change ones Social Security Number. Unlike simply walking into court and convincing a judge that you're tired of the name Moon Unit that your ex-hippie father laid on you during a particularly intense acid trip, one has to have a reason for changing ones SSN. Lets take a look right out of the SSN handbook on how to discourage an applicant and if one can't discourage said applicant, how to issue a new SSN. It is important to remember that this "new" number *will be* cross referenced with your old number if you do this legally.

Application Interview For Second SSN's

Since requests for second SSN's are considered original applications, an in-person interview is mandatory when the individual is age 18 or older.

- What to tell applicant:

1. Potential problems with multiple SSN's –

During the interview explain the potential problems associated with assigning a second number since many organizations, both public and private, may have records under the old number.

Examples:

- IRS
- Banks
- Department of Motor Vehicles
- Other Federal and State agencies
- Schools
- Credit bureaus

2. SSN's will be cross-referenced –

Also explain that the original SSN will remain assigned to the number holder (NH). The old and new numbers will be cross-referenced so that the earnings can be properly credited, and misuse of the SSN can be prevented. The information on both numbers is confidential unless disclosure is required by law or allowed by the NH. Explain that we will not void, delete, or cancel the original SSN.

Required Documentation

A. Applicant's statement –

Get the individual's signed statement (Form SST-795) explaining the reasons for wanting a second SSN.

B. Report of contact –

Prepare a report of contact (Form SST-5002) to document the interview. Include your observations and/or reactions to the individual's allegations.

C. Evidence of problem –

1. General.

Ask the applicant to submit documentary evidence showing how the SSN is disadvantaging him/her and that he/she is not at fault. This shall include third party cooperation of the problem, if possible (e.g., police report regarding misrepresentation by another individual using the NH's SSN.) If there is no evidence the, applicants' statement must give the full reason for the request.

2. Applicant alleges that credit record is affected.

When the applicant alleges that someone has used his/her SSN to gain access to and/or affect his/her credit, ask the applicant for copies of the credit record, correspondence showing the applicant's attempts to correct the credit record, and other evidence supporting the allegations. A statement from the credit bureau and/or creditors should show:

- How the applicant's SSN was used (If the applicant already has one or more SSN's on record, advise the applicant to use the cross-referred multiple
- Death threats or stalking
- Misuses of SSN to fraudulently obtain credit, public benefits, employment, etc.

Reasons For Denial Of Second SSN Requests

Deny the request if the individual gives one of the following reasons:

- Avoidance of the law or legal responsibility
- Poor credit record when the applicant is at fault (When the applicant is not at fault, see RM 00205.030.)

- Bankruptcy
- Lost or stolen SSN card and there is no evidence of misuse
- Desire for a specific number
- Use of SSN by other government agencies and /or by private companies
- Fails to submit documentary evidence which should be available (RM 00205.030)

Summary Of Official Requirements For Changing SSN

1. Determine your reason for requesting a second SSN.

2. Obtain corroborating evidence to prove how the SSN is disadvantaging you at no fault of your own.

3. Complete a form SS-5 (available at all SSA offices).

4. Present all documentation to the Social Security office (preferably a supervisor).

Although it's a bit difficult to track anyone through the use of a SSN (especially attempting to go through the Social Security agency itself), it is possible to see whether the owner of a particular number is still among the living. A number of years ago the Social Security Administration sold its entire death record to a company called Cambridge Researchers. Cambridge in turn broke this database down allowing individual investigators, or simply curious people, to, for a small fee, to check to see whether the individual using a particular number had been reported as deceased to the SSA.

The primary reason for this databank is, of course, to ensure government types that no incidences of fraud are being employed by the use of a deceased person's number to collect benefits, apply for loans, or other schemes.

Recently it has become possible to access the complete SSA death data base on line by going to www.familytreemaker.com/fto_ssdisearch.html.

As this is written, it is still possible for a non-infant to be issued a new, legal SSN by the friendly SSA. Problems with this concept include the fact that you must have good supporting documentation including a birth certificate (or baptismal certificate). Apply in person if you are over 18 years old, and have a damn good story as to why you have never had a SSN issued to you.

There are some valid excuses for ones finding oneself in this situation. Including:

- You lived outside the United States since infancy with your over-indulgent, rich parents in a castle in Spain and they were dead set against their only living protegee taking a job

- You were given life in prison at an early age and due to the tearful pleas from your wife, the governor has just pardoned you

- You joined a ministry, the Moonies or that weird Monk-thing, where the members are not allowed to speak to each other, just dropped out and decided to rejoin legit society

- You have a gay lover that supported you all your life (although this could get you in a little trouble with the IRS because you are supposed to report income as income, but we'll deal with that later)

- You have been mentally ill and institutionalized, but thank God for Prozac, you are completely well now

If you're going to try and pull any of these somewhat oblique schemes on a SSA clerk, who has waited all her life for someone like you to walk in, I suggest you take a Valium and a couple of drinks before wandering down to the office.

In plain English while it is legal under these circumstances to apply for your first card, it is damn unusual, and you can bet that there is going to be some sort of little file started on the 36-year-old gay, parolee who just dropped out of the ministry.

A little-known "secondary" type of Social Security card is also issued by the SSA. This card is issued to aliens (preferably those from other countries, not planets) that are spending some time in the United States and expect to generate some income. Note that income generation does not necessarily mean "take a job" because if one doesn't have a Visa that allows one to work in the states you ain't gonna be working anyway...

Travelers from other nations might, for instance, wish to play the American stock market while here expecting to make a fortune during their stay. By law, this income should be reported to the IRS, even though the individual has not actually obtained gainful employment. This minor gap in the SSA procedure is taken up by a special card, identical to the normal SS card, except for a stamp across the front which says "Not Valid For Employment." This is a valid SSN number with no expiration date, but it cannot be used for the purposes of employment.

What makes this special? Many smaller Social Security Offices do not maintain a list of all foreign residency documents that is to say that a person applying for this number with a driving permit, residency permit, or other official appearing document from some country that does not generate a lot of activity for the Social Security Administration (I don't know, be creative here: Ethiopia, some small Russian state, Finland, Bolivia, etc.) may be recognized as genuine and a real SSN will be issued to the bearer.

Believe me, this has happened more than once. Of course, it helps if one speaks some form of Russian when arriving from a Russian country...

I should point out that because some of the things covered above, the Social Security Administration recommends that you request a copy of your file from them every few years to make sure that your records are correct (your income and "contributions" are being recorded for you, and no one else's are). As a result of a recent court case, the SSA has agreed to accept corrections of errors when there isn't any contradictory evidence, SSA has records for the year before or after the error, and the claimed earnings are consistent with earlier and later wages. Call the Social Security Administration at (800) 772-1213 and ask for From 7004, (Request for Earnings and Benefit Estimate Statement.) The forms are available online on the SSA's website www.ssa.gov. You can also pick up a copy at any SSA office.

How to Verify Social Security Numbers and Earnings – A Trick

Correct names and Social Security numbers (SSN) on W-2 wage reports are the keys to successful processing of your annual wage report submission. Not only can you be subject to penalties when employee names and SSNs don't match our records, but also unmatched wage reports can cause additional processing costs for you, and earnings that are not posted to your employees' records. Social Security offers employers two convenient methods for verifying employee SSNs. All methods are free:

To verify up to 5 names/SSNs – Just call our toll-free number for employers – 1-800-772-6270 – weekdays from 7:00 a.m. to 7:00 p.m. EST. You'll need the following information to verify each name/SSN: (1) SSN (2) last name (3) first name (4) middle initial (if applicable) (5) date of birth, and (6) sex.

To verify up to 50 names/SSNs – Submit a paper listing containing the data listed above to your local Social Security Office. Some offices accept faxed listings. To find the office nearest you, check your local phone book or visit SSA's Internet Home Page at www.ssa.gov.

To verify over 50 names/SSNs – A simple registration process is required for requests of more than 50 names/SSNs or requests submitted on magnetic media (regardless of how many items you want verified). Just follow the instructions in the registration package.

Enumeration Verification Service (EVS)

Social Security Number Allocations – Knowing what Social Security Numbers have been allocated will help you determine if a SSN is valid. We have two guides that will help you make this determination:

Social Security Number Allocations – How SSNs are assigned and a list of number areas by State. *

High Group List – This list shows the SSN area and group numbers that are in the process of being issued and are updated monthly.

The Social Security Administration recommends that you request a copy of your file from them every few years to make sure that your records are correct (your income and "contributions" are being recorded for you, and no one else's are.) As a result of a recent court case, the SSA has agreed to accept corrections of errors when there isn't any contradictory evidence, SSA has records for the year before or after the error, and the claimed earnings are consistent with earlier and later wages. Call the Social Security Administration at (800) 772-1213 and ask for Form 7004 (Request for Earnings and Benefit Estimate Statement.) The forms are available online on the SSA's website. You can also pick up a copy at any office of the SSA.

*This is a great, and one might add, free method to upgrade the listings I have provided in this book.

Social Security General Information and Significant Points

In 1982, SSA introduced a new system called District Office Direct Input (DODI), which allows the SSA field offices to input SSN application data via a telecommunications system. DODI was developed as a faster way to process requests for original and replacement SSN cards. Usually, SSN cards are delivered to applicants within 10 days.

Counterfeit-Resistant Card

The 1983 Social Security Amendments required SSA to begin issuing "counterfeit-resistant" Social Security cards by October 31, 1983. Accordingly, on that date, SSA began issuing new and replacement Social Security cards on special counterfeit-resistant banknote paper.

The new SSN card appears quite different from the prior card issued, although the same size. The front of the entire form (card and stub) has a marbleized light blue tint with the words "Social Security" in white. The entire form contains small multicolored discs. Offset and intaglic printing are used, and the card is issued on banknote paper. All of the cards are issued from Social Security Headquarters in Baltimore, and the card stock is kept securely in one location.

The new cards appear very different from those issued previously and contain many altering considerably more difficult. However, cards issued before October 31, 1983 remain valid.

The above is important as one can produce an older, easier to fake card if one appears to be of the appropriate age BUT not after the pertinent dates.

Fundamentals – Summary

In summary, the Social Security number is commonly referred to as the "SSN." The Social Security card is frequently referred to as the "SSN card." The SSN only identifies a particular record, and the SSN card indicates the name of a person whose record is identified by that SSN.

Pocketbook Numbers

SSN 078-05-1120 was the first of many numbers now referred to as "pocketbook" numbers. If first appeared on a sample SSN card contained in wallets sold nationwide in 1938 Many people who purchased the wallets assumed the number to be their own personal SSN. Since then, it has been reported thousands of times on employers' reports of wages, and many times on taxpayer returns.

There are now over 20 different "pocketbook" SSN's, each caused by some organization displaying an actual number in its advertising. The following are the most common "pocketbook" SSN's;

022-28-1852	141-18-6941	212-09-7694
042-10-3580	165-16-7999	219-09-9999
062-36-0749	165-18-7999	306-30-2348
078-05-1120	165-20-7999	308-12-5070
095-07-3645	165-22-7999	468-28-8779
128-03-6045	165-24-7999	549-24-1889
135-01-6629	189-02-2294	987-65-4320

Authorized Uses Of The SSN

Program Uses:

The SSN card was never intended to be an identification document. As noted above, the SSN identifies a particular record only, and the SSN card indicates the person whose record is identified by that number. SSA intended that the SSN be used for record keeping purposes in SSA program-related matters only, i.e., to:

- Control the record of all earnings an individual has in covered employment or self-employment
- Control the claim when someone applies for a benefit under one of SCI's programs
- Control records of monthly benefits and Medicare and Medicaid claims
- Enforce certain other aspects of the Social Security law

Non-program Uses:

Although the SSN and the SSN card were originally intended for SSA program purposes, their use has increased greatly over the years. Some non-program uses are:

State Unemployment Insurance Agencies

The SSN is used by State unemployment insurance agencies in their numerical identifications system for the State unemployment insurance program.

Office of Personnel Management (OPM)

Executive Order 9397, issued on November 30, 1943 and still in effect, provided authority for use of the SSN by the Civil Service Commission (CSC), forerunner of the OPM, to identify records kept on civil service employees. The Order requires any Federal agency establishing a new system of permanent numbers for employee record purposes to use the SSN. In November 1961, the CSC registration program got underway as an adjunct to the IRS taxpayer identification program. In June 1965, the CSC began to add SSN's to the retirement records of their annuitants.

Internal Revenue Service (IRS)

Public law 87-397, enacted on October 5, 1961, required each taxpayer to furnish an identifying number for tax reporting purposes. The IRS, after discussions with SSA, reached a decision to use the SSN for taxpayer identification purposes.

School Data Processing Systems

The rapid development of electronic data processing capability brought with it requests from schools, colleges, and universities for permission to use the SSN in numbering systems. These systems were to be used to trace the progress of pupils throughout their school lives across district, county, and State lines. (E.g. for transcript purposes). Many school systems wanted to assign SSN's beginning with kindergarten or the first grade.

In a decision dated April 16, 1964, the Commissioner of Social Security approved the assignment of SSN's to pupils in the ninth grade and above if the school requested such issuance and indicated a willingness to cooperate in the effort. (Students and parents are given the opportunity to decline such enumeration).

Department of Defense

By memo dated January 30, 1967, the Department of Defense advised SSA of a decision to use the SSN in place of the military service number.

Veterans Administration (VA)

Effective January 1, 1966, the VA began using the SSN as a hospital admission number and for other record keeping purposes.

Indian Health Service

On April 7, 1966, the Commissioner of Social Security approved the use of the SSN by the Division of Indian Health of Public Health Service as a means of identifying and keeping records of Indians in its beneficiary population.

Parent Locator Service

The Parent Locator Service (PLS) was established by the Social Security Amendment of 1974 The functions of the PLS may require the disclosure of limited information (such as the whereabouts) contained in Social Security records.

Aid To Families With Dependent Children

Effective August 1,1975, supplying one's SSN became a condition of eligibility for title IV-A (Aid to Families with Dependent Children) benefits under the Social Security Act.

Food Stamp Program

A SSN must also be furnished for certain household members as a condition of eligibility for food stamps. (P. L. 96-58, Section 4).

State Governments

State governments are authorized by Section 205 (c) (2) (C) of the Social Security Act to use the SSN as an identifier for any tax, public assistance, and drivers license or vehicle registration programs under their jurisdictions.

All violations of section 208 of the Social Security Act committed after December 29, 1981, are felonies with penalties of up to $5,000 fine, up to 5 years in jail, or both.(Prior to that date such violations were classes as misdemeanors and carried lesser penalties.)

An interesting test of the "one must give one's SS Number in order to get a drivers license" recently took place in Los Angeles where 5 sheriff's deputies refused to provide their SS number for "religious reasons."

Lower court threw it out, waiting for appellate decision.

Still, an interesting idea...

Text of Social Security Act Penalty Provisions

The full text of sections 208 (f), (g), and (h) of the Social Security Act is as follows:

"Whoever –

(f) willfully, knowingly, and with intent to deceive the Secretary as to his true identity (or the true identity of any other person) furnishes or causes to be furnished false information to the Secretary with respect to any information required by the Secretary in connection with the establishment and maintenance of the records provided for in sections 205 (c) or (2); or

(g) for the purpose of causing an increase in any payment authorized under this title (or any other program financed in whole or in part from Federal funds), or for the purpose of causing a payment under this title (or any such other program) to be made when no payment is authorized thereunder, or for the purpose of obtaining (for himself or any other person) any payment or any other benefit to which he (or such other person) is not entitled, or for the purpose of obtaining anything of value from any person, or for any other purpose –

willfully, knowingly, and with intent to deceive, uses a Social Security account number assigned by the Secretary (in the exercise of his authority under section 205 (c) (2) to establish land maintain records on the basis of false information furnished to the Secretary by him or by any other person; or

with intent to deceive, falsely represents a number to be the Social Security account number assigned by the Secretary to him or to another person, when in fact such number is not the Social Security account number assigned by the Secretary to him or to such other person; or

knowingly alters a Social Security card issued by the Secretary, buys or sells a card that is, or purports to be, a card so issued, counterfeits a Social Security card, or possesses a Social Security card or counterfeit Social Security card with intent to sell or alter it or;

(g) discloses, uses, or compels the disclosure of the Social Security number of any person in violation of the laws of the United States; shall be guilty of a felony and conviction thereof shall be fined not more than $5,000 or imprisoned for not more than five years, or both."

False Identification Crime Control Act of 1982

The False Identification Crime Control Act of 1982 added a new section to Title 18 of the U.S. Code: Section 1028, Fraud and Related Activity in Connection with Identification Documents. This law became effective December 31, 1982 It provides a penalty of not more than $25,000, or not more than five years in jail, or both, for certain acts involving the production, transfer or possession of false or stolen identification documents.

While many Social Security cards bear the legend "not for identification purposes," the statute nevertheless appears applicable in cases involving their use, since the term "identification document" commonly includes documents accepted (as the SSN card is) for purposes of identification of individuals.

The Act also amended Title 18 of the U.S. Code by adding section 1738, Mailing Private Identification Documents Without a Disclaimer, which provides a penalty of not more than $1,000, or not more than one year in jail, or both.

Types of SSN Fraud

SSN fraud occurs under an extremely wide variety of circumstances, a few of which are noted below.

- Using multiple false SSN's to receive various types of benefits under fictitious Identities
- Using another person's name and SSN to cash U.S. government bonds illegally
- Obtaining an SSN under false pretenses
- Selling false SSN cards as part of fake identification packages, in connection with illegal immigration and other schemes
- Presenting fraudulent evidence to obtain SSN
- Making, possessing, buying, or selling counterfeit SSN cards
- Using another person's name and SSN to receive benefits on that person's record
- Using fraudulent SSN's to set up fictitious credit histories and to apply for bank loans
- Working under an incorrect SSN to conceal income while receiving disability insurance benefits, retirement insurance benefits, supplemental security income, or welfare payments
- Using a false SSN to conceal receipt of Veterans Administration payments
- Using bogus SSN's to file fraudulent requests for tax refunds (multiple-filer scheme)

- Using bogus SSN's to obtain a "circuit-breaker" refund under a State program which helps low-income elderly and disabled retain private housing
- Using bogus SSN's to illegally obtain food stamps
- Using false SSN's and false identities to apply for unemployment compensation
- Using false SSN's to obtain Federal Workers' Compensation payments
- Using fraudulent SSN's to obtain Federally guaranteed student loans
- As previously stated, other types of violations, e.g., bribery and conspiracy, sometimes occur along with the SSN fraud.

How SSN's Are Fraudulently Obtained

The SSN and the SSN card are often used in criminal schemes involving fraudulent identity. Usually, the SSN card is one part of a large packet of false identification documents used in such schemes.

Otherwise valid SSN's and SSN cards are fraudulently obtained through means which include:

- Using false documents and making false statements when applying for an SSN
- Buying, borrowing, or stealing another person's SSN card
- Bribing an SSA employee to cause issuance of a valid SSN card, or to obtain a valid SSN card stock

Counterfeit SSN cards are also used in connection with various false identity crimes. The counterfeit cards may bear real or fictitious names and SSN's.

Detection of SSN Violations

Detection of SSN fraud occurs in many different ways. Such cases are discovered;

By OIG, through its conduct of special investigations and projects relative to the integrity of the SSN process.

By other law enforcement agencies in the course of investigations and arrests in connection with crimes under their jurisdiction. These include:

- Immigration and Naturalization Service – Immigration violations
- Border Patrol – Immigration violations
- Postal Inspection Service – Mail frauds.

What Your Government Is Doing About The Social Security Card

New Counterfeit-Resistant SSN Card:

On October 31,1983, the SSA began issuing new, more counterfeit-resistant SSN cards. A provision in the 1983 Social Security Amendments requires that new and replacement cards be made of banknote paper and, to the maximum extent practicable, no non-counterfeitable.

Fraud Awareness:

SSA has trained the Social Security filed employees who take SSN applications to recognize counterfeit or altered immigration documents and other documents indicating age or citizenship. Employees are encouraged to report suspected violations to OIG.

Electronic Process to Issue SSN's:

SSA tightened controls and reviews of SSN applications through the implementation of a new electronic process which speeds the issuance of SSN's by transmitting the application data by wire directly from the local Social Security office to the central processing system. This new process, called District Office Direct Input (DODI), reduced the possibility of obtaining cards fraudulently by increasing the difficulty of bypassing any part of the issuance process.

Removal of Blank SSN Card Stock from Field Offices:

The new electronic SSN issuance system (DODI) also allowed SSA to remove all blank SSN card stock from field offices where it could be lost or stolen more easily. The entire supply is now kept in one central, secure location.

Deletion of SSN from SSN Card Stub:

SSA stopped printing the SSN on the tear-off stub of SSN cards. The stubs of other individuals' SSN cards were being fraudulently used by some people to get a job or establish a false identity.

Recent Security Programs Affecting the SSN

Project Clean Data:

Two computer programs called "Project Clean Data" have been designed to help State and Federal agencies identify either incorrect or fraudulent SSN's. One program identifies SSN's that have not been issued; the second program detects SSN's being used fraudulently.

The programs have been distributed to more than 60 agencies in 40 States and to several Federal agencies. Many States reported using the program to identity thousands of incorrect SSN's in their data files. SSN's being used fraudulently also have been identified.

Project Baltimore:

This ongoing project began in 1978 It is a joint investigative effort by the OIG, INS, and SSA focusing on criminal conspiracies to obtain SSN's for illegal aliens.

Many conspiracies have been identified, and criminal convictions obtained relative to crimes such as bribery; mail fraud; visa fraud; the concealment, harboring or shielding of illegal aliens; submission of false INS documents; and forgery of official seals.

The project also has led to deportation proceedings against hundreds of illegal aliens.

Project SSAMANS:

OIG and the FBI are cooperating in a project to investigate suspected widespread fraud involving Social Security and other benefits and assistance fraud in New York Project SSAMANS (SSA Multiple Account Numbers) involves examining thousands of records bearing SSN's which are suspected for a variety of reasons. Cases which appear to involve fraud are shared with State and local agencies for matching against their beneficiary rolls and any necessary investigation and prosecution.

AFDC Benefits Project – Verification Of The Accuracy Of SSN's:

The AFDC Benefits Project was established by OIG to assist State and local agencies in the detection and prosecution of fraud against Federal/State income maintenance and benefit programs. State and local agencies may obtain information concerning:

- The accuracy of SSN's provided by applicants for benefits
- Eligibility for and payment of benefits under Title II and Title XVI of the Social Security Act
- The issuance of Title II and Title XVI benefit checks by the Treasury Department

Specially Annotated SSN Cards:

In May 1982, SSA began annotating the face of SSN cards issued to legal aliens who are not authorized to work in this country, with the prominent legend "Not Valid For Employment." This is to advise employers that individuals presenting such SSN cards are not authorized to work in this country.

The AFDC Benefits Project will provide information from SCI's records to verify whether the SSN provided by an application for State or local income maintenance or medical assistance benefits if the number issued to that individual. The requesting agency will be notified that the name and number provided do or do not match with SCI's records. The Project cannot operate to provide a name to match a number, nor a number to match a name. The requester must provide both the name and SSN which are to be verified.

Project Map:

Under this project, a search is conducted of SSN mailing address information to identify and list addresses which receive ten or more SSN cards during a specific period. The address listings are forwarded to OIG field offices for review and possible use as investigative leads. The review helps identify suspected ineligible beneficiaries or organized illegal schemes.

Nothing under federal law says you must give a private company your Social Security number, you can not be prosecuted for not providing it. Now as far as being prosecuted for providing another number, that's a gray area. If it's simply a mistake, and maybe your hand just slipped, nobody can say that you were purposefully appropriating somebody else's Social Security number to get a benefit. That's a practical matter. Very few people have ever been prosecuted for the fact that they got insurance but used a different Social Security number to get it.

The following article is reproduced with permission from a very good privacy advocate and writer –

What To Do When They Ask For Your Social Security Number

By Chris Hibbert: Computer Professionals for Social Responsibility.
(Used with his permission.)

Many people are concerned about the number of organizations asking for their Social Security Numbers. They worry about invasions of privacy and the oppressive feeling of being treated as just a number. unfortunately can't offer any hope about the dehumanizing effects of identifying you with your numbers. I can try to help you keep your Social Security Number from being used as a tool in the invasion of your privacy. The advice in this FAQ deals primarily with the Social Security Number used in the U.S., though the privacy considerations are equally applicable in many other countries. The laws explained here are U.S. laws. The advice about dealing with bureaucrats and clerks is universal.

The Privacy Act of 1974 (Pub. L. 93-579, in section 7), which is the primary law affecting the use of SSN's, requires that any Federal, State, or Local government agency that requests your Social Security Number has to tell you four things:

- Whether disclosure of your Social Security number is required or optional
- What statute or other authority they have for asking for your number
- How you're Social Security number will be used if you give it to them
- The consequences of failure to provide a SSN

In addition, the Act says that only Federal law can make use of the Social Security number mandatory (at 5 USC 552a note). So anytime you're dealing with a government institution, and you're asked for your Social Security number, look for the Privacy Act Statement.

If there isn't one, complain and don't give your number. If the statement is present, read it. Once you've read the explanation of whether the number is optional or required, and the consequences of refusing to give your number, you'll be able to decide for yourself whether to fill in the number.

There are several kinds of governmental organizations (see the list in the "Short History" section below) that usually have authority to request your number, but they are all required to provide the Privacy Act Statement described above. The only time you should be willing to give your number without reading that notice is when the organization you are dealing with is not a part of the government.

Why You May Want To Resist Requests For Your SSN

When you give out your number, you are providing access to information about yourself. You're providing access to information that you don't have the ability or the legal right to correct or rebut.

You provide access to data that are irrelevant to most transactions but that will occasionally trigger prejudice. Worst of all, since you provided the key (and did so "voluntarily"), all the info discovered under your number will be presumed to be true, about you, and relevant. A major problem with the use of SSN's as identifiers is that it makes it hard to control access to personal information.

Even assuming you want someone to be able to find out some things about you, there's no reason to believe that you want to make all records concerning yourself available. When multiple record systems are all keyed by the same identifier, and all are intended to be easily accessible to some users, it becomes difficult to allow someone access to some of the information about a person while restricting them to specific topics.

Unfortunately, far too many organizations assume that anyone who presents your SSN must be you. When more than one person uses the same number, it clouds up the records. If someone intended to hide their activities, it's likely that it'll look bad on whichever record it shows up on.

When it happens accidentally, it can be unexpected, embarrassing, or worse.

What You Can Do to Protect Your Number

It's not a good idea to carry your SSN card with you (or other documents that contain your SSN). If you should lose your wallet or purse, your SSN would make it easier for a thief to apply for credit in your name or otherwise, fraudulently use your number. Some states that normally use SSN's as the drivers license number will give you a different number if you ask.

If your health insurance plan uses your SSN for an ID number, it's probably on your insurance card. If you are unable to get the insurance plan to change your number, you may want to photocopy your card with your SSN covered and carry the copy. You can then give a health care provider your number separately. Here are some suggestions for negotiating with people who don't want to give you what you want.

They work whether the problem has to do with SSN's (your number is added to a database without your consent, someone refuses to give you service without getting your number, etc.) or is any other problem with a clerk or bureaucrat who doesn't want to do things any way other than what works for 99% of the people they see.

Start by politely, explaining your position and expecting them to understand and cooperate. If that doesn't work, there are several more things to try:

- Talk to people higher up in the organization. This often works simply because the organization has a standard way of dealing with requests not to use the SSN, and the first person you deal with just hasn't been around long enough to know what it is

- Enlist the aid of your employer. You have to decide whether talking to someone in personnel, and possibly trying to change corporate policy is going to get back to your supervisor and affect your job. The people in the personnel and benefits departments often carry a lot of weight when dealing with health insurance companies

- Threaten to complain to a consumer affair bureau Most newspapers can get a quick response. Ask for their "Action Line" or the equivalent. If you're dealing with a local government agency, look in the state or local government section of the phone book under "consumer affairs"

- Insist that they document a corporate policy requiring the number. When someone can't find a written policy or doesn't want to push hard enough to get it, they'll often realize that they don't know what the policy is, and they've just been following tradition

- Ask what they need it for and suggest alternatives. If you're talking to someone who has some independence, and they'd like to help, they will sometimes admit that they know the reason the company wants it, and you can satisfy that requirement a different way

- Tell them you'll take your business elsewhere (and follow through if they don't cooperate)

If it's a case where you've gotten service already, but someone insists that you have to provide your number in order to have a continuing relationship, you can choose to ignore the request in hopes that they'll forget or find another solution before you get tired of the interruption.

How to Find Out If Someone Is Using Your Number

There are two good places to look to find out if someone else is using your number: the Social Security Administration's (SSA) database, and your credit report. If anyone else used your number when applying for a job, their earnings will appear under your name in the SSA's files.

If someone uses your SSN (or name and address) to apply for credit, it will show up in the files of the big three credit reporting agencies. The Social Security Administration recommends that you request a copy of your file from them every few years to make sure that your records are correct (your income and "contributions" are being recorded for you, and no one else's are.) As a result of a recent court case, the SSA has agreed to accept corrections of errors when there isn't any contradictory evidence, SSA has records for the year before or after the error, and the claimed earnings are consistent with earlier and later wages.

Call the Social Security Administration and ask for Form 7004 (Request for Earnings and Benefit Estimate Statement.) The forms are available online at the SSA's website: http://www.ssa.gov/online/forms.html. One can also pick up a copy at any office of the SSA.

Choosing A Key For New Databases

Most organizations that have studied the issue have concluded that a simple combination of Name, Address, and Phone number are usually sufficient. In cases where you are likely to be dealing with several members of the same family (and thus, Jr. and Sr. might have matching records), you can add date of birth.

If the database saves an old address and the date of the move that will usually be sufficient to identify particular clients uniquely. If you're designing a database or have an existing one that currently uses SSN's and wants to use numbers other than SSN's, it's useful to have the identifiers use some pattern other than 9 digits.

You can make them longer or shorter than that, or include letters. That way it won't be mistaken for a SSN. Robert Ellis Smith, the publisher of the *Privacy*

Journal, recently asked people to suggest alternatives to the SSN for indexing databases.

Some of the qualities that are (often) useful in a key and that people think they are getting from the SSN are uniqueness, universality, security, and identification. When designing a database, it is instructive to consider which of these qualities are actually important in your application; many designers assume unwisely that they are all useful for every application, when in fact, each is occasionally a drawback. The SSN provides none of them, so designs predicated on the assumption that it does provide them will fail in a variety of ways.

Uniqueness

Many people assume that Social Security numbers are unique. They were intended by the Social Security Administration to be unique, but the SSA didn't take sufficient precautions to ensure that it would be so. They have several times given a previously issued number to someone with the same name and birth date as the original recipient, thinking it was the same person asking again.

There are a few numbers that were used by thousands of people because they were on sample cards shipped in wallets by their manufacturers. The passage of the Immigration reform law in 1986 caused an increase in the duplicate use of SSN's. Since the SSN is now required for employment, illegal immigrants must find a valid name/SSN pair in order to fool the INS and IRS long enough to collect a paycheck.

Using the SSN when you can't cross-check your database with the SSA means you can count on getting some false numbers mixed in with the good ones. Universality not everyone has a Social Security Number. Foreigners are the primary exception (though the SSA will now assign a number to a legal immigrant without connecting that to the authority to work), but many children don't get SSN's until they're in school (and some not until they get jobs).

They were only designed to be able to cover people who were eligible for Social Security. If your database will keep records on organizations as well as individuals, you should realize that they're not covered either.

Identification

Few people ever ask to see a SSN card; they believe whatever you say. The ability to recite nine digits provides little evidence that you're associated with the number in anyone else's database. There's little reason to carry your card with you anyway. It isn't a good form of identification, and if your wallet is lost or stolen, it provides another way for the thief to hurt you.

Security

Older cards are not at all forgery-resistant, even if anyone did ever ask for it. (Recent cards are more resistant to forgery.) The numbers don't have any redundancy (no check-digits) so any 9-digit number in the range of numbers that have been issued is a valid number. It's relatively easy to write down the number incorrectly, and there's no way to tell that you've done so. In most cases, there is no cross-checking that a number is valid.

Credit card and checking account numbers are checked against a database almost every time they are used. If you write down someone's phone number incorrectly, you find out the first time you try to use it. An incorrect SSN might go unnoticed for years in some databases. In others, it will likely be caught at tax time, but could cause a variety of headaches.

Dealing With Government Organizations

Surprisingly enough, government agencies are reasonably easy to deal with; private organizations are much more troublesome. Few agencies are allowed to request the number, and all agencies are required to give a disclosure complete enough that you can find the law that empowers them. There are no comparable Federal laws either restricting the uses non-government organizations can make of the SSN, or compelling them to tell you anything about their plans. Some states have recently enacted regulations on collection of SSN's by private entities. (Usually in cases of consumers making payments with checks or credit cards.) With private institutions, your main recourse is refusing to do business with anyone whose terms you don't like. They, in turn, are allowed to refuse to deal with you on those terms.

Public Schools

Public schools that accept federal funds are subject to the Family Educational Rights and Privacy Act of (It's also known as FERPA or the "Buckley Amendment") which prohibits them from giving out personal information on students without permission.

There is an exception for directory information, which is limited to names, addresses, and phone numbers, and another exception for release of information to the parents of minors. There is no exception for Social Security numbers, so covered Universities aren't allowed to reveal students' numbers without their permission. In addition, state universities are bound by the requirements of the Privacy Act (so they have to give a Privacy Act notice if they ask for a SSN).

If they make uses of the SSN which aren't covered by the disclosure, they are in violation. The National Coalition of Advocates for Students (100 Boylston Street, Suite 737, Boston, MA 02116, 617-357-8507) has some literature on what information a school can ask you for based on a Supreme Court decision [Plyler v. Doe 457 U.S. 202 (1982)] that held that requiring SSN's from all students would discriminate illegally against undocumented students.

Even if you are a citizen, this ruling prevents schools from requiring your Social Security number.

U.S. Passports

Some forms for applying for U.S. Passports (DSP-11 12/87) request a Social Security Number, but don't give enough information in their Privacy Act notice to verify that the Passport office has the authority to request it. There is a reference to "Federal Tax Law" and a misquotation of Section 6039E of the 1986 Internal Revenue Code, claiming that that section requires that you provide your name, mailing address, date of birth, and Social Security Number.

The referenced section only requires TIN (SSN), and it only requires that it be sent to the IRS (not to the Passport office). It appears that when you apply for a passport, you can refuse to reveal your SSN to the passport office, and instead mail a notice to the IRS, give only your SSN (other identifying info optional) and notify them that you are applying for a passport.

The latest passport application asks for a SSN, but states that failure to provide it isn't grounds to deny a passport. It warns that the SSN is used to verify the other information on the form, and processing of the application may be delayed if the number is not provided.

However, I have also found a different notice that implies (in a same roundabout way) that the SSN is required by the above mentioned laws, and says passports will be refused if the number is not included.

Requirement for Disclosing Employee's Children's SSN's Repealed The Omnibus Budget Reconciliation Act of 1993 required all employers to collect Social Security numbers for everyone covered by their health plans, including all dependents. After not being pursued actively by the government for a few years, legislation (PL 104-226) was passed in October, 1996 repealing the Medicare and Medicaid Coverage Data Bank. Children The Family Support Act of 1988 (Pub. L. 100-485) requires states to require parents to give their Social Security Numbers in order to get a birth certificate issued for a newborn.

The law allows the requirement to be waived for "good cause," but there's no indication of what may qualify. Section 1615 of the Small Business Job Protection Act of 1996 strengthened the requirement for taxpayers to report SSN's for dependents over one year of age when they are claimed as a deduction. (H.R. 3448, became PL104-188 8/20/96).

The new law allows the IRS to treat listing a dependent without including a SSN as if it were an arithmetic error. This apparently means that the taxpayer isn't allowed to petition the tax court.

Private Organizations

The guidelines for dealing with non-governmental institutions are much more tenuous than those for government departments. Most of the time private organizations that request your Social Security Number can get by quite well without your number, and if you can find the right person to negotiate with, they'll willingly admit it.

The problem is finding that right person. The person behind the counter is often told no more than "get the customers to fill out the form completely. " Most of the time, you can convince them to use some other number.

Usually the simplest way to refuse to give your Social Security number is simply to leave the appropriate space blank. One of the times when this isn't a strong enough statement of your desire to conceal your number is when dealing with institutions which have direct contact with your employer. Most employers have no policy against revealing your Social Security Number; they apparently believe that it must be an unintentional slip when an employee doesn't provide a SSN to everyone who asks.

Employers

Employers are required by the IRS to get the SSN's of people they hire. They often ask for it during the interview process, but there are good reasons to refuse if you can afford to argue with the potential employer. Some of them use the SSN to check credit records, to look for criminal history, and otherwise, to delve into your past in areas you might object to.

Tell them you'll give them your SSN when you accept their offer. They have no legitimate use for it before then. At one point I needed a security badge from a company that wasn't my employer (my employer was contracting to the host.)

The host company used SSN's to do background checks on applicants for security badges. I asked if there was a way I could keep my SSN out of their database, and we worked things out so I gave my number directly to the person who ran the background check, and he used it for that and then destroyed it.

I may have been the only person working at this very large company who didn't have a SSN on file.

Utilities Public

Utilities (gas, electric, phone, etc.) are considered to be private organizations under the laws regulating SSN's. Most of the time they ask for a SSN, and aren't prohibited from asking for it, but they will usually relent if you insist.

Most banks will refuse to open safe deposit boxes without a SSN, though there is no direct governmental requirement that they collect it. One correspondent reported that he was able to open a non-interest bearing account at a U.S. bank by presenting a passport and international drivers license.

Many banks, brokerages, and other financial institutions have started implementing automated systems to let you check your balance. All too often, they are using SSN's as the PIN that lets you get access to your personal account information If your bank does this, write them a letter pointing out how common it is for the people with whom you have financial business to know your SSN. Ask them to change your PIN, and if you feel like doing a good deed, ask them to stop using the SSN as a default identifier for their other customers. Some customers will believe that there's some security in it and be insufficiently protective of their account numbers. Nearly every financial institution I have asked has been willing to use a password I supplied.

I don't know why they don't advertise this rather than relying on the SSN. Sometimes banks provide for a customer-supplied password, but are reluctant to advertise it. The only way to find out is to ask whether they'll let you provide a password. (This is true of Citibank Visa, for instance. They ask for a phone number but are willing to accept any password.)

When buying (or refinancing) a house, you have to give your SSN, because the bank is required to report the interest you pay. Most banks will now ask for your Social Security number on the Deed of Trust. This is because the Federal National Mortgage Association wants it. The fine print in their regulation admits that some consumers won't want to give their number, and allows banks to leave it out when pressed. (It first recommends getting it on the loan note, but then admits that it's already on various other forms that are a required part of the package, so they already know it).

The Deed is a public document, so there are good reasons to refuse to put it there, especially since all parties to the agreement already have access to your numbers.

Insurers, hospitals, doctors: no laws require private medical service providers to use your Social Security number as an ID number.

They often use it because it's convenient or because your employer uses it to identify employees to its group's health plan. In the latter case, you have to get your employer to make an exception to their standard practices. Often, the people who work in personnel assume that the employer or insurance company requires use of the SSN when that's not really the case.

When a previous employer asked for my SSN for an insurance form, I asked them to find out if they had to use it. After a week they reported that the insurance company had gone along with my request and told me what number to use. Insurance companies often require the SSN for underwriting purposes, but don't usually use it for underwriting personal property or personal auto insurance policies. You may be able to get them to leave the number out of their data base, even if they want to use it when deciding whether to cover you.
They may call every few years to ask for it again. Insurance companies share information with one another that they have collected while evaluating applications for life, health, or disability insurance. They do this by sending the information to an organization called the Medical Information Bureau (MIB). The information they share includes test results and brief descriptions of conditions

relevant to health or longevity. MIB rules prohibit the reporting of claims information.

If an insurance agent asks for your Social Security number in order to "check your credit," point out that the contract is invalid if your check bounces or your payment is late. Insurance is always prepaid, so they don't need to know what your credit is like, just whether your check cleared.

Blood Banks

Blood banks also ask for the number but are willing to do without if pressed on the issue. After I asked politely and persistently, the (non-Red Cross) blood bank I go to agreed that they didn't have any use for the number. They've now expunged my SSN from their database, and they seem to have taught their receptionists not to request the number. I've gotten one report that some branches of the Red Cross will issue a "file number" in lieu of your SSN if you insist.

It's probably the case that not all branches (and especially not all receptionists) know about this possibility, so it will pay to be persistent. Blood banks have changed their policies back and forth a few times in the last several years. When the AIDS epidemic first hit, they started using SSN's to identify all donors, so someone who was identified as HIV-positive at one blood bank wouldn't be able to contaminate the blood supply by donating at a different site.

For a few years, they were a little more loose, and though they usually asked for SSN's, some would allow you to donate if you provided proof of your identity. (I showed a drivers license, but didn't let them copy down the number).

Now the Federal Government has declared blood banks to be "manufacturers" of a medical product, and imposed various Quality Control processes on them. The Blood bank I go to now ask for SSN's, and if you refuse, allows you to give a Drivers license number. I balked at that, since I hadn't had to give it before. They let me donate, but while I was eating cookies, the director of Quality Control came down and talked to me. After a little bit of discussion, she was satisfied to have me pick an ID number that I promised to remember and provide when I visited again.

So, once again, if you want to protect your SSN and your privacy, it pays to push back when they ask.

Landlords

Landlords often request SSN's from prospective tenants. There are two things they usually want it for: a credit check, and in some parts of the country, landlords apparently have access to a database of "bad tenants" as reported by other landlords.

There don't seem to be any laws restricting the use of these kinds of databases, which leaves renters in a precarious situation If a landlord makes a mistake, or a prior tenant gave an incorrect number, the prospective tenant may be unable to find out why no landlord will rent to him or her. The applicant can refuse to supply the number, but in a seller's market, the landlord often has many other applicants to choose from.

There aren't many avenues of recourse, except to politely inquire if the landlord will accept a letter of reference from a previous landlord or if there are other ways that you can demonstrate your creditworthiness.

The tenant is almost powerless if the landlord doesn't want to go along.

Using A False Social Security Number

If someone absolutely insists on getting your Social Security number, you may want to give a fake number.

I have never needed to give a fake number; at least one of the remedies described above has always worked for me. There are legal penalties for providing a false number when you expect to gain some benefit from it. For example, a federal court of appeals ruled that using a false SSN to get a Drivers license violates federal law. Making a 9-digit number up at random is a bad idea, as it may coincide with someone's real number and cause them some amount of grief.

It's better to use a number like 078-05-1120, which was printed on "sample" cards inserted in thousands of new wallets sold in the 40's and 50's. It's been used so widely that both the IRS and SSA recognize it immediately as bogus, while most clerks haven't heard of it.

There were at least 40 different people in the Selective Service database at one point who gave this number as their SSN.

The Social Security Administration recommends that people showing Social Security cards in advertisements use numbers in the range 987-65-4320 through 987-65-4329. There are several patterns that have never been assigned, and which therefore don't conflict with anyone's real number.

They include numbers with any field all zeroes, and numbers with a first digit of 8 or 9. For more details on the structure of SSN's and how they are assigned. Giving a number with an unused pattern rather than your own number isn't very useful if there's anything serious at stake since it's likely to be noticed.

Collecting SSN's Yourself

There aren't any federal laws that explicitly forbid the collection of SSN's. However, there is a body of law, intended to prohibit the misuse of credit cards that are written vaguely enough that it could be interpreted to cover personal collections of SSN's.

The laws are at 18 USC 1029, and cover what is called "access device fraud." An access device is "any card, plate, code, account number or other means of access that can be used, alone or in conjunction with another access device, to obtain money, goods, services, or any other thing of value, or that can be used to initiate a transfer of value." The law forbids the possession, "knowingly and with intent to defraud" of fifteen or more devices which are counterfeit or unauthorized access devices." If interstate commerce is involved, penalties are up to $10,000 and 10 years in prison.

Secrets of the Social Security Card Itself

The first SSA cards issued were unique in a way, beneficial, to anyone seriously considering the use of more than one card.

Two common methods of obtaining a false Social Security card exist: one involves doctoring an existing card, while the other the other consists in securing an actual, valid new card through fraudulent means.

Series one cards were printed on thin cardboard which contained none of the modern anti-forgery safe guards we have come to know and love; no magnetic ink, no special paper, no threads and no security strips. In fact, pretty much the only security device built in series one cards, was the fact they were printed in a special color known as NON-PHOTO BLUE.

NPB is\was a color specifically designed to go unseen by printing cameras. This attribute allowed printers, layout artists and makeup people to make notations and positioning marks directly on a book, magazine, or anything else that was to be printed for their own reference. When the printing camera "shot" the material prior to printing it, the NPB markings would simply disappear. Thus, printing the cards themselves in this hue provided a first step against mass counterfeiting.

Today's print cameras, not to mention scanners, see NPB quite well, thank you. Modern printers are not overly fond of layout artists who mark up copy with NPB marks as they will have to attempt to adjust the sensitivity of their camera to avoid the markings coming out as if they were written in black.

It is now possible to take a series one card; whiteout the name and number and reprint it on thin cardboard stock in non-photo blue.

A quick note (well, two quick notes); the first one is that this is probably illegal and I do not advise you to do it; secondly the numbers on the early cards were normally typed with a Selectric typewriter.

The success of this method can be further ensured by laminating the card, which will help hide any defects. Laminating was very common on older cards, since their card stock composition did not hold up very well; as a result, a laminated older-issue card will not raise any suspicions. (Note: newer-issue Social Security cards contain design features that make this method of forgery much more difficult).

Keep in mind that the creation of an older issue fraudulent card would only work for an adult of at least 25 years of age, since the Social Security Administration switched to a new design in the 1970s.

In 1983 the government, apparently tired of the influx of phony SS cards, mandated the SSA to begin new counterfeit-resistant replacements. The new cards have a number of built-in features making them far more difficult to successfully imitate.

The SSA also changed the method of application submission and implementation by employing an electronic only process which not only speeds up the issuance of a new SSN by transmitting the data via modem directly from the local office to the central processing system, and also reduces any chance of obtaining a fraudulent card. The Administration also removed all blank SSN card stock from their field offices where one could be "misplaced" and now stores it in a secured, guarded, central location.

The second method of procuring a false Social Security card involves a great deal of prep work, on the one hand; but if it succeeds, it also leads to an almost foolproof form of ID. This method requires the person seeking a Social Security card to obtain or create a fraudulent birth certificate.

Once a certified birth certificate has been obtained, the bearer uses this document to obtain a form of primary ID such as a drivers license. With this primary ID in hand, obtaining an actual government-issued Social Security card complete with valid SSN is only a matter of filling out a simple form.

A loophole in the application process even makes the intermediate step of obtaining a primary ID unnecessary. For persons under 18 years of age, the Social Security card can be applied for by mail. As long as the appropriate document (i.e., copy of certified birth certificate) accompanies the application, no primary form of ID is necessary. Since the Social Security card contains no other information than the name and SSN of the bearer, it is feasible that a person of any age could apply for a card using this method. However, since the possibility of cross-checking exists, this approach is less foolproof than the one just detailed.

As mentioned above, Social Security cards, especially older ones, are extremely easy to counterfeit. If someone takes the time to carefully doctor an existing card especially, if they go to the relatively easy step of laminating it, it is very difficult to determine whether or not the copy is a forgery.

In addition, the use of a falsified birth certificate and, even more so, a primary ID obtained with such a certificate makes it quite simple to obtain a valid Social

Security card. The safeguards against this process are few, and protection against fraud in this area rests in catching the falsified birth document before it is accepted to receive an ID.

How To Obtain A Fraudulent Social Security Card

- Don't bother. Most clerks from the DMV to your local bank simply ask you for your SSN or at worst have you write it down on a form. If you're prepared and can rattle off the nine digits like you own them, you will very, very seldom be questioned

If you are questioned, advise the person that you do not believe in carrying the card with you as it would be subject to loss, theft and it wears the card out and you know the number perfectly well without prompts.

- Find a friendly printer who will print you one or more (it's easier to do them in a sheet) blank series one SS cards on thin cardboard in NPB

- Buy a copy that looks remarkably close to a series two card from a number of sources. This card is usually good enough to pass anything but close government scrutiny

- Have the chuptaz to ignore the format and obtain a completely different card. This is marginally legal, or at least isn't counterfeiting, because the SS is *not* a government issued ID and there is really no law that says you have to carry the original government produced document. One of our examples was purchased from an ID vendor for $5

This particular "card" is pressed into a thin metal with a gold-like coating and includes the American flag is in full color. It has been used numerous times by its owner at banks, stores and even DMV's without incidence. In fact, the typical comment from official clerks has been something to the effect of, "what a nice card, I've never seen one like that before".

> Under section 1029, title 18 of the U.S. Code, it is a criminal offense (punishable by up to 15 years in prison, or a fine, or both) to, among other things, knowingly and with intent to defraud, traffic in or use one or more unauthorized access devices (such as credit cards) during any 1-year period and by such conduct obtain anything of value aggregating $1,000 or more during that period.
>
> Under section 408(a)(7), title 42 of the U.S. Code, a penalty for up to 5 years in prison, or a fine, or both, can result from, among other things, falsely representing – with intent to deceive – a number as the Social Security account number assigned by the Commissioner of Social Security to him or to another person.

The Road Less Taken

Or if you can't baffle 'em with bullshit; bribe 'em

Recently, several employees of the Social Security Administration passed information on more than 11,000 citizens to a credit-card fraud ring, according to federal prosecutors in New York.

That information included Social Security numbers and mothers' maiden names, and allowed the ring to activate cards stolen from the mail and run up huge bills at merchants ranging from J&R Music World to Bergdorf Goodman.

The court papers do not name the Social Security employees who prosecutors said stole the information from the agency. But the documents refer to an unidentified female employee of the Brooklyn office of the agency who pointed investigators to Emanuel Nwogu, a New York City employee who was charged last week with fraud in federal court.

A spokesman for the U.S. attorney in Manhattan said that the investigation is ongoing, and that others are likely to be charged.

The agency is "shocked and disheartened" by the case, a spokesperson said, and will look for ways that its security can be improved.

The case is also part of an increasing number nationwide in which information is stolen from business, medical and government files. While much attention has been paid to hackers who break into electronic databases through high-tech back doors, experts say most computer crime is committed by employees who are authorized to use the systems.

"The human link is the weakest link in any information security program," said Ira Winkler, technical director for the National Computer Security Association. "If you are a clerk making $12,000 or $18,000 a year, and someone offers you a few hundred to a few thousand dollars every so often to look up some specific information, it's a tempting offer."

Are We Really Going To Get a Counterfeit Proof SS Card?

In 1996, under the Illegal Immigration Reform and Immigrant Responsibility Act, the Congress included a mandate requiring SSA to develop a prototype counterfeit-resistant card made of a durable tamper-resistant material with various security features that could be used in establishing reliable proof of citizenship or legal non-citizenship status.

The mandate also required SSA and GAO to estimate and compare the cost of producing and disseminating several types of enhanced cards to all living number holders over 3, 5, and 10-year periods. These estimates were to include an evaluation of the cost of imposing a user fee on those who request a replacement of the enhanced card and enhanced cards requested prior to the time individuals were scheduled to receive them.

Earlier that year, a Member of Congress asked GAO to estimate the cost of issuing a counterfeit-resistant card, believing an earlier SSA estimate of producing such a card was high for work eligibility verification purposes. States renew these documents every few years and already include security features and a photograph.

Also, the states could obtain current citizenship information from SSA for up to 87 million individuals for work authorization purposes. This option would avoid the enormous costs associated with reissuing the current Social Security card but would likely impose a significant burden on the states to make work eligibility determinations for the remaining 190 million individuals.

The government could produce a tamper-proof Social Security card with an individual worker's picture, but it could cost as much as $10 billion and take as long as 10 years to generate new cards for every person, the Social Security Administration said in a recent report.

The study, which comes amid growing concerns over fraudulent use of cards by undocumented workers, represents the most serious examination so far of making Social Security cards more resistant to counterfeiting. Issued in response to a request by Congress in last year's immigration and welfare reforms, the report does not make any recommendations on whether new cards should be issued. An "enhanced" card of this type also "raises policy issues about privacy and the potential for the card to be used as a national identification card," the agency acknowledged in a report to Congress.

About 277 million cards are currently outstanding; most are printed on paper with few security features. The issuance of new cards would be a massive job, particularly with the addition of information on an individual's citizenship status, a picture, or a fingerprint. All these additional features would make it considerably more difficult to obtain cards illegally.

But the production of cards would become more costly, and the card itself could be employed as a national identification document.

Many Americans strongly oppose the concept of a national ID card as "a violation of privacy and a threat to their civil liberties." The total of 277 million cardholders, which exceeds the U.S. population of 268 million, includes cards issued to people who have died but whose deaths have not been reported to Social Security, and cards held by non-citizens who have left the country.

To produce the new cards, the agency would mail at least two pieces of correspondence to each cardholder: a general announcement and then a specific letter asking for documentation about the individual, according to the report. The most secure, and expensive, card considered in the report would include the individual's picture, fingerprint, and complete information on work history and earnings. It would cost almost $10 billion for this approach. A basic plastic card with limited security features, and without an individual photograph, would cost about $3.9 billion.

Congress also asked the Social Security Administration to look into the idea of charging people for their card. Costs to the public would range from $18.70 for a basic plastic card to $37.90 for a card with optical storage, containing information on the worker's earnings, the report said.

As of now, no fee is charged for issuing the cards, and any new fee undoubtedly would stir considerable public opposition. The Social Security Administration has always opposed charging a fee because Social Security is a mandatory program for all workers.

Moreover, a new card would not necessarily enhance public confidence in the Social Security system. Alternatives to the high costs associated with a mass issuance of new cards do, however, exist. These alternatives may provide a more cost-effective approach to handling work eligibility verification, although they may not address all concerns about public confidence in the Social Security system.

One alternative would be to issue a new enhanced Social Security card only to those who need it to verify work eligibility. Bureau of Labor Statistics (BLS) data suggest this approach could involve up to an estimated 118 million individuals - about 43 percent of the 277 million current number holders.

This option would help maximize control over illegal workers while significantly reducing SSA's costs. However, many additional individuals may choose to apply for such a card instead of waiting until they seek employment or change jobs. If this occurs, the savings attributable to this alternative would be reduced.

In a second approach, SSA could issue the new card only to those applying for a new Social Security number and those who normally request replacement cards. This option would also substantially reduce the cost of card issuance but provides no new employment authorization internal controls for many current number holders.

A third alternative could use state drivers licenses, and identity cards instead of Social Security cards for Businesses and governments are not limited to using SSN's only for purposes required by federal law. Officials of all the organizations we reviewed – businesses that sell personal information, those that offer financial and health care services, and state personal income tax and driver licensing agencies – routinely choose to use SSN's as a management tool to conduct their business or program activities.

These uses can affect large numbers of people. Credit bureau and state personal income tax officials, for example, said they use the SSN as a primary record identifier for internal activities, such as maintaining individual consumer credit histories and identifying income tax filers, whereas officials of the other organizations said they generally assign their own identifiers for internal activities.

Officials of all the organizations we contacted said they use SSN's to match records with those of other organizations to carry out the data exchanges necessary to conduct their business. Data exchanges are conducted for such purposes as obtaining information to assess credit risk, locate assets, and ensure compliance with program rules and regulations.

Both private business and government officials said their organizations could be adversely affected if the federal government passed laws that limited their use of SSN's. Credit bureau officials and state tax administrators said federal restrictions could impede their ability to conduct routine internal activities, such as maintaining consumer histories and identifying tax filers, activities for which members of their industries use the SSN as the primary record identifier.

American Association of Motor Vehicle Administrators (AAMVA) officials said such restrictions could make it difficult for states to detect noncommercial drivers who were trying to conceal driving infractions under other state licenses. In general, credit bureau and other officials said that if credit reports could not be requested using SSN's, organizations would have less assurance of receiving information on the individuals in question.

For changes to information contained in SSA's records (such as a legal name change after marriage), SSA issues a replacement card. However, unlike the process for issuing original cards, SSA does not verify the citizenship of individuals who indicate to SSA that they were born in the United States, as long as the information they previously provided to SSA supports their assertion.

As a result, the process for issuing replacement cards does not provide for the cards to be reliable proof of the number holder's entitlement to work in the United States.

To receive a replacement card, an individual completes an application for a Social Security number and provides proof of identity, such as a drivers license, government or state identification, or school records. If, however, an individual is foreign-born and has not become a naturalized U.S. citizen, additional documents must be shown.

These applicants must provide evidence of current lawful alien status, and either INS work authorization or a valid non-work reason for needing a number.

SSA has issued new versions of Social Security cards while allowing existing cards to remain valid. As a result, current number holders may conceivably have one of 47 valid versions of the card that SSA has issued since the inception of the program.

For example, cards issued before 1982 to non-citizens without work authorization do not contain legends indicating their lack of work authorization. The 40 versions of cards issued before 1983 lack counterfeit-resistant and tamper-proof security features. Likewise, cards issued before 1992 to non-citizens authorized to work for a limited time do not bear legends indicating their temporary work authorization.

The Proposed Options For A New "Tamper Resistant Card" Include:

- Option 1: Basic plastic card with the number holder's name and Social Security number printed on the front of the card. There are two versions of this card: one with and one without a statement concerning the number holder's citizenship/non-citizen status

- Option 2: Plastic card with the number holder's name and Social Security number printed on the front of the card, and an electronically captured picture, sex, and date of birth on the back of the card

- Option 3: Plastic card with the number holder's name and Social Security number on the front of the card and a secure bar code data storage stripe on the back to hold identifying information and a Biometric identifier

- Option 4: Plastic card with the number holder's name and Social Security number on the front of the card and an optical data storage stripe on the back that can store large amounts of identifying information about the number holder

- Option 5: Plastic card with the number holder's name and Social Security number on the front of the card and a magnetic stripe on the back

- Option 6: Plastic card with the number holder's name, Social Security Number, and picture on the front of the card and a magnetic stripe on the back

- Option 7: Plastic card with the number holder's name, Social Security number, and a microprocessor (computer chip) on the front of the card, a magnetic stripe on the back and a picture

(Ed. note: Biometric identifiers are mechanisms to capture a living personal characteristic such as a fingerprint in a digital or analog format).

In order to issue the new version of the SS card the SSA assumes that out of the total number of number holders, it would add the verification of citizenship for about 190 million individuals who would need to provide to SSA proof of their work eligibility status.

SSA field offices would review applications and documents establishing the number holders' identity; verify their citizenship status, as appropriate; and take pictures, capture fingerprints, or both, if required for the new card.

For the remaining people, SSA would only need to take new applications, establish identity, and take the individuals picture because SSA has already documented their citizenship status.

SSA has also proposed mailing at least two correspondences to inform number holders of the re-issuance and request that they contact the agency. SSA estimates that this effort will require a total expenditure of up to 73,000 work years, or about 7,000 to 24,000 work years annually, depending on the issuance period and option selected.

To put this effort into perspective, SSA currently has a total workforce of about 65,500 employees. The mass re-issuance of Social Security cards to all number holders would have a significant impact on SSA's resources and potentially cost billions of dollars.

One popular alternative to reissuing the Social Security card would be to enhance state drivers licenses so that they could be used to verify workers employment eligibility. This approach could save significant SSA resources, and could make the re-issuance of an enhanced Social Security card unnecessary.

States already issue to residents drivers licenses and state identification cards, which are renewed every few years. According to the American Association of Motor Vehicle Administrators (AAMVA), an organization that helps establish uniform licensing standards and practices for state Motor Vehicle Administrations (MVA), most people already have drivers licenses or state identification cards.

All licenses include the individual's picture, have various security features, and are already widely accepted as identification documents. Currently, 40 states use digital pictures as a security feature on their licenses. This digital technology allows an individual's image to be viewed electronically from a database in order to help ensure the proper identification of an individual whose license has been lost or stolen.

This alternative, however, would impose a significant burden on state MVAs, because they would have to review original documents to prove an individual's citizenship or alien status and indicate their status on drivers' licenses.

States would have the same difficulty SSA would have in securing original documentation from older and foreign-born individuals to support their claim of citizenship and work eligibility in order to certify their work status.

In addition, state MVA workloads would increase because individuals who do not currently have a license or identification card may need one for work purposes. Except for the fact that the SS people have become increasingly suspicious about late-in-life cards...

A loophole in the application process even makes the intermediate step of obtaining a primary ID unnecessary.

The use of a falsified birth certificate and, even more so, a primary ID obtained with such a certificate, makes it quite simple to obtain a valid Social Security card. The safeguards against this process are few, and protection against fraud in this area rests in catching the falsified birth document before it becomes an acceptable form of ID.

Changes to the design of the card itself have made forging of cards more difficult. Instead of the old card stock issues, cards since the 1970s have been issued on paper that contains a background of intersecting blue and white discs, on which the seal of the Social Security Administration is printed. This background creates a marbleized effect to the card, which is very difficult to copy or reproduce by computer methods.

Also, cards are now printed with the label, "do not laminate," which prevents would-be counterfeiters from hiding behind the protection that lamination provides.

One procedure that was instituted to help stem the tide of fraudulent Social Security cards was put in place by the Internal Revenue Service in 1995. Working with the Social Security Administration, the IRS now cross-checks the SSN's provided on tax returns with the name listed on the return. If the name and number do not match official records, the return is not processed, and an investigation may be initiated.

How to Open a Bank Account Without a Social Security Number

Anyone opening a bank account, broker's account or other financial instrument which will contain assets and provides a SSN can expect the account to be monitored and drained at any given point by the IRS, a lawyer representing one's ex-spouse or anyone who can produce a subpoena.

There is a method (as of this writing) which allows one to open an account at any institution w/o SS number and stay within the law.

- Fill out and read the Constructive Notice shown. This simply outlines the law that permits you to open a bank account without a SSN
- Take the Constructive Notice to a bank where no one knows you
- Show a passable form of ID that does not have a (or at least your) SSN on it
- Inform the bank representative of your intention to open a bank account without giving the bank your Social Security Number
- Open a non-interest bearing account
- If the nice bank official refuses to open your account, provide a copy of the Constructive Notice and remind them it is a legal offense not to follow this procedure and you have a lawyer on retainer who has nothing better to do with his time but file suits

Will the above work?

Probably.

Will the bank take special notice of your presence and perhaps pass it on to some nice federal agency?

Well, they shouldn't. As the laws now stand unless you approach any IRS or CTR guidelines there is no reason to report your existence to anyone.

But nothing's perfect.

Constructive Notice

TO: ____________________
(Person Being Served)

FROM: ____________________

____
(Name and address of Institution)

You are being made aware by this Constructive Notice that it is a violation of Federal lay to refuse to:

a) Open a non-interest bearing bank account if the party wanting to open the account does not provide a Social Security account number or a taxpayer identification number; or
b) To provide your services to a client or potential client because the client or potential client does not provide a Social Security account number or a taxpayer identification number.

You personally, and the institution you represent, may be liable for damages and attorney's fees.

In accordance with Section 1 of Pub L. 93-579 also known as the Privacy Act of 1974, and Title 5 of U.S. Code Annotated 552 (a), also known as the Privacy Act, you are being informed of the following:

The right to privacy is a personal and fundamental right protected by the Constitution of the United States. You may maintain in your records only such information about an individual's as is relevant and necessary to accomplish a purpose required by statute or by executive order of the President of the United States.

Section 7 of the Privacy Act of 1974 specifically provides that it shall be unlawful for any Federal, State, or Local government agency to deny any individual any right, benefit, or privilege provided by law because of such individual's refusal to disclose his Social Security account number.

"Right of Privacy is a personal right designed to protect persons from unwanted disclosure of personal information..." CNA Financial Corporation v. Local 743; 515 F. Supp. 943.

"In enacting Section 7 (Privacy Act of 1974), Congress sought to curtail the expanding use of s by Federal and Local agencies and, by so doing, to eliminate the threat to individual privacy and confidentiality of information posed by common numerical identifiers." Doyle v Wilson; 529 F. Supp. 1343.

"It shall be unlawful for any Federal, State, or Local government agency to deny any individual any right, benefit, or privilege provided by law because of such individual's refusal to disclose his ." Doyle v. Wilson; 529 F. Supp 1343.

An "agency is a relation created by express or implied contract or by law, whereby one party delegates the transaction of some lawful business with more or less discretionary power to another." State Ex Real. Cities Service Gas v. Public Service Commission; 85 SW 2d 890.

If the institution you represent is a bank, you are advised that if such bank routinely collects information and provides such information to Federal, State, or Local government agencies, then such bank is an agency of government.

The 1976 amendment to the Social Security Act, codified at 42 U.S.C.A., Section 301 et seq., 405 (c) (2) (i, iii), states that there are only four instances where Social Security account numbers may be demanded. These are:

1. For tax matter
2. To receive public assistance
3. To obtain and use a drivers license
4. To register a motor vehicle

You are advised that a non-interest bearing account does not pertain to any of the above. Because the account pays no interest, there is no "need-to-know" on the part of the government.

In accordance with the Privacy Act of 1974, whenever an agency fails to comply with the law, the party wronged may bring civil action in the district court of the United States against such agency. Should the court determine that the agency acted in a manner which was intentionally or willful, the agency shall be liable to the wronged party in an amount equal to the sum of:

Actual damages sustained, but in no case less than $1,000; and
The cost of the action together with reasonable attorney's fees.

Constructive Notice issued by: ______________________________

Representing: ______________________________________

Witness: ________________________ Date: _______________

National ID the Real Story

In 1999 the so-called "national ID" bill was defeated due to the efforts of a few smart legislators. This demise was healded in countless privacy oriented publications. Mr. McDonald is a top expert on this subject and has some interesting facts about the, perhaps, premature death of the national ID.

The following article is used with permission by the author Scott McDonald, editor of the *Scan This News* email newsletter and of the host the Fight the Fingerprint web site http://www.networkusa.org/fingerprint.shtml.

I (ed. Note: in 1999) explained that the now-defunct section of law prohibited federal agencies from accepting identification documents that did not incorporate certain fraud-prevention and other security features. It also stated that, in order for an "identification document" to be "accepted" by a federal agency the issuing agency must have obtained the applicant's Social Security number at the time of issuance. The "national ID law" was slated to go into effect on October 1, 2000. It specifically referred to drivers licenses.

State-issued drivers licenses are the "national identification documents." But, you should not think of the "national ID" so much in terms of "Identification Documents." A more appropriate concept is the "National Identification Database." The actual "documents" themselves will prove to be of only secondary importance once biometrics identification systems come on line later this year. It is the "identification database" that is the key to the national identification system. The real "national ID," is the national identification database which has now been made possible via the Drivers Privacy Protection Act of 1994 (DPPA) which requires states to send driver records to a federal driver registry.

I commented in that October message that the repeal of section 656(b) represented "the epitome of symbolism over substance," as Rush Limbaugh might say. It had no substantive effect, and would not serve as a deterrent to establishment of a national ID system.

Not wanting to sound too negative, however, the message also stated that there were beneficial aspects about the repeal. It stated that the "victory" was an excellent opportunity to educate others about what is really going on behind the scenes. The repeal effort was a great start at getting people to "just say no" to government monitoring and tracking schemes.

But, the message emphatically warned, "make no mistake about it, the national ID is proceeding forth without interruption."

Lately, messages have begun to circulate around the Internet warning about a bill now under consideration in Congress, HR 3429, the Legal Employment Authentication Program (LEAP) Act of 1999, which, the message states, "will completely reinstate the federal ID system."

The bill in question would simply further implement the Illegal Immigration Reform and Immigrant Responsibility Act of 1996 (PL 104-208) which instituted "pilot citizenship attestation and employment eligibility confirmation programs."

These are already underway in some states:

Enforcement Of Regulations Sources

http://www.networkusa.org/fingerprint/page2/fp-employment-eligibility-208.html.

http://www.networkusa.org/fingerprint/page2/fp-ssa-employment-elegibility.html.

Our web sites have been warning about these programs for years.

Claire Wolfe first warned about the numerous laws that would ultimately result in a national ID system way back in early 1997 in her article "Land Mine Legislation."

Let me repeat, the federal national ID was never "uninstated." The federal national ID system is moving full-steam-ahead. It has never even been slowed down. The national ID is not dead; it never was. To stop it would require the repeal of somewhere between 20 and 30 individual federal laws; the first of which would have to be the DPPA. As long as the DPPA is in place, states will be forced to supply driver records to a central federal database which will be the national identification database.

Almost all of the states went ahead and adopted the Identification Document (ID) standards established under section 656(b) of the IIRIRA of 1996 out of fear that the law would be enforced and they would not be in compliance. To stop the national ID now would require states to somehow be forced to "de-standardize" their drivers license documents – which is not going to happen.

Fight the Fingerprint maintains a chart that is regularly updated showing the progression of the national ID.

http://www.networkusa.org/fingerprint/page4/fp-04-page4-winners-losers.html. In other words: The identification document standardization law, section 656(b), was enacted in Congress in 1996, slated to go into effect in 2000. States immediately began the process to bring their state-issued IDs (drivers licenses) into compliance. By 1999, most states had already purchased new equipment and were producing standard identification documents. In the fall of 1999 the law was repealed. It had served its purpose – compelled standardization.

A paper describing the national ID standard features which most states have now adopted is available here:

http://www.networkusa.org/fingerprint/page4/aamva-dl-standards.htm.

In that earlier message, we also referenced the American Association of Motor Vehicle Administrators (AAMVA) which is working with state agencies and the federal Department of Transportation (DOT) to make certain that the states adopt the national ID standards. We quoted from their material which describes the "B.10" effort for developing the national ID.

The AAMVA's web page states:

"Through ANSI's Accredited Standards Committee, National Committee for Information Technology Standards (NCITS), is a committee dedicated to identification cards and related devices known as B10. A Working-Group was formed in B10 for Drivers license/identification cards (DL/ID) and designated B10.8. The Working-Group is comprised of industry (vendors) and jurisdictional representation (AAMVA's members). The development involves broad-based project teams including state driver license agencies, government, equipment and software suppliers, card vendors, and consultants (Our Partners)."

AAMVA's Standards Development Program

http://www.aamva.org/aamvanet/indexMVISecommerce.html.

They go on to say (regarding standardized DL/IDs):

"The main body of the standard will contain general information which does not relate to any specific technology but includes: card size; data standards on human and machine readable information; physical security features; etc. Most of this information reflects work that was already done between AAMVA and the National Highway Traffic Safety Administration in developing the Uniform Identification Practices Model Program: in 1996. The [standards] document will also include a set of: annexes for each applicable technology such as bar code, digital imaging, integrated circuit cards, magnetic stripe, and optical memory. Much of the information in the bar code, digital imaging, and magnetic stripe annexes comes directly from AAMVA's Best Practices. Other annexes will cover topics such as biometrics, durability & test methods, and possibly some historical information."

AAMVA's "Best Practices" web page states:

In recent years many AAMVA Jurisdictions have been converting to technology-based DL/ID (drivers license/identification cards). "Technology-based" refers to the concept that the information contained on the drivers license document is machine-readable. Two machine-readable formats are magnetic stripe and bar code. The MVIS Standing Committee and other standing committees recognized in 1991 the need to standardize the use of these technologies, to gain the greatest utility for use of the data.

It goes on:

There is a growing need for driver identification information to assist law enforcement in processing traffic citations and other NCIC 2000 compliant reports in a more efficient manner through the use of technology.

In conclusion, the Best Practices page states:

Jurisdictions were also moving toward employing digital image technology to capture and store driver license information. Within the jurisdiction, this digital image data may be captured remotely, stored, transmitted to a central database, restored and printed. This entire process may be implemented in a number of ways. In the future, it was foreseen that jurisdictions would want to communicate with each other and exchange data....

Beyond the specific requirements of section 656(b), the AAMVA is also pushing aggressively for the standardization of biometrics technology for identification purposes in driver licensing programs.

The B10.8 Proposed American National DL/ID Standard Draft was prepared by the American National Standard for Information Technology (NSIT), Driver License Cards - Identification Cards Secretariat, Information Technology Industry Council (ITI). It states:

"The purpose of the Driver License Card standard is to provide a uniform means to identify (a) issuers and (b) holders of Driver License cards within the United States.

The standard specifies minimum requirements for the presentation of identification information in human-readable form, and it specifies the format and data content of identification in the following technologies: magnetic stripe, bar code, integrated circuit cards, optical memory, and digital imaging."

It further states:

"This standard is a U.S. Driver License application of existing international identification card standards that relate to physical characteristics, layout, data access and storage techniques, physical security requirements, and to registration procedures for identification of card issuers."

Work on this standard began in 1997 and is a result of cooperation between ANSI NCITS B10, the American Association of Motor Vehicle Administrators (AAMVA) and their Industry Advisory Board. The development involved broad-based project teams including state driver license agencies, government, equipment and software suppliers, card vendors, and consultants.

This standard meets the following objectives:

- Uniquely identifies the card issuer and cardholder
- Brings uniformity to the millions of driver license cards now in circulation
- Encourages transition from existing practice to the new standard
- Assists administrative efficiency and accuracy through machine readable identification within a foundation that encourages future applications
- Facilitates future development in technology and application

Under the DL/ID standards described above, item 15 is called the "ISO Issuer Identifier Number (IIN)" which, it states, is "the assigned identification number from ISO." It says that this number "shall always begin with a "6" with a six-place field.

Item 17 is for digital photograph.

Item is 24 is the card holder's Social Security number.

Interestingly, item 51 is the "Driver 'AKA' Social Security number" for alternate SSNs used by the card holder.

There are 57 multi-length data fields in all.

The NIST report also provides standards for micro-chip imbedded cards, biometrics (finger imaging), and machine-readable technologies.

You can download the "B10.8" report from this page: http://www.aamva.org/aamvanet/indexMVISecommerce.html.

Also, section 404 of P.L. 104-208 establishes the "Employment Eligibility Confirmation" pilot program wherein there was established the "citizenship attestation" pilot program.

Under these two programs participating employers in participating states must obtain approval from the Attorney General before hiring any new employee. The AG-designated federal agency must first confirm (with the SSA) that the applicant is a citizen or otherwise, eligible to work in the U.S., and then issue approval before any employee can be hired. Section 401(b)(2)(A) states that, "the Attorney General may not provide for the operation of the citizen attestation pilot program in a State unless each drivers license or similar identification document contains a photograph of the individual involved; has been determined by the Attorney General to have security features; and [is] issued through application and issuance procedures which make such document sufficiently resistant to counterfeiting, tampering, and fraudulent use that it is a reliable means of identification for purposes of this section."

Furthermore, section 403(c) put into motion the development of what is referred to as the "machine-readable-document pilot program" for automated employment eligibility confirmation and approval. It states that, under the pilot program, the applicant's drivers license or similar identification document must be "machine-readable" and must include the person's Social Security account number.

Although these are only limited "pilot programs" presently, these are the test beds where the technology is developed for application to everyone.

In addition to the IIRIRA, another major piece of legislation adopted by the very same Republican Congress in 1996 was the PRWORA; PL 104-193. This law amended Title 42 USC section 666 so as to force all states to institute policies to require SSN's from all license applicants as a condition for the state to receive welfare funding.

Currently, 31 states have complied. With the threat of losing federal funding hanging over their heads the rest are likewise beginning to require SSN's as part of the license application process.

Is The National ID Dead? No!

Does your state drivers license include the following: Digital photos? Digital signatures? Tamper-resistant features? Machine-readable capability? Does the licensing agency require applicants to supply their SSN?

If you live in any one of the county's most densely-populated states - such as California, Texas, Florida, New York, Illinois, Pennsylvania, or Ohio, among many others – then you would have answered yes to all of the above which means you already have a conforming "national ID" document.

Drivers licenses are "scanned" through the readers which record every sale. The stores find them beneficial because they can be used to "prove" to the state that they did not make any "illegal" sales.

The national ID will be "dead" when the states disband their drivers license/identification databases – not before.

Scott McDonald

Drivers License

This section also covers the state ID card, which is identical in method of issue, information contained, and, for ID purposes, use. (The difference, of course, is that the drivers license permits the bearer to drive, whereas the state ID form serves purposes of identification only.) The term "drivers license" is used exclusively throughout for conciseness; however, all issues discussed here apply equally to the state ID as well.

DRIVERS LICENSE AT A GLANCE	
Type	▪ Primary ID
Method of Issuance	▪ Issued by state departments of motor vehicles (DMV's) ▪ Varies by state ▪ Required documents: varies by state
Information Contained	▪ Bearer's name ▪ Bearer's address ▪ Bearer's sex ▪ Date of birth ▪ Physical characteristics ▪ Bearer's photo ▪ State of issue ▪ Drivers license number ▪ Expiration date ▪ Signature of bearer
Use	▪ Single most common form of ID for U.S. citizens in general ▪ Accepted across states for purposes of employment, obtaining other identification documents, and so on
Method of Fraud	▪ Valid drivers license may be obtained with use of fraudulent birth certificate ▪ Possible to create "fake IDs"

Security Issues	▪ -: Obtaining a drivers license with a falsified birth certificate almost foolproof ▪ +: Newer designs of drivers license make counterfeiting more difficult

Type

The drivers license is a form of primary ID; that is, in and of itself the drivers license is considered verification of the identity of the person bearing it. No other documents are needed to support the drivers license as a proof of identity.

Method of Issuance

The drivers license is issued by the state department of motor vehicles (DMV). No universal standard exists to regulate the procedures of the various DMV's; thus, a wide variance exists in the application and issuance procedures for drivers licenses from state to state.

However, some general rules do apply. For example, almost all states require the applicant to provide a copy of their birth certificate; some require a second document showing the applicant's name and signature as well. A few states go further, requiring the applicant to show their Social Security card before issuing them a license.

Information Contained

Part of the drivers license's value as a primary ID lies in the relatively detailed amount of identifying information it contains. In addition to the bearer's name, address, and signature, most drivers' licenses list the following physical characteristics:

Sex
Hair Color
Eye Color
Height
Weight

Perhaps more important, the license carries a photo of the bearer, taken at the DMV itself, as well.

The license also contains some miscellaneous information, such as the state of issue, the drivers license number, and the expiration date of the current license.

Use

Other than its obvious purpose in indicating that its bearer is legally entitled to drive, the drivers license has taken on a whole separate area of significance: it is the single most commonly recognized form of ID used in the United States. Armed with a drivers license, the bearer has access to employment, other identification documents, memberships, bank accounts, and so on. Drivers licenses from any given state are accepted country-wide, making them a very potent form of ID indeed.

Method of Fraud

Because of their power as a form of ID, a well-made drivers license has a very high value in the market of falsified documents. Most high school students have had experience creating "fake IDs," with varying degrees of success. However, a more successful form of fraud involves using other falsified documents to obtain an authentic, state-issued drivers license.

As discussed in the chapter on Social Security cards, a person who has obtained or created a false birth certificate is in perfect position to procure a valid drivers license. Since most states require only a birth certificate for issuing the license, it is a simple matter to go to the DMV with one's certified fake document and fill in the applicable forms.

Security Issues

A person who obtains a legitimate drivers license using a falsified birth certificate has just provided himself with an ID that will be virtually fail-safe. Since the license itself is officially state-issued and authentic, it is impossible to detect it as a fraud. Only if someone were to question the identity of the applicant presenting the birth certificate in the first place could the fraud potentially be detected.

Otherwise, the only current safeguard against counterfeiting rests in the design of the license itself, which has made uses of hologram technology and sturdier materials to make simple duplicating or doctoring less likely to succeed.

The Drivers License Itself

The Department of Motor Vehicles in all states, countries and providence's issue their own standard driver license to those who feel may be qualified individuals.

When initially used the license is to show that the person operating the vehicle had passed the tests required for driving a vehicle. Recently these cards have served as an unofficial national ID card.

Even with the close repeal of the National Identity law, some states have carried the concept a bit further by adding additional information on the cards which include photographs, Social Security numbers, height weight and fingerprints may be obtained when the license is applied for. The addition of holograms and magnetic stripes helps to prevent fraudulent cards.

Some states are just beginning to toy with the idea of implanting one's fingerprint within the mag stripe; others are implanting the idea of implanting a "smart" chip in the card.

Should/when this comes to pass any person with the correct reader will be able to check a driver's ID features as well as his driving record on the spot.

Hard to tell the cop you've never had a speeding ticket before when the damn chip says you drift through school zones at a 100+ on a regular basis.

Remember This

Most states and providence's and countries have no idea what the other states drivers licenses look like.

If one is applying for a license for the *"first time"* and is over the age of 18, one needs to do the following:

Submit a notarized or certified statement stating that you have never had a drivers license in any state and therefor do not have one to turn in.

This statement should state one's situation, what state one is applying for a license in what state one moved from, a signature, the signature of the person verifying your statement and a written warning about the penalties for making false statements.

It is the issuing state's responsibilities to further check whether the person applying for the license has ever been licensed in any state.

Wait, calm down, listen to what I'm going to tell you.

There are several organizations and groups that collect information from traffic violations in one state and relay the information to a state who may inquire further information about a licensed driver.

This is very important to anyone seeking a DL for any but the strictest legitimate purposes.

AAMVA

Throughout this five star publication the reader will find various references to a group, known as the AAMVA.

It is *extremely* important to understand whom this group is and what the hell they do.

My version –

The AAMVA is a group which attempts to establish and promote standards among those responsible for the nation's driving and driver license issuing and enforcement.

They also publish a series of publications, which, although aimed at administrators which can be very informative to the average driver.

The following is a mission statement directly from the AAMVA:

"Welcome to the American Association of Motor Vehicle Administrators (AAMVA). Founded in 1933, AAMVA is a voluntary association of public service executives responsible for motor vehicle administration, driver licensing issues and the enforcement of state and national laws that govern the safe use of vehicles on the roads in the United States and Canada.

The Association's mission seeks to improve the administration of motor vehicle and law enforcement agencies by providing educational forums for its jurisdictional members to exchange ideas; to more effectively serve the driving public by encouraging jurisdictions to implement uniform laws and regulations; and to foster excellence in service to its diverse customer base by providing jurisdictional service delivery best practices."

American Association of Motor Vehicle Administrators
4301 Wilson Blvd. Suite 400 Arlington, VA 22203
webmail@aamva.org
www.aamva.org

The following a few of what I consider their more useful publications:

The Bulletin A newsletter published by AAMVA; the Bulletin provides quick updates and information for motor vehicle administrators and law enforcement officers. Published monthly. Member: free Nonmember: $25/year (US); $30 (Canada); $40 (Other).

State/Provincial Licensing Systems – Comparative Data
Member: $5.00 Nonmember $20.00.

Driver License Administration Requirements & Fees (NHTSA)
Member: $5.00 Nonmember: $10.00.

Driver License Compact Administrative Procedures
Manual (1990, NHTSA) Member: $5.00 Nonmember: $10.00.

Uniform Identification Practices – Model Practices (AAMVA)
Member: $5.00 Nonmember: $10.00

Fast Track to Vehicle Services Facts – What jurisdictions issue their own VIN? Who administers emission inspections? Which jurisdictions use the Internet?

Rely on this book for quick, accurate and current answers to answer your questions. It is an easy-to-use source of information on titling, fees, registration, specialty license plates, emissions and safety inspections, and other vehicle – related issues.

In addition, it also gives you a leading edge on current trends in the motor vehicle administration field.
Special Pricing Member: $12.50 Nonmember: $25.00

Best Practices for Mag Stripe – Version 2.0 (April AAMVA)
Member: free Nonmember: $5.00

Best Practices for Digital Image & Signatures (AAMVA)
Member: free Nonmember: $5.00

Best Practices for Bar Code – Version 2.0 (April AAMVA)
Member: free Nonmember: $5.00

The Driver License Compact

Maybe the original database to help ferret out folks who should not have a license because of previous violations, the DLC is administered by the American Association of Motor Vehicle Administrators. (AAMVA) (www.aamva.org.)

States belonging to the DLC, exchange information about drivers who have been convicted of serious offenses in the state in which they are applying for a license as compared to the applicant's home state.

If found, the charges are then applied to the person as if the offense occurred in their home state.

According to the American Association of Motor Vehicle Association, the home state has the authority to prosecute the driver as if the offense occurred in their own state for the following offenses:

a) Manslaughter or negligent homicide resulting from the operation of a motor vehicle.

b) Driving under a motor vehicle while under the influence of alcoholic beverages or a narcotic to a degree which renders the driver incapable of safely driving a motor vehicle.

c) Any felon in the commission of which a motor vehicle is used.

d) Failure to stop and render aid in the event of a motor accident resulting in the death or personal injury of another.

The participating states also check to see whether the applicant holds a license in another state and/or has had that license suspended or revoked.

States that do NOT belong to the Driver License Compact:

Georgia
Tennessee
Massachusetts
Michigan
Wisconsin

In the Queen's English this means is you have a license from any state EXCEPT one of the above states, and you are foolish enough to commit manslaughter/homicide, drunken driving and/or throwing your wife from a moving car for talking back, these particular states will not be able to access the report.

National Driver Register (NDR)
(www.nhtsa.gov/people/perform/driver)

Here's another heavy agency, in fact maybe the heaviest, one be cognizant of; The National Driver Register (NDR). Who are they? – According to the National Highway Transportation Safety Administration:

"The National Driver Register (NDR) is a computerized database of information about drivers who have had their licenses revoked or suspended or who have convicted of serious traffic violations such as driving while impaired by alcohol or drugs."

State motor vehicle agencies provide NDR with the names of individuals who have lost their privileges or who have been convicted of a serious traffic violation. When a person applies for a drivers license, the state checks to see whether the name is on the NDR file. If a person has been reported to the NDR as a problem driver, the license will be denied.

How to Find Out If One Is Listed In The NDR

Everyone is entitled, under the provisions of the Privacy Act, to request a file search to see whether you have a record on the NDR.

The "paperwork" can be downloaded by requesting the Individual Request Form, (http:// www.nhtsa.dot.gov/people/perform/driver/ndrform.htm#iform) then one must complete it, have it notarized, and mail it to the NDR.

What NDR Records Contain

NDR results for employers will contain only the identification of the state(s) which have reported information on the driver to the NDR and only information reported within the past 3 years from the date of the inquiry. Driver control actions initiated prior to that time, even if still in effect, will not be included. Detailed information to confirm identity or to describe the contents of the driver record can be obtained only from the state(s) listed when probable matches are reported. The name and address of the licensing official will be provided for each state listed.

How to Request an NDR Record Check

Using this form, which may be completed by either the current or prospective employer or the current or prospective employee;

- The driver must certify his or her identity
- The driver must authorize the request by his or her signature or mark as witnessed

Any mailed NDR record checks request must be notarized to certify identity. Requests made in person require certification of identity acceptable to the state through one or more documents issued by a recognized organization (e.g., a drivers license or a credit card) which contains a means of verification such as a photograph or a signature.

Requests must be made to the state in which the driver is licensed.

Location of NDR Records

Records on individuals can be made available to those individuals, within a reasonable time after request, for personal inspection and copying during regular working hours at 7:45 a.m. to 4:15 p.m., each day except Saturdays, Sundays, and Federal legal holidays. The address for requesting record information in writing directly from the NDR or for making requests in person is:

National Driver Register
Nassif Building
400 7th Street, SW
Washington, DC 20590

Problem Driver Pointer System

According to Public Law 97-364, the NDR is converting to the Problem Driver Pointer System. (PDPS) This is a computerized system that "points" from the drivers home state to a state where a traffic conviction or violation has occurred. This is of major importance, as it *requires* all states to access the NDR through this relatively new database.

Even though it is required by law that all states have to belong to the PDPS, due to the cost of the service, beararacy, and other reasons, at this time, NOT all states participate in the PDPS system. If a state does not belong to the PDPS, they do not have access to the PDPS central site and no records from that state will be available.

How to Get A Drivers License Even If Yours Has Been Suspended: A Trick

As of *this time* the following states DO NOT use the PDPS system to check driver records on NEW licenses.

Alabama
Louisiana
Puerto Rico
South Carolina
Utah

This means one can lose (revoke or suspension) one's license in any state in the union (except the above 5) and take the following steps:

- Become a resident of one of the above states. One might use a mail drop for a residency, buy house, become a roommate, whatever. This step may or may not require a trip to the state in question
- One might be wise to have minimal proof of residency such as a postmarked letter to one, although a good ID card is always better (see this topic under ID theft)
- Go to the DMV and apply for an in-state license, as you just moved in-state
- One should be able to surrender the last state's DL, BECAUSE they won't check the PDPS, or one can use alternate ID such as a birth certificate and "move" from which ever state pleases one
- Take whatever tests are necessary and one should have a new drivers license delivered by an agent of the Federal government in a matter of weeks

A trick within a trick here is to change one vital piece of information IF POSSIBLE such as one's DOB on the application form so if by some act of God one is stopped in the original state of suspension with the new and improved license it will not pull up some other person with the same name who should not be driving.

Another important fact is that at this time, the following states do NOT check the PDPS system to check driver license on license when one is renewing a license.

So even if one has some minor interactions with a non-local DMV, if one's license is in one of the following states and license is due for renewal soon one can wait and renew with confidence.

Alabama
Colorado
Connecticut
Georgia
Illinois
Indiana
Iowa
Louisiana
Michigan
Missouri
New Jersey
Oklahoma
Pennsylvania
Utah
Vermont
Washington

Driver License Reciprocity (DLR)

Is an automated way for a state to check whether the applicant has had any convictions, or failure to comply with another states conviction. According to AAMVA, "the DLR is designed to assist jurisdictions in meeting the basic tenet...that each driver, nationwide have only one driver license and one record through the cooperative interstate exchange of state-issued driver license." If a person has had their drivers license suspended in New Jersey, it will be suspended in California.

Not signed on to this are the following states:

Georgia
Massachusetts
Michigan
Tennessee
Wisconsin

Translated this means that if you commit a big mistake in any state in the union EXCEPT for the above list, the DLR system WILL alert your state to the problem and enforce the penalty.

Non Resident Violation Compact (NRVC)

Is much like the above, except for minor violations. Developed in 1977, when a non resident driver receives a minor traffic violation, in a state belonging to the NRVC, the driver is treated as if their violation occurred in the drivers state of residence.

These states exchange information on violations that occur in their states by out of state drivers. The state informs the person's home licensing state when the resident does not comply with the violation's terms. The person is treated as if the offense occurred in their home state. If the person does not comply with the citation, their license may be suspended by their home state until the terms of the citation are met.

States which are NOT members of the NRVC are :

Alaska
California
Michigan
Montana
Oregon
Wisconsin

Example if you get a speeding ticket in Nevada, and your drivers license is from California; the information will not be sent to California's DMV.

Social Security and DL's

Although a number of laws are in the works to stop states from requiring a Social Security number for the issuance of a drivers license many either require a number and/or use the number as the actual DL number.

Presently there are 14 states that use the drivers SSN as their drivers license number, these are:

Hawaii
Iowa
Kansas
Mississippi
Montana
North Carolina
North Dakota
Oklahoma
South Dakota
Virginia

Arkansas offers a nine digit number beginning with a nine.

Georgia (has the option of using the SSN as their DL number or not).

Massachusetts is one of the few states that issues a DI with a state issued number.

Missouri (will assign a DL number, requires SSN for their records).

The following states have a driver license number, but also the SSN on their licenses.

Alabama
Alaska
Arizona
Colorado
District of Columbia
Illinois
Indiana
Louisiana
Nevada
Ohio
Tennessee
Utah
West Virginia
Wyoming

Note that all states will put a person's SSN on their license if he requests it.

Social Security and Drivers Licenses

Although the issue of whether states are/will be required to collect a drivers applicant Social Security number, either for inclusion as the actual DL number, or simply as an identifier on the application is undergoing numerous court tests there's something you should know...

As of this writing 7 states subscribe to a system called SSOLV which automatically checks a person's SS number for validity and ownership when they apply for a DL.

In real time.

In other words, one shows up, applies for the license, shows a card, or rattles off an SS number from memory, the computers link up and inform the nice clerk if this number belongs , has ever been issued, has been issued to a dead person, or possibly issued to an applicant wanted by the law enforcement community.

Or possibly even behind in his child support.

These particular DMV's don't advertise this fact, but trust me, they will do it.

Iowa
Maine
Missouri
Mississippi
South Dakota
Tennessee
Wyoming

Now for the other Great Truth in this arena. Even though the law requires a SS number many states (such as California), the unwritten law is that the DMV clerk is God.

If you happen to have blond hair and blue eyes, or anything vaguely close, they will often accept any card or number provided.

If you look Hispanic, prepare for trouble.

In many states the SS number is simply used as a "citizen verifier."

One of the best ways to stay abreast of the changing laws and regulations that concern Drivers Licenses and National ID cards is to visit a fantastic web site www.networkusa.org. The following 3 pages are current as this is written and is used with the permission of the site owner.

Icon Legend

	Social Security Number **required upon application.**
	Fingerprint or Thumbprint **required upon application.**
	Machine Readable **driver's license card.** **MS = Magnetic Stripe** **PDF = 2D Bar-code PDF417** **1D = 1D Bar-code 3/9 or 128** **SMART = Chip Card**
	Digital Photograph **included on driver's license card.**

This table is a compilation of information collected from various sources with varying degrees of reliability. It is intended as a general guide only. Please remember: Each States' laws are in a continual state of flux - they change all the time. Check your own State's laws to determine the requirements that are being imposed at any given time.

If you know of any state's driver's license requirements that are not reflected here please let me know.

fingerprint@networkusa.org

Magnetic License States

1. Arizona, July 1995
2. Arkansas, October 1994
3. California, March 1991
4. Colorado, February 1994
5. Florida, March 1993
6. Iowa, October 1993
7. Kansas, June 1994
8. Louisiana, May 1995
9. Maryland, January 1994
10. Minnesota, February 1995
11. Missouri, Unknown
12. Montana, March 1994
13. New Mexico 1997
14. New Hampshire, March 1995
15. New York, November 1992
16. Ohio, May 1995
17. Pennsylvania, December 1994
18. South Carolina, January 1994
19. Texas, July 1993
20. Vermont, January 1994

States that either "request" or "require" a SSN are included on this chart.

STATE:	SSN Required	Fingerprint Required	Machine Readable	Digital Photograph	State Links	Notes
Alabama		defeated	PDF			
Alaska	requested					
Arizona	requested, not required		PDF/MS			
Arkansas			MS			
California			MS/1D			
Colorado			MS			
Connecticut			1D			
Delaware			PDF			
Florida	"if issued"		MS			
Georgia	ssn prohibited		PDF			
Hawaii	ssn is dl#		1D			
Idaho			PDF			
Illinois	religious objection form		PDF			
Indiana			PDF			
Iowa			PDF/MS			

Kansas			MS		●	
Kentucky					●	
Louisiana	"optional?"		MS		●	●
Maine			PDF		●	
Maryland	not required		ID		●	
Massachusetts			MS		●	●
Michigan			MS/ID		●	
Minnesota			MS/ID		●	●
Mississippi						
Missouri	religious obj.		MS	religious obj.	●	●
Montana			MS/ID			
Nebraska					●	
Nevada			MS/PDF			●
New Hampshire			PDF		●	●
New Jersey						●
New Mexico			MS		●	
New York			PDF/ID		●	●
North Carolina			PDF		●	
North Dakota			PDF			

Ohio	"if the person has one"		MS/ID		●	●
Oklahoma					●	
Oregon			PDF		●	●
Pennsylvania			MS/PDF		●	●
Rhode Island					●	●
South Carolina			MS	optional?	●	●
South Dakota			PDF			
Tennessee					●	●
Texas			PDF		●	●
Utah			PDF		●	
Vermont			?	optional	●	
Virginia	"if you have one"		PDF		●	●
Washington State	No longer required!	defeated	PDF	defeated twice	●	●
West Virginia		optional?	PDF	recognition	●	
Wisconsin	voluntary		MS		●	
Wyoming			PDF		●	●

Additional links to state licensing agencies.

Drivers License Security And Manufacture

The DL is the primary piece of ID for most Americans (hey, how many of you carry your passport around?) It not only allows the owner to operate a motor vehicle, it facilitates check cashing, alcoholic consumption, and generally convinces anyone from a Sears clerk to a DEA agent that you are who you say your are.

One would think it would be the most sought after counterfeit document; which it is. The problem is that it is *very* difficult to purchase a license that even vaguely reassembles the real thing (at least to someone that knows what to look for).

Why?

Well let's take a look at just some of the built-in security features used in today's licenses:

California – Current format includes a patter of the state seal and the DMV logo in variable gold ink. The bottom of the license has a machine readable bar code that verifies the information on document as well as a magnetic stripe on the reverse confirming some of the data.

Prior licenses had a see through hologram of both the state and DMV seals as well as hidden reproductions of the state seal and logos.

Also, note most of the licenses are printed on plastic, usually PVC.

To make a single, good hologram or changing light seal, can run $20,000-$50,000 in equipment alone.

All right, let's look at Connecticut's license. Laminated, digitized, with a shadow image of the drivers commissioner's signature over lapping the photo.

Add to that a row of state seals on the bottom that is visible under black light, plus the ghost image, state seal in lower right hand corner as well as a 3 digit camera code in the same area.

Wonder why all those lovely net sites promise "exact duplicates of any state's drivers license" then send you paper copies of go kart licenses once your check clears?

The idea with phony DL's is to get one as far from where one plans to exercise one's drivers rights and pray the nice highway patrolman doesn't know that New Brunswick, Canada DL has a holographic overlay on the front and readable mag stripe on the reverse.

It does help to overload the senses with an International Drivers Permit, New Brunswick library cards and police benevolent associations (see section on ancillary ID), but the real test of one's character comes when the cop looks at the proffered license and goes, "uh, huh" or starts laughing.

A more prevalent forgery of DL's is to change the picture to match the new owner. Works sometimes but the problem is that the original photo was incorporated into the PVC while the forger is simply gluing on a replacement.

If anyone slips their fingernail under the new and improved photo, it will, of course come right off.

The best protection here is to laminate the license even though many states now print "do not laminate" on the obverse.

It's easier to explain to a cop why you laminated an ID ("my wife washed it, it was all ragged, no I didn't see the do not laminate line, I'm sorry officer") than it is to explain why you look absolutely nothing like the person pictured on the license.

The second most common alteration is probably kids changing the date as to appear to be of drinking age.

Difficult, but not impossible – again think lamination afterwards...

Here's an excellent example of a hip driver license format, including security features not only current in Michigan but about to be adopted by almost every state.

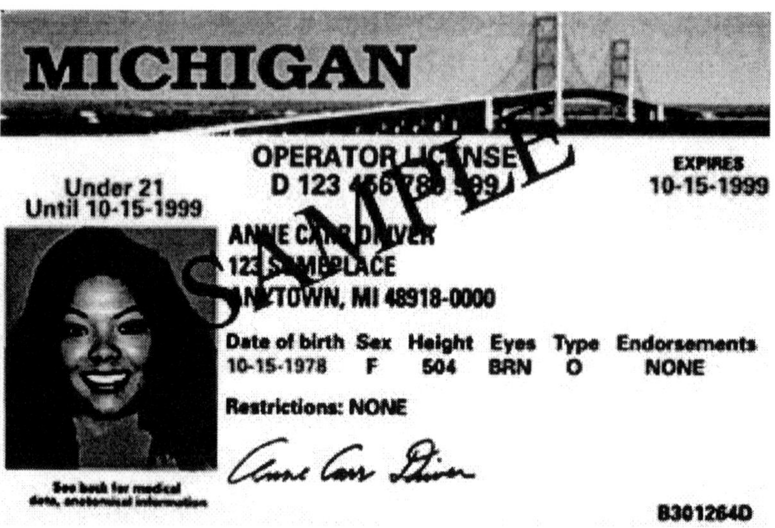

The New Michigan Driver License And Identification Card

The Michigan driver license has a whole new look and feel, and opens the door to customer benefits never available before with Michigan's driver license.

Unlike any license ever issued by the state; the new Michigan driver license represents the latest in driver licensing technology. With its superior quality photograph, state-of-the-art security features and attractive design, the new driver license is a high quality, tamper-resistant product designed to meet the needs of residents, retailers and law enforcement.

Imagine your driver license being mailed within 2 weeks after you apply for it. Imagine being able to scan the license to retrieve the driver license number rather than having to write or key in numbers. The new driver license offers these advantages and much more.

The new driver license is produced for the Secretary of State by the Polaroid Corporation and is available at all Secretary of State branch offices.

The Michigan Secretary of State is proud to offer the new Michigan driver license and remains committed to continuing efforts to deliver customer service you can count on.

Customer Benefits

The new Michigan driver license offers a number of exciting benefits which include:

- Faster delivery time. The number of days to mail a driver license after an application is made is shortened from 4 to 6 weeks to within 2 weeks

- State-of-the-art security features to prevent the license from being altered or copied

- Improved photographs. Secretary of State branch office staff can immediately check the quality of an applicant's photograph

- A magnetic stripe and bar code which allow for a more accurate exchange of information

- Space for writing organ donor and medical information

The Magnetic Stripe And Bar Code

On the back of the new driver license and state identification card is a magnetic stripe and bar code. Under Michigan law, the information on the magnetic stripe and bar code is restricted to only the:

- Drivers license or state ID number
- Holder's date of birth
- License expiration date

It is important to note that Michigan's law limiting the amount of information on the magnetic stripe and bar code is one of the strictest in the nation. (ed. note, this is true, other states are considering adding a digitally compressed photo of the applicant, a computer readable fingerprint and/or a recent history of traffic violations).

Security Features

The new driver license offers several innovative security features. In fact, Michigan's driver license is first in the world to carry **PolaPrime UV**, a unique security feature only visible under black light. Created with special primary colored inks, the PolaPrime UV image of the state seal will deter copying or reproduction of the license.

Another security feature is the optical variable device known as **PolaSecure®**, which is imprinted on the laminate to protect the portrait and data from counterfeiting, scanning or color copying. The outline of the state and the word "MICHIGAN" on the license are created with the PolaSecure® technology.

Because driver licenses are used for everything from cashing a check to showing proof of age, it is important that residents have a license that is secure and tamper resistant. With its state-of-the-art security features offering the latest in tamper-resistant design, Michigan residents can rest assured that the new driver license is a secure, fraud-resistant product.

It's For You

The new Michigan driver license earns an important place in the history of the Michigan driver license. The new driver license is the first license to take advantage of several new technological innovations. Its tamper-resistant features, easy-to-read format, and magnetic stripe and bar code provides many benefits to residents, law enforcement officers and retailers.

With more than 6.7 million licensed Michigan drivers, it will take about eight years to completely remove the old driver license from circulation and replace it with the new one.

Magnetic Stripes – A Trick

The mag stripe on the back of a DL normally just verifies the data on the front of the same card – although this is changing with "smart" cards which imbed a chip or can even implant one's fingerprints in a mag strip.

At any rate, no one really expects to read the stripe. A couple of different encoding schemes are utilized (on can purchase a stripe reader for one's PC for a $200 output and a programmer for not much more) but it looks really great if it works.

To make a stripe not work, simply walk through the check out line of any store that has an anti-magnetic shoplifting counter, you may note the wording DO NOT RUN A CREDIT CARD THROUGH THIS.

Just smile at the nice clerk and ask him/her to activate the wiper while you run your DL over it several times.

If act this embarrasses you, go to Radio Shack and spend $20 on a video demagnetizer which will do the same exact thing.

Want to duplicate the mag stripe on a DL? Take a VHS vide cartridge and an Exacto knife and cut out a duplicate of the strip.

Glue it on.

Of course it's not programmed unless you do so, but is a real mag stripe on the back of a DL.

Please also note that a number of states are using non-mag stripes in place of the traditional data giver.

A NMS looks the same as its predecessor, contains the same, or more information, but *cannot* be erased!

Makes it hard to claim the old eel skin wallet wiped out all your cards.

How to Get A New Drivers License

Okay, let's say, for the sake of conversation that you lose "your" drivers license. How do you get a replacement?

Go to the DMV (or AAA in some places) and explain the situation. If you have your birth certificate handy there will be no problem.

If you, don't have a copy right within reach, the DMV would like to see some proof that you are who you say you are.

But this is not actually necessary in many situations. The last time I actually needed to replace a lost license I didn't bring anything because I didn't know that rule existed.

Clerk - "Then how do we know it's really you?"

Me - "Well you've got my photo and fingerprint on file, just take a look."

Clerk - "I can't access that database, don't you have anything with you, electric bill, water bill, vehicle registration, library card?"

Me - "No, gosh I'm sorry I assumed you had ways to validate my identity. I didn't think to bring anything."

Clerk - "Okay step behind the line so I can take a new photo. Do you still live at 678 Laughing Cow Lane?"

Me - "Yes, ma'am, I really appreciate this."

Three weeks later I had my new license and new and improved photo. Yes, I did have to re-supply my fingerprints, which could someday be a problem.

A year or so ago the Federal government "suggested" all states run their DMV fingerprint database through a program that would identify duplicates. So far this has not happened, partly due to lack of funds, partly because of the new and improved climate or privacy in matters of national identifiers.

But this doesn't mean it won't happen.

A Trick

If you misplace your license and, you successfully apply for a replacement you will be issued a temporary license until the permanent copy arrives. Most temporaries these days are nothing more than computer print outs showing you have paid the necessary fees should you have a conversation with a member of the law enforcement profession, they don't contain many, if any security features (sometimes a pre-printed state seal in light blue on the paper itself).

If one were to move to another state during this lapse between temporary license and permanent replacement, one would find most states accept this as proof to apply for an in-state license.

Want an even neater trick? I tell this with a bit of trepidation because it really is a secret. Most states have a very simple form which they send to any DL applicant when something screws up in the manufacturing process.

Normally this is because the applicant's photo did not print well.

So, one receives a small piece of paper explaining there was a problem and the applicant's permanent license will be delayed.

In the Interim (and this is usually what the document is called) the license is valid.

No photo, no security features, black ink (maybe with a state seal, but also in black), and the beauty is most DMV's have no idea in hell what this piece of paper is supposed to look like, or even if it exists.

Many will accept the information contained and gospel and most won't even bother to send it back to the issuing state, because it's "not my job."

Or as I like to say, good enough for government work.

Either of the above techniques can conceivably create a new person without the nine months gestation period normally required.

Although federal law takes precedence over state regulations, all states have a say in not only what laws are passed, but which they will actually enforce.

Below is a sampling of actual letters from 3 states to the feds detailing not only what the state officials would like to see in the way of drivers license controls but what they actually will (probably) do in spite of federal guidelines.

Bottom line is check the web sites, and organizations I have mentioned in order to stay informed about what is actually in force as well as being enforced at any particular time.

STATE OF CAIFORNIA
PETE WILSON, Governor
BUSINESS, TRANSPORTATION AND HOUSING AGENCY
DEPARTMENT OF MOTOR VEHICLES
LICENSING OPERATIONS DIVISION P. O. BOX 932345
SACRAMENTO, CA 94282-3450

William Holden, Chief
Driver Register and Traffic Records Division
National Highway Traffic Safety Administration
Docket Management, Room PL-401
400 Seventh Street, SW

Washington, D.C. 20590 Re: Docket #NHTSA-98-3945-506
Notice RIN 2127-AG-91

Dear Mr. Holden:

This is in response to the above-referenced rulemaking proposal which affects state-issued driver licenses and identification (DL/ID) card documents. The California Department of Motor Vehicles is or will be in compliance with most of the proposed requirements by the year 2000.

Following are our comments on the five major provisions:

Evidence of Identity

The California Department of Motor Vehicles (DMV) opposes the requirement to provide two forms of identity for original and duplicate DL/ID cards.

We have developed a comprehensive document list that includes only those documents issued officially and/or requiring evidence of identity before they can be issued. We do not believe there is any benefit in requiring a second form of identification. In fact, it is our experience that the relatively small percentage of individuals intent on fraudulently acquiring DL/ID cards have become very sophisticated at acquiring multiple fraudulent forms of identification. To routinely require two documents from every applicant for an original or duplicate DL/ID card imposes a burden on the majority of honest customers, while doing nothing to deter the individual intent on committing fraud.

DMV places the highest priority on the security and integrity of the DL/ID cards we issue. We are currently implementing several new features that will enhance the integrity of these documents. We are in the process of adopting regulations to ensure that only the true full name of the applicant appears on the document.

Page 2

Form and Security Features

We support this proposal, and currently issue DL/ID cards containing security features that limit tampering, counterfeiting and duplication for fraudulent purposes. Our new photo contract includes even more security features.

Social Security Number

We support this proposal.

Social Security numbers (SSN) have been collected on all DL/ID card applications in California since 1992. For privacy reasons, the SSN does not appear on the document itself, but is retained on the subject's record. Contracts have been draped to allow this department to begin electronic verification of SSN's with the Social Security Administration (SSA) as soon as programming can be completed.

For applicants who claim not to hold an SSN, rather than requiring a signed certification to that effect, we intend to require the applicant to present a form from the SSA that documents that fact. We believe this process puts us in compliance with the proposed rule, and in fact has more integrity than a signed certification by the applicant. We request that this process be allowed as an option for compliance to the proposed rule.

We appreciate the opportunity to respond to this proposal. If you have any questions or comments about any of the information provided, please contact me..
Sincerely,

SUSAN C. LARSON, Chief
Policy and Automation Branch

cc: Brendan M. Peter, AAMVA

STATE OF DELAWARE
DEPARTMENT OF PUBLIC SAFETY
DIVISION OF MOTOR VEHICLES
P.O. BOX 698

DOVER, DELAWARE 19903
Phone: 302-739-5669
Fax: 302-739-2602

Docket Management
Room PL-401
National Highway Traffic Safety Administration,
Nassif Building,
400 Seventh Street, SW
Washington, D.C. 20590

RE: Docket No. NHTSA-98-3945 -1527

Dear Sir:

This letter addresses the Department of Transportation, National Highway Traffic Safety Administration's Notice of Proposed Rulemaking titled "State-Issued Drivers License and Comparable Identification Documents," reference 23 CFR Part 1331, Docket Number NHTSA-98-3945, RIN 2127-AG-91. This regulation implements section 656(b) of the Illegal Immigration Reform and Immigrant Responsibility Act of 1996.

Every state will benefit from this proposal. It standardizes licensing and identification card personal identification procedures, defines minimum standards for license document format and security features and requires all states to verify the applicant's Social Security number. This will reduce fraud and set national identification standards.

The following are Delaware's comments on specific provisions contained within the Notice of Proposed Rulemaking:

1. Reference Subpart B-Procedures, §1881.4(b), "If the current license or document is unavailable, the applicant would be required to submit instead a primary and secondary document."

The requirement to present a primary and secondary document to obtain a duplicate drivers license or identification card is too restrictive for the average citizen who has an immediate need for these documents. We recommend each state determine individual policies when obtaining a duplicate license.

Page 2

Most persons seeking duplicate drivers licenses or identification cards are honest people who lost these documents as a result of theft. At the same time they may lose all other forms of personal identification such as credit cards, employment ID cards, military ID, health card, etc. Surprisingly few people keep copies of these documents at home. Primary and secondary identification documents can take weeks to obtain if the person does not have them in their possession. To increase the identification standards invites customer dissatisfaction.

The Division of Motor Vehicle (DMV) computer files contains information on every document holder and many of the states now have digitized images of the person's face and signature. If the digitized image and signature on file matches the applicant's facial features and signature, then no other primary or secondary documents may be necessary when issuing a duplicate document.

By Delaware State policy, duplicate licenses are issued if the applicant brings in three identification documents of which one must have their signature. We ask personal identification questions such as address and Social Security card number and compare their response against the information on file. Other technology changes such as biometric identifiers will make this provision obsolete over time. Therefore, recommend that the policy for issuing duplicate licenses be left up to the issuing state.

2. Reference §1881.6(d), "States shall require each applicant who claims not to hold a Social Security number to sign a certifying statement to that effect."

Requiring a signature to certify that an applicant does not hold a Social Security number adds to the time and complexity of the licensing process but it does not add validity to the process. Dishonest people will sign anything to get a document. A better approach is to require the applicant to present DMV with a letter from the Social Security Administration stating that the applicant is not eligible for a Social Security number. An alternative approach is to require the applicant to show a document from Appendix D to prove that they are ineligible for a Social Security number.

3. Reference §1881.6(e), "States may require licenses and documents issued to individuals who do not possess social security numbers to contain an alternative numeric identifier that can be read visually or by electronic means."

This provision is unclear. If a state assigns a driver license number that is not the applicant's Social Security number and the applicant does not have a Social Security number, is the driver license number or identification card number considered a viable alternative to the Social Security number? If each state must make up a 9 digit numeric number and insert it in the social security number position in the computer data base, the national driving records will contain inaccurate and conflicting records. The potential for duplicate alternative Social Security numbers is great. Recommend that the Social Security number position be coded 999-99-9999 or left blank when the applicant does not have a Social Security number; the driver license or identification card number assigned by the state then becomes the unique identifier.

4. Reference Appendix A (8), "Microfilm/copy of a State issued or Canadian drivers license or identification card that has not been expired for more than one year that is certified by the issuing agency."

Page 3

Recommend the word "Record" be inserted after the words "License" and "Card" in the above sentence. States do not keep copies of the actual driver license or identification card document. They already exchange certified driving license records with other states.

The cost estimates for implementing the proposed rules are attached.

However, this is contingent upon the degree of cooperation by the Social Security Administration and by the availability of computer programming. Currently, the implementation of some federal and state programs are delayed up to two years because of limited computer programming support. Delaware supports the Oct 1, 2000 deadline as long as extensions are available through NHTSA. Given our experiences implementing PDPS and other federally mandated programs, it is necessary to allow for exceptions in the planning process. Exceptions will occur during execution.
Sincerely,

Arthur G. Ericson
Chief of Driver Services

AGE/ccm

Attachment

c: Brendan M. Peter, AAMVA (Faxed)
Docket Management

STATE OF MICHIGAN

CANDICE S. MILLER, Secretary of State
MICHIGAN DEPARTMENT OF STATE

TREASURY BUILDING, LANSING, MICHIGAN 48918

Mr. Rodney Slater
Secretary of Transportation
400 Seventh Street, SW
Washington, D.C. 20590

Subject: 23 CFR Part 1331 - Docket No. NHTSA-98-3945 (-3945)

State-issued Driver Licenses R Comparable Identification Documents
Proposed Rule

Dear Mr. Slater:

I am writing to voice my deep and abiding concern with the federal government mandating a person to disclose his or her Social Security number in order to obtain a driver license or personal identification card. I firmly and unequivocally oppose the wholesale collection, retention, and use of Social Security numbers for driver licensing activities as an unnecessary infringement on personal privacy. The proposed rules for the Immigration Reform and Immigrant Responsibility Act of 1996 ignore the legitimate privacy concerns of Michigan's citizens and require disclosure of their most important personal identification number, their Social Security number. This requirement is an unnecessary government intrusion into the lives of private citizens.

As Michigan's chief motor vehicle administrator, I would be remiss if I did not express my strong concern with any federal mandate that requires an individual to disclose his or her Social Security number in order to obtain a driver license or personal identification card. I ask you to envision what will happen in our branch offices when we must demand disclosure of social security numbers. There will be an extremely negative reaction from our citizens who view collection and possible retention of Social Security numbers as an invasion of their privacy.

Discrepancies in spelling of names, more than one person sharing the same Social Security number, multiple Social Security numbers for the same individual, and incorrect date of birth are well-documented problems. If someone cannot remember, does not know, or is unwilling to provide a Social Security number, or if we are not able to verify that number, that person will be refused service. The probable delays in serving customers due to systematic problems attributable to the Social Security number verification process, not to mention the cost to build the appropriate systems infrastructure and ongoing transaction costs, make the proposed changes an inconceivable nightmare.

If any of the above-mentioned problems occur, citizens will lose their privilege to drive and earn their living. And for what purpose? The basic tenets for these rules, and the Welfare Reform Act of 1996 which contained a similar requirement, are to curb illegal immigration and delinquent child support payments. Requiring all citizens to disclose their Social Security number, when the vast majority of them are not a part of this target population, is a waste of effort on our part, as well as an unneeded

Page 2

invasion of everyone's privacy. Moreover, identifying and verifying social security numbers has no connection to a person's ability to operate a motor vehicle.

I should also note that Michigan already complies with the Welfare Reform Act of 1996 by suspending the driver licenses of people who are delinquent in their child support payments. The court orders imposing these sanctions use the person's driver license number, not the Social Security number - proving there are other ways to meet these goals.

Public perceptions regarding the retention and accessibility of personal information remain skeptical, and public sentiment is against government intrusion into daily lives. These opinions escalate with any type of change. Michigan's new driver license, implemented this Spring, offers the latest in driver licensing technology with state-of-the-art security features. The license features a digital photo, magnetic stripe and bar code with limited encoded information as defined by law (driver license number, date of birth, and license expiration date), and is tamper resistant with special colored inks to prevent copying. Despite my efforts to build in statutory restrictions for access to information on driver licenses, some citizens are concerned and have refused to provide a signature or have their photos captured electronically. To now mandate that everyone furnish a Social Security number when applying for a driver license or personal identification card is a betrayal of the public trust.

On a related note, it is likely that these requirements will further lead the public into believing the federal government is headed toward the establishment of a "national identity card". This concept is something that has been feared for years by privacy advocates, and will likely be fought vehemently on the state as well as the federal level. The Social Security number is a "national identity number". A driver license or personal identification card that is mandated to include collection and verification of the Social Security number will no doubt create this perception.

Citizens, the vast majority whom have never had any type of brush with the law, should not have to face this intrusion into their lives. Furthermore, motor vehicle administrations should not be required to verify the accuracy of the records for the Social Security Administration.

The proposed rules for the Immigration Reform Act should be rewritten to eliminate the requirement that motor vehicle administrations collect or verify Social Security numbers.

Thank you for your consideration of this matter.

Sincerely,

Candice S. Miller
Secretary of State

International Drivers Permit: A True Story

International Driving Permit – The Trick

The IDP is issued in one's home country prior to taking a trip. In the U.S. the AAA is the issuing agency. One goes to the local office, has a couple of passport sized photos taken, fills out a form, pays the nice clerk $10.00 and walks away with a permit that "allows" one to drive in a number of countries.

Problem being, see, one is supposed to also present one's U.S. driving license along with the permit in order for it to be valid.

No drivers license, no valid permit.

Many "privacy" agencies will provide you with an IDP from another country for $100 or so. I talked to one of the issuing agents and said, "yeah but when I get stopped in Bakersfield and he asks for my Bolivian license, what do I say?"

His reaction was, "how many cops in the U.S. do you think they know you're required to have a "local" license to go along with the permit?"

My reaction is that I have never liked jail.

So, a number of agencies have taken this concept one step farther along the golden road and issued the applicant a "local driving license" as well as the IDP.

A real one?

Sure...

But now you are in the "if you can't dazzle 'em with brilliance, baffle them with bullshit" category. How many U.S. cops do know what a Bolivian driving license looks like?

The average officer will run "your" name for local violations, give you a warning and let you go.

So will the average bank clerk.

Of course this does not work forever – if you are here on vacation, or just moving to town, great, but most states want to see a local ID within a set number of days.

Also most states like to see the tag of the car match the state/country of the driving license.

Second or third time the same officer notices you in the same area during a 3 month period he may have some questions.

Some hard questions.

For those of you wishing to save the issuing agent's fee I should point out the AAA will NOT issue an IDP to your cousin from Spain who forgot to get one before he came to America, even though he has his "drivers license" with him.

This is a great piece of ancillary ID, especially if you look like you might actually be from the country in question.

Since the IDP is a standardized format the only difference between issuing "agents" is the price and what they are going to furnish for back up ID.

I might also suggest one do a bit of research on the country one is "from" because, God and Murphy's law withstanding, your first chat with a official will be with the one who lived in Bolivia for 6 years during his stint with the Peace Corps.

APPLICATION FOR
INTERNATIONAL DRIVING PERMIT
OR
INTER-AMERICAN DRIVING PERMIT

FEE FOR EACH PERMIT $10.00

Issuance of Permit is restricted to persons EIGHTEEN YEARS or over who hold a valid U.S.A. or Territorial License.
PERMIT VALID FOR ONE YEAR. Not renewable.

CHECK DESIRED PERMIT	MANDATORY REQUIREMENTS
☐ International Driving Permit (fee $10.00 and 2 signed photos.) ☐ Inter-American driving Permit ***(See reverse side) (Fee $10.00 and 2 signed photos.	1) Attach 2 recent signed passport-type photos (2"x2") 2) Enclose permit fee of $10.00. (DO NOT MAIL CASH)

NOTE: IT IS IMPORTANT THAT YOUR VALID U.S.A. OR TERRITORIAL LICENSE BE CARRIED WITH THE PERMIT AT ALL TIMES. The International or Inter-American Driving Permit is not valid for driving in the United States.

Print name in full. No Initials

FIRST	MIDDLE	LAST
DAYTIME PHONE	HOME STREET ADDRESS	
CITY	STATE	ZIP CODE
U.S. DRIVER'S LICENSE NO.	STATE OF ISSUE	EXPIRATION DATE (MO. DAY YEAR)
BIRTHPLACE: CITY *	STATE OR COUNTRY	BIRTH DATE (MO. DAY YEAR)
DATE PERMIT TO BE EFFECTIVE (MO. DAY YEAR) / DEPARTURE DATE FROM U.S. (MO. DAY YEAR)	COUNTRIES TO BE VISITED	

Please check the appropriate box below to indicate the type of vehicle for which you now hold a valid U.S.A. or territorial driver's license, and for which you desire this permit:

☐ Motorcycle ☐ Passenger Car ☐ Vehicle over 7,700 lbs. ☐ Vehicle over 8 seats ☐ Vehicle with heavy trailer

I certify that the above information is true and correct, and that the license indicated has not been suspended nor revoked.

I further certify that I understand that a valid state driver's license must accompany this permit, and that this permit is valid only as long as the state license is valid, but not to exceed one year from the date the permit is issued.

SIGNATURE (SIGNATURE MANDATORY FOR ISSUANCE OF PERMIT)	DATE

WE ARE PLEASED TO ENCLOSE YOUR INTERNATIONAL DRIVING PERMIT.

KINDLY SIGN YOUR NAME ON THE LINE PROVIDED BENEATH YOUR PHOTOGRAPH.

IMPORTANT: YOUR VALID U.S.A. STATE OR TERRITORIAL DRIVER'S LICENSE MUST BE CARRIED WITH THE INTERNATIONAL DRIVING PERMIT AT ALL TIMES.

IMPORTANT: THIS IS YOUR MAILING LABEL.
PLEASE PRINT LEGIBLY TO ENSURE PROMPT DELIVERY. THANK YOU.

NAME ....

ADDRESS ....
CITY
STATE, ZIP
COUNTRY ....

MAIL ENTIRE APPLICATION TO:

YOUR NEAREST AAA DISTRICT OFFICE

F567A (Rev. Jul 1998)

Contracting States Which Honor International Driving Permits (Convention on Road Traffic; United Nations, Geneva 194
of May 1980.

AFGHANISTAN*
ALBANIA
ALGERIA
ANDORRA
ANGOLA
ANTIGUA*
ARGENTINA***
AUSTRALIA
AUSTRIA
BAHAMAS
BANGLADESH*
BARBADOS**
BELGIUM
BELIZE
BHUTAN*
BOLIVIA* and ***
BOTSWANA
BRUNEI*
BULGARIA
BURMA*
BURUNDI*
CAMEROON*
CANADA
CAYMEN ISLANDS
CENTRAL AFRICAN REPUBLIC
CHAD*
CHILE***
CHINA (NATIONAL REPUBLIC)
COLOMBIA* and ***
CONGO (BRAZZAVILLE)
COSTA RICA* and ***
CUBA
CURACAO
CYPRUS
CZECHOSLOVAKIA
DAHOMEY
DENMARK
DOMINICA*
DOMINICAN REPUBLIC*
ECUADOR*
EGYPT
EL SALVADOR* and ***
ETHIOPIA*
FIJI
FINLAND
FRANCE (INCLUDING FRENCH
OVERSEAS TERRITORIES)
GABON*
GAMBIA*
GERMANY*
GHANA
GIBRALTAR
GREECE
GRENADA
GUATAMALA*
GUERNSEY
GUINEA-BISSAU*
GUINEA*
GUYANA*
HAITI***
HONDURAS* and ***
HONG KONG
HUNGARY
INDIA
INDONESIA*
IRAN*
IRELAND
ISRAEL
ITALY
IVORY COAST
JAMAICA
JAPAN
JERSEY
JORDAN
KENYA*
KHMER (REPUBLIC)
KOREA (REPUBLIC)
KUWAIT*
LAOS
LEBANON
LESOTHO
LIECHTENSTEIN*
LUXEMBOURG
MALAGASY REPUBLIC
MALAWI
MALAYSIA
MALI
MALTA
MAURITANIA*
MAURITIUS*
MONACO
MONTSERRAT*
MOROCCO
MOZAMBIQUE*
NEPAL*
NETHERLANDS
NEW ZEALAND
NICARAGUA* and ***
NIGER
NORWAY
PAKISTAN*
PANAMA* and ***
PAPUA AND NEW GUINEA
PARAGUAY***
PERU***
PHILIPPINES
POLAND
PORTUGAL
QATAR*
RHODESIA
ROMANIA
RWANDA
ST. CHRISTOPHER, NEVIS
AND ANGUILLA*
ST. LUCIA
ST. VINCENT
SAN MARINO
SAUDI ARABIA*
SENEGAL
SEYCHELLES
SIERRA LEONE
SINGAPORE
SOUTH AFRICA
SOUTH WEST AFRICA
SPAIN
SRI LANKA
SUDAN*
SURINAM
SWAZILAND
SWEDEN
SWITZERLAND*
SYRIA
TANZANIA*
THAILAND
TOGO
TRINIDAD AND TOBAGO
TUNISIA
TURKEY
UGANDA
UNITED KINGDOM
U.S.S.R.
UPPER VOLTA*
VENEZUELA***
VIETNAM
WESTERN SAMOA*
YEMEN ARAB REPUBLIC*
YEMEN (PEOPLE'S DEM. REP.)
YUGOSLAVIA
ZAIRE
ZAMBIA*

*International Driving Permit honored, although country not a party to 1949 Convention.

**U.S. driver's license and International Driving Permit recognized on presentation to local police and payment of a Soc
Registration Fee upon arrival.

***Contracting States Which Also Honor Inter-American Driving Permits (Convention on Regulation of Inter-American M
Vehicle Traffic, Organization of American States, Washington, D.C. 1943) as of February 1985. If you intend to drive in a
the following countries be sure to check INTER-AMERICAN DRIVING PERMIT box page 1:
Brazil and Uruguay.

(FOR OFFICE USE ONLY)

AMOUNT	RECEIPT NO.	PERMIT NO.	DATE ISSUED

SENT TO:

UNITED STATES OF AMERICA

INTERNATIONAL MOTOR TRAFFIC

FEE
$10.00

International Driving Permit

Convention on International Road Traffic of 19 September 1949
(United Nations)

Issued at HEATHROW, FLORIDA 32746-5063, U.S.A.
Valid For One Year From:

Date ______________________________

IMPORTANT— This permit is not valid for driving in the United States

Authorized signature of the empowered authority

67297484

Back-Up's – Ancillary ID

An important and often overlooked segment of identification, whether it be a created personal or borrowed life, is back up documents.

Most police, federal agents, and custom's personnel are taught to look at more than just the main ID in order to assess the validity of the initial identification. Bank personnel are also counseled to recognize secondary ID documents.

A person with a state ID and nothing else, had better have a good story and expect his ID to be severely scrutinized.

For many, many years Polaroid Corporation was the answer to this dilemma, and in some ways they still qualify.

Polaroid pioneered instant ID cards – their cameras, which many of you can probably remember resting comfortably on the counter of the local DMV, were designed to photograph a person and then "imbed" it in a pre-designed ID card.

Many states used the Polaroid system to issue their drivers license and official ID's and many, many private organizations used the machine to issue membership or company ID cards.

The original system (301 as I recall) let the operator design their own card, leaving a space for the photo and the machine combined the two into one authentic ID.

Very close personal friends of mine have used this system to create a whole wallet full of realistic ID cards; a little red ink, a little black typesetting and you have a membership to the NRA, the National Bowling Association, Body Guards International, whatever.

Polaroid has continued this tradition by simplifying their systems and expanding their sales to make it easier for "corporate" clients to procure the equipment.

One can now choose from such diverse systems as the ID-4 Instant Photo Identification System, the ID-100 Instant Photo ID System (for those horizontal, wallet sized cards), to the portable BadgeCam, a handheld card/badge maker to the Idware which will whip up an ID that includes a bar code, and fingerprint storage.

There are a few storefront ID shops that still use various Polaroid ID systems for on-the spot cards, but most of these look fairly rudimentary.

The concept for a serious ID person would be to locate an organization that utilizes one of the Polaroid systems and make a deal with the operator or actually purchase a unit for one's own organization or personal use.

With the advances in computer aided design, incorporating programs such as PhotoShop, etc., any component graphic artist can design a more realistic card than the real ones used for government agencies and private corporations.

Remember this system is not a laminating process (which shouts "fake" to any knowledgeable examiner), but actually produces an integrated ID card.

Here are some other, perhaps easier choices for ancillary ID's. Some are obviously much more valid than others. Point being, each card adds a layer of respectability to the holder, and, oddly enough, the more "expensive" cards don't necessarily appear more legitimate than the low priced, or even free examples.

It tends to be the card itself that demands respect, not the issuing agency.

- Join the NRA. It's cheap, provides a great plastic membership card with which many law enforcement folk can identify
- Gasoline credit cards are notoriously easy to obtain if one has any credit history at all
- A number of chain vitamin and book stores offer a 15% off card after a small membership fee
- Library cards, obviously, are a must
- Any association from the National Ocean Water Skiers to the Save The Children Foundation that has a photo card is a gem
- No down payment, 100% credit, balsa wood furniture stores are easy on handing out credit (well, let's be honest, Macy's and other department stores are right there also)
- Join AAA. Hell it's worth it anyway
- AARP
- Join clubs

- Purchase ID's from places like NIC – look don't buy something that says CIA, okay, but some of the press credentials look pretty authentic, especially if the examiner really has no idea what a press credential is supposed to look like

- Costco, Price Club, Sam's and B. J.'s, depending on what area of the country you reside in, all issue Polaroid cards including your photo when you join. Most do not require any ID to "join" except the required $25

- Any ATM card is a help, those from banks that include the customer's photo are even more impressive

- My own personal opinion is to join any Friend's of Law Enforcement, The Nurse's Brotherhood, Candy Stripers; any benevolent organization that has a photo card and will get a cop and/or official talking about what a interesting organization you belong to" is a plus, plus

The next page shows a modern ID maker.

ID card & badge systems

◆ ID-4 Instant Photo Identification System

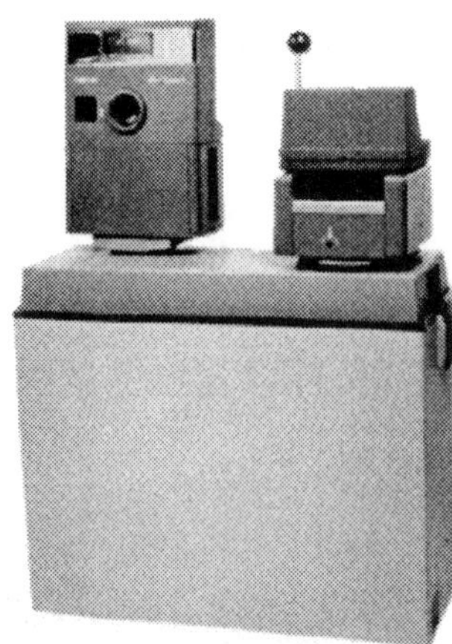

A self-contained system offering a variety of portrait sizes and formats, and a choice of over 40 security laminates.

Municipalities, housing project security departments and prisons will find the Polaroid ID-4 system to be a secure choice. Issue up to 125 full-color "all-photo" ID cards per hour. No special training is needed. The system is completely self-contained and designed for optimal performance and reliability. LED indicators guide operation, sonar ranging assures correct camera-to-subject distance, an aiming light assures accurate portrait composition, and electronic timers keep track of picture development.

Order #614477

Other system configurations available upon request.
(Polacolor ID Ultraviolet film recommended)

Gary
Blue Ridge Fire Department
Gary Smith
Blue Ridge, MA
Station # 48

◆ Captiva BadgeCam

The fastest, easiest way to make temporary photo badges. Ideal for fire, accident and rescue scenes.

Make high quality badges, passes and short-term ID's quickly, easily, on the spot, virtually anywhere. This lightweight, fully-automatic, aim-and-shoot camera produces full-color photo badges at the touch of a button. The 2.5 x 4.4-inch badges are ready to wear — and show the unique (and non-transferable) image of the individual. No laminating or diecutting is needed. BadgeCam images combine individual portraits with custom artwork produced from any design.

Order #619410 (BadgeCam)

Order #619411 (BadgeCam Date)

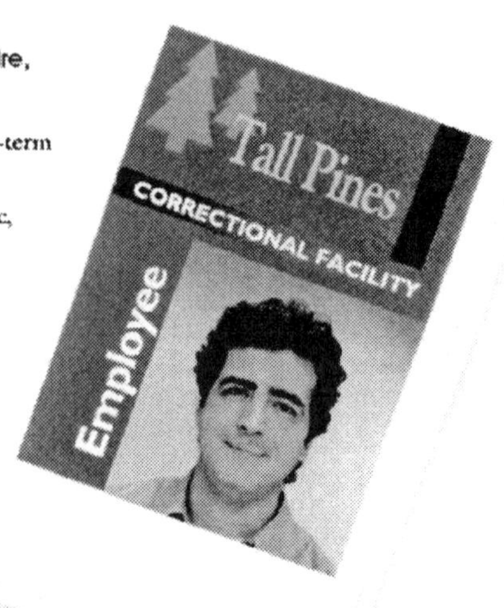

Ancillary ID – A Trick With Guns

One of the very nicest, coolest, secondary ID's one can obtain is not only impressive, but completely free.

Regardless of your political position you should think about getting on the mailing list of the National Rifle Association.

Notice I didn't say you had to join the NRA – just get on their mailing list. The NRA will send anyone they feel might contribute to their cause, a beautiful PVC, credit card sized "membership" card.

The plastic card is a thing of red, white and blue beauty. It features an eagle grasping a rifle while sitting on a stars and stripes shield with the words, "National Rifle Association 2000."

Beneath that comes "your" membership number in raised gold embossed figures followed by your name.

The reverse has a space for one's signature as well as a nice quote from Amendment II of the Bill of Rights:

"A well-regulated Militia, being necessary to the security of a free State, the right of the people to keep and bear Arms shall not be infringed."

The NRA would appreciate a donation, but even if you choose to keep your money belt cinched up, you still get the card.

I would be remiss if I did not point out that my card has done me far more good than harm when "accidentally" pulled out along with my license during a traffic stop.

NRA
11250 Waples Mill Road
Fairfax, VA 22030

Voters Registration Card

VOTER'S REGISTRATION CARD AT A GLANCE	
Type	Secondary ID
Method of Issuance	▪ Issued by city or county board of elections ▪ Can apply by mail in some cities/counties ▪ Required document: varies; none in some cases
Information Contained	▪ Bearer's name ▪ Bearer's address ▪ Bearer's voting precinct ▪ Bearer's political party ▪ Date of issue ▪ Date on which card becomes effective
Use	▪ Indicates that bearer has the right to vote in the U.S. ▪ Indirect proof of U.S. citizenship, since voting is a right extended only to U.S. citizens
Method of Fraud	▪ Authentic voter registration cards may be easily obtained illegally in areas where they are obtained by mail and/or without any prior identification
Security Issues +/-	▪ -: Ease of obtaining voter registration cards makes them easy targets for fraud

Type

The voter registration card is considered to be a secondary ID that is, a document that can support a claim to identification but must be used in conjunction with other forms or cards to verify the holder's identity. This document does not normally stand alone as a proof of identification.

Method of Issuance

Voter registration cards are generally issued by county boards of elections, or by city boards for very large cities. As with all forms of ID that is issued in a decentralized fashion, a wide variation exists from place to place in the procedures for obtaining a voter registration card.

With regard to fraud, two methods of issue are important – in some locales, voter registration cards may be applied for and obtained via mail; and in others, *absolutely NO* identification is required to obtain a voter registration card.

The voter registration card serves one primary and one secondary purpose, as follows:

As its name implies, the voter registration card signals that its holder is eligible to vote in the United States. Persons wishing to vote are required to bring this card, and, generally a picture ID with them to the polls.

The voter registration card also performs a very important secondary function: it serves as indirect proof that its bearer is a U.S. citizen. The reason for this is simple: only U.S. citizens aged 18 years or older are eligible to vote in this country. Therefore, anyone holding a voter registration card is assumed to have U.S. citizenship. It is this function that makes the voter registration card so valuable as a forgery.

Method of Fraud

Because of its indirect value as a citizenship-proving document, it would seem reasonable to expect that the rules governing the issuance procedures of voter registration cards would be relatively strict.

Surprisingly, this is not the case. As mentioned, issuance procedures vary from county to county (or city to city); however, in those jurisdictions that issue voter registration cards by mail, or, alternately, those that require no ID to obtain a card, it is a piece of cake to gain possession of a perfectly valid, officially issue card – even using a false identity.

This card then serves as a key document to enjoying the rights and privileges of U.S. citizenship.

Security Issues

Taking the above into account, it is not surprising that the security value of a voter registration card is extremely low. The incredible ease with which an individual may illicitly obtain an authentic voter registration card make it virtually impossible to distinguish the real article from a fake.

Passports

PASSPORT AT A GLANCE	
Type	Primary ID
Method of Issuance	▪ Issued by the U.S. State Department ▪ Standard, involved application process ▪ Required documents: birth certificate, drivers license or state ID
Information Contained	▪ Bearer's name ▪ Bearer's nationality ▪ Bearer's sex ▪ Date of birth ▪ Place of birth ▪ Bearer's photo ▪ Place of issue ▪ Passport number ▪ Issue date ▪ Expiration date ▪ Signature of bearer
Use	▪ Widely accepted as a form of ID, though not as universal as the drivers license
Method of Fraud	▪ Very difficult currently to obtain or create a fraudulent passport
Security Issues +/-	▪ +: Methods of issue and design combine to make the passport a highly secure document.

Type

The passport is a form of primary ID; that is, in and of itself the passport is considered verification of the identity of the person bearing it. No other documents are needed to support the passport as a proof of identity.

Method of Issuance

Issued by the U.S. State Department, passports are regulated by a very detailed, controlled application procedure. Along with the application form, an individual seeking a passport must show a certified copy of his or her birth certificate and a copy of his or her drivers license/state ID as well. Passport workers handling the application receive special training, so they know what to look for on the various documents to verify their authenticity. What's more, passport agents are instructed to hold conversations with applicants to see whether their verbal comments correspond with the information written on the documents. Any discrepancies will indicate potential fraud and will cause an inquiry into the application.

In some instances, especially when one applies for an expedited passport, the agency will actually call the references one has listed on the application and ask them personal questions, such as your weight, hair color, how long they have known you, etc.

Use

As do drivers licenses, passports have both a functional use and a value as a form of ID. The functional use, of course, is that the passport allows the bearer to travel between this country and those other nations that recognize the U.S. passport. The passport's ID value lies in the fact that the passport is accepted throughout this country as a form of primary ID, for many the same purposes as a drivers licenses. However, it should be noted that in specific cases a passport may not be accepted as readily as a license as proof of ID, or at all.

Method of Fraud

Given the issuance procedures governing the passport – which, ironically, were instituted by the State Department in response to widespread passport fraud in the 1960s and 1970s – it is extremely difficult to create a fraudulent passport today; as a result, no common method for obtaining fake passports is in use.

Security Issues

Digital Passport Security

Starting in January 1999 The **Image Trac** scanner from Imaging Business Machines, LLC became a critical piece of the U.S. State Department's new passport issuance system.

The Image Trac scans the passport application and create a digital version.

Instead of pasting and laminating the 2-inch head shot to the passport, the digitized photo will print out as a part of the passport document.

This improves the security and integrity of the passport as well as eliminating labor costs.
At full production, systems will be installed in Portsmouth NH, New Orleans, Boston, New York, Philadelphia, Washington DC, Miami, Houston, Chicago, Los Angles, San Francisco, Seattle, Honolulu, Charleston SC, and Stanford CT.

Where passports are concerned, security is extremely high. If one comes across a U.S. passport, it is probably legitimate; if one is attempting to create a false passport, the odds of success are low.

How to Get A Real Passport

The difficulty in applying for a US passport in a "created" name (they will check a bunch of databases) or attempting to falsify one (I'll come see you on Sunday's and bring cigarettes) leaves only a couple of options for the determined international mover and shaker.

Remember every US citizen is entitled to a passport – if an Identity Assumer happened to pick a person that had never applied for a passport, and he had done his homework, the document would probably be issued.

Guess wrong and one will be in small room with several people wearing white socks, black shoes and gold badges.

There is really no guaranteed method to discover if a person has applied for a passport, except, of course, to ask the person in question.

That is to say, it's not out of the question to inquire, after a little research, if a person would mind you becoming them, for passport purposes only.

The agreement is shaky at best; you are pledging not to take over any other part of John Smith's life, while he reciprocates with a promise to never apply for a passport.

Plan on spending some money to seal this mutual agreement.

Probably best done between trusting friends.

One other option is to hit up the passport agency for a quickie immediately after the target died and his demise probably hasn't made its way into many databases yet.

Please note I am NOT advising anyone to attempt this; I just don't know and I would add, if it works (on an expedited basis, get in, get out) and I would not plan on coming back to the U.S. for my dear old grandmother's birthday.

Second Passports

U.S. citizens, as well as those from many other countries have the legal option of being a citizen of more than one country at a time. Not too long ago, as the crow flies, this was not the case and a second passport, if discovered, could have led to fairly unpleasant legal action. There are as many ways to get a second passport as there are reasons for desiring one. Some legitimate, some, well, some not so legitimate.

In this section we are going to take a look why a person would want a second passport – everything from "investing" nontaxable money offshore, to running from someone who wants you badly, be them the FBI, Mafia, or just the ex-wife-with-a-great-lawyer.

The following information has been complied from some of the best experts in the business, plus my own efforts. Take it for what it is worth – it should answer many questions and set the reader on the path that won't leave him broke, mad and maybe busted.

There are many avenues into a second citizenship, from those of a top level diplomat to a bottom feeder citizen. Each requires some effort, usually in the form of introductions and cash, although some countries will accept the cash in the form of the would-be-citizen purchasing land or domiciles in the target country.

Some countries, if one can prove correct ancestry, will issue a second passport, flat-out free (Ireland has always been good, Israel was founded on this very principle).

And they both kept their word.

A few other nations have similar programs that alleviate nearly all the hassle and cost factor involved in becoming a second citizen.

Let's start the reader's education with a composition of by Dr. Georg Adem of Financial Privacy Consultants, Inc. (an attorney who specializes in this type of work) used with his permission :http://www.privacy-consultants.com email contact: counselor@privacy-consultants.com, and little old me.

First, thing little old me would like to present is that if you are serious about a 2nd passport, understand there are countless web sites, dealers, "attorney's" and other people of indifferent credentials that can "smooth the way for you and your new life".

Okay, so you cough up anywhere between $4,000 and $50,000 and hand it over to a web contact who claims to be a Costa Rican attorney.

How exactly do you plan on recovering your cash once disappeared to into a diplomatic tangle in some third world county?

International small claims court?

So, right off the bat I have to say that I favor a term known as "escrow", wherein a mutually acceptable bank holds all funds until the deal has been successfully completed.

Most brokers/attorneys will try to talk you out of this idea.

Dr. Adem separates the various available programs into a number of categories; the first, and best he delegates "white glove" programs, for obvious reasons.

When we're talking of passports, we're really talking citizenships. A passport is an, easily recognizable evidence of citizenship. Every country in this world has more or less well defined parameters how you may become naturalized in their nation. However, 99.9% do not advertise their programs or are keen to promote them – it's more or less a "find-the-loophole-task" and then take advantage of it. If you are an outstanding sportsman or a charismatic entrepreneur it is usually easier and faster to obtain a certain citizenship within a short amount of time - and probably no money (or bribe) involved. There exist numerous examples for fast naturalizations in the USA, Switzerland, Germany, Luxembourg – usually countries in high demand, but difficult to access.

The same rules apply for smaller countries, especially for countries which are classified 3rd or 2nd world, BUT here you can upgrade very often your appearance with the help of well spent 'donations'. Albeit you have to find the best deals, money wise and visa-free-travel-wise if you have been a dual citizen from birth or childhood, or else became a citizen of another country after already having U.S. citizenship, and the other country in question does not have any laws or regulations requiring you to formally renounce your U.S. citizenship before U.S. consular officials, then current U.S. law unambiguously assures your right to keep both citizenship's for life.

Remember each level of accessibility and ease of application raises the ante on the hand.

White Glove programs typically range from a $5000 starter kit to $150,000 for a top drawer first class country.

The cheapest white glove program is Grenada at $54,000. You can have Dominica for $75,000, mas o menos, or St. Kitts/Nevis for $250,000, of course, it comes with a condo.

You can have the U.S., Canada, New Zealand, or Australia for free if you can jump through all the hoops and don't need it anytime soon and are willing to pay 50% of everything you earn for the privilege.

White glove programs are not suitable to someone who has had legal entanglements that make him or her less than welcome in a white glove country, yet, ironically, the seeker is often most enthusiastic about relocation. A tainted past can be anything from bad credit, to a felony conviction for a something that is not a crime in most civilized countries, to unacceptable political views, or to someone who has ever been the target of an FBI or Interpol investigation. Front door programs require fingerprinting.

If you've got problems, none of the "free" countries will take you, and neither will Grenada or the others, even for a lot of money.

All economic programs use licensed agents to vet the applicants. The program facilitator will often say that "no one ever recommended by the company has been turned down". This is true. This doesn't mean they're slipping someone an extra $500 to get you in. It means they review the application and when they find you come from a blacklisted country or can't submit a police clearance, or you put on the application that you were arrested in 1965 for smoking a joint or your credit report doesn't equal six figures or shows a bankruptcy; they will flush you out before they submit you.

Therefore, no one is ever turned down. White Glove programs are not suitable for someone who wants a 'fresh start' for any reason, including fleeing an abusive spouse, because all white glove programs require a very straight forward posting of one's past and, therefore, a finger pointing right smack into your future.

Just as alternative programs have the chance of being fraudulent, so do PT programs have the potential for going sour when a new government takes over and wishes to rid itself of all those wealth robbing foreigners who entered under the previously constitutional programs enacted by an elitist parliament who is no longer in power.

The political undesirables who received economic citizenship are all on one list, duly entered into the official rolls. But for the rest of us poor devils, blood might not be blessed us with a Belizean/Canadian mother and a Cypriot father and an Italian grandfather!

Fortunately, there are alternatives.

Aside: two useful genealogy/citizenship sites: for Ireland:

http://www.amireland.com , for Italy, http:// www.daddezio.com. and http://www.phoenix.net/~joe/itans.

Persons who live in countries from which they wish to emigrate, say old Soviet Bloc countries or Asian countries in flux, may not be willing to queue up for years awaiting first world permission to immigrate or may not be able afford the high cost of first world economic citizenship.

By acquiring discretionary citizenship in a civilized South American country, the immigrant increases a family's chances ten fold for approval into its first world target country, say the U.S., or a country of the EU and has escaped poor conditions and can safely live and work and amass capital to continue its journey, or perhaps find that they have found paradise in a country it never knew much about until it 'bought' its way in.

A number of years ago Dr. Hill (not his real name) wrote a series of very expensive books and offered consolation for persons wishing to becomes "PT's" (Perpetual Travelers), i.e., free world citizens that kept no real home base.

PT advocates generally are not looking for a country for immigration purposes since they are operating under the "Five Flags" theory, one of tenets being never live in the same country as your passport (thereby nominally living outside the system of the country of residency).

A PT is urged to view a residency country as an innkeeper. If the services are commensurate with the tariff, you keep your room at the inn. If the rate goes up or services fall or the climate sours, one moves on.

In this scenario, one's new citizenship is not for the purpose of finding employment or a home, but for the convenience it offers to visit and linger within 'innkeeper' countries.

In this solution matrix, an alternate citizenship can provide the means to visit and stay in countries without acquiring visas (thereby not checking into the system). By carefully looking at the list of visa free countries approved by a potential 'innkeeper' country, one might find alternative citizenship's that are more useful or more affordable than "front door" programs.

There are persons who are using some of Dr. Hill's advice, who simply wish to acquire a "banking passport" under a name other than one's given name, in order to hold assets anonymously without the bother and cost of international business corporations (IBC's) and registered agents and nominee directors and annual renewal fees or trusts with yearly trustee fees and the attendant risk of someone else having a hand on your funds.

Crudely put, it might be better to spend $25,000 once and have no risk whatsoever, than $3000 per year for 20 years with some risk of misappropriation or discovery.

There is also an even nastier reason. If one is trying to use such a contrivance to escape the jurisdiction a high-tax country, the IBC/trust route to anonymity is, in 99.9% of cases, just as potentially unlawful as the anonymous banking passport and a lot more likely to be discovered.

How dare I say that? Because if you can afford international tax advice, which includes citizenship portfolios, from competent lawyers and accountancy firms and your track record is clean enough, your bank account is fat enough, you are probably not going to benefit from this advice.

And tax-avoidance-international – planning is a dicey bit of business for the do-it-yourselfer. If you don't have assets in the millions and you're not paying $50,000 for the advice, chances are the advice you're getting is just mucking up already muddy waters. And, Lord forgive me for saying this, but firms who offer advice for a large fee to help you avoid tax or hide assets, will usually set up programs which require their watchful eye and a yearly retainer.

I'm equally sure that none of them receive commissions from the companies abroad who actually set up the accounts and manages them on behalf of the client.

Less it be said that I unreasonably besmirch the carriage trade practice (since I too have plied that trade), may I remind the reader that any of us who offer this type of tax or asset protection advice are either officers of some court or have otherwise sworn oaths to uphold national and state laws and we fear a disgruntled, revenge minded client as much as the long arm of the law. Put practically, no one can afford to offer anything less than upper crust white bread advice with the threat of lawsuits from errors and omissions and criminal prosecution for 'structuring' held over our heads.

Can you imagine how vulnerable a lawyer would be if he were to have the gall to tell you to forget the whole international planning route and instead buy a Mozambique passport for $5000 in any other name except yours, get a mail drop address with 24 hour access based on your new passport and a $200 international driver's license to match.

Then he might be so bold as to suggest his customer open a bank account in his own country as a foreigner here temporarily on vacation from his missionary practice in a town not less than a thirty-minute drive from where one really lives (since deposits held by foreigners are not reported to the government), regularly deposit by mail or at another branch in a town not your own, cash under $5000 or small money orders available for a buck at the local grocers and forget international tax planning since it is possible to move about a million dollars per year this way.

Of course, one can visit one's funds with an ATM/Visa debit card that one will most likely leave the bank with the day this account is opened. And if one wanted to be extra safe, he could buy a $25,000 second passport and in a new name with supporting ID including driver's license and birth certificate, in a territorially based tax country (no tax unless the income is made in the country) and then move the funds to a new bank near, but not in, the new homeland.

Then one could withdraw the funds with a Visa debit card, or if one is willing to spend a miserly $50,000 on your new citizenship, an EU passport in the new family name and one could live in, say, London, on the fruits of the ill-gotten gains.

Can you imagine any lawyer saying this? Why not?

Because if the client doesn't do everything exactly right or tells his wife or soon-to-be-ex-wife, or brags to the girls at the club about the great advice he got from the "smart" lawyer, and someone takes offense, or tries it themselves and forgets some of the steps and blows it, they're going to call some crew cut government official whose going to lean on one's person until one names one's lawyer in about 10 seconds as the guy who gave you this allegedly felonious advice and next thing, the lawyer knows, he's in prison or spending every cent he has to stay out.

All that for $300 worth of honest advice? No, dear reader, it's much better to charge you $50,000 up front and $10,000 a year and make sure that you have properly avoided tax under Subpart F of Revenue Code Section 954. We can both sleep better at night. In conclusion, there is a host of alternative citizenship's available that may be more affordable and more useful than 'front door' programs and for persons whose credentials are not impeccable or whose pockets are not full, these programs can mean the difference between slavery and freedom but they may take a little more work on the part of the client.

For a starter, here's a list of countries available with a waiting period not longer than 90 days and with total costs not exceeding $40,000:

Guatemala
Costa Rica
Honduras
Venezuela
Paraguay .
Nicaragua .
Dominican Republic

Along with the 7 examples above, one must consider the usual requirements including if one needs to travel to the issuing country or spend any amount of time there.

I (Dr. Adem) have personal experiences with a similar program from Panama. This worked very well, and there was no obligation at all to travel there, although I did go to visit my new country once I had my new passport.

With most countries the entire process can be done by mail, one does not even have to spend time there, but of course are always invited to visit your new country. I have worked and am still working with all of the countries listed.

The easiest of the bunch to deal with are Guatemala and Costa Rica.

Requirements are generally easy to meet (application form, photos, in CR a police certificate are needed).

If you are serious about the second passport concept I would advise you to check out Dr. Adem's site as well as check out a number of the references I have indicated in the offshore section before making any final decision.

Top 10 Benefits From Owning a Second Passport

1. Visa free travel to areas that may be difficult to travel to with your current passport.

2. Travel freely, without creating a permanent record on your current passport.

3. You can get a fresh start with a legal name change.

4. Open offshore bank or brokerage accounts more privately.

5. You don't risk being singled out, due to your current nationality, by terrorists, thieves, terrocrats, etc.

6. You'll be able to distance yourself from potential problems due to a nasty divorce, bad partnership, a run away jury verdict, etc.

7. Tax advantages. Becoming a citizen of a country that does not impose taxes on world wide income, capital gains, estate or death taxes on her citizens, may have significant value when one is considering estate planning. This area should be discussed with your legal or accounting professional.

8. Enjoy complete peace of mind knowing that should it become necessary, due to some political, social or financial disaster, to relocate elsewhere, your right to permanent residency in another country is guaranteed and protected under law, by virtue of your acquired citizenship.

9. You should seriously consider that at some future date, high taxation countries may elect to impose punitive "exit" or "departure" taxes on citizens who become citizens of "tax haven" countries. Taxing authorities may determine your purpose for obtaining a second citizenship followed by your "renunciation", was primarily

done for tax "related / avoidance" matters, and continue to impose taxes on your worldwide income, well into the future. U.S. citizens, in particular, should consult with knowledgeable legal and or accounting professionals, concerning these matters.

10. You're living in a country ruled by totalitarians or communists and want to leave safely? One of the very few safe ways to do so is by becoming citizen of another country first. (Dr. Adem).

As long as we are being fair about this sharing thing let's take a look at some advice from another source that specializes in second passport placement and advice:

PT Shamrock Ltd.
EBC House
Townsend Lane
London NW9 8LL
Great Britain
E-mail PT Shamrock Limited, ptshamrock@ptshamrock.com

Where Do I Take Delivery Of My Passport?

Delivery is normally made in Europe which is greatly to your benefit. For instance Switzerland is the easiest country to enter on your present passport and if you like you can travel out of Switzerland on your new passport. The Swiss do not stamp visa-free passports either upon entry or exit. Passports that need visas like St.Kitts/Nevis and the Bahamas will be stamped.

Why Is There An Additional Cost For Family Members?

A few countries such as Argentina and Bolivia allow additional family members to be included in the original passport which greatly reduces the cost to additional family members. However the countries currently on offer issue a separate passport for each family member and the processing time is the same for each. Remember a passport is for life, so even if a child is newly born, he will need a passport to travel and the cost is the same. There are however reduced rates, in some cases, for children under the age of 18 years. If family members are processed at a later date than when the original application was processed then the cost is the same as the original, as the processing implications are the same.

How Long Are Passports Valid And Can They Be Renewed?

Most passports are valid for ten years, but may have to be extended at the end of five years. This is not a formal renewing process requiring new forms and photographs. Your present passport is simply taken to any Consulate and is stamped, extending it for a further five years, usually while you wait. At the end of ten years a new passport will be issued through a Consulate or Embassy, new forms and photographs are required. The process will take a few days depending on Consular policy and upon passport traffic at the particular office.

Are There Any Countries on Offer But That You Do Not Recommend?

As a last resort, we will offer Paraguay, Chile and Peru. We will not however accept any responsibility for these countries because of constant political and legal changes. There are also potential problems related to customs, immigration and passport renewal procedures.

Remain skeptical, Investigate thoroughly before you part with your money.

Obtaining a second passport is a major step, and you must choose the firm with which you deal as carefully as you would choose a surgeon. Avoid any firm which asks for advance up front consulting fees. You will never again see your money or any documents. Your money must go into a protected account with a reliable bank where it takes your signature to release any funds. This is the only way your money is safe.

Is It Possible For Me To Obtain Documents Under A Different Name?

The question often arises from Middle Eastern clients whose surname might subject them to terrorism. Therefore once we are satisfied that your record is free of criminal convictions, it is possible to apply under a different name, by using a deed-poll legal name change procedure. We can legally change your name in the country from where your new passport will be issued.

To do this we must file the documents necessary for a legal name change in the issuing country, which will then allow us to apply for the passport in the new name. The name change will only be recorded in the issuing country and nowhere else. The additional fee is U.S. $7,500 but we must emphasize that although it is perfectly legal to carry out this task, we must first be satisfied that your intentions are proper.

What Advantages Do Latin American Passports Have Over Other Passports?

Legally every Latin American has two last names. Firstly, his or her father's last name, followed by his or her mother's last name. For example if your name is John Doe because your father's name was Jacob Doe and your mother's maiden name was Sarah Smith then your full legal name, carried in your Latin American passport is John Doe Smith.

Legally you may call yourself John Doe or John Smith or John Doe-Smith, and legally you may travel in any of these names, open bank accounts in any of the se names, hold assets in any of these names and maintain credit cards in any of these names. Since most people (i.e. creditors, friends, associates, tax authorities, and even ex-spouses) have no idea what your mother's maiden name was this is a perfect opportunity to protect your assets by using a legal alternative name.

In addition, certain Central American Countries that were former Spanish colonies have a special law. This special law may allow you to parlay your Central American citizenship into a Spanish, i.e., EU passport, should you qualify.

Camouflage Passports – The Real Story

Besides legitimate, fraudulent, diplomatic and second another category of passports exists.

At least they're passports in name if in nothing else.

Camouflage passports are counterfeit documents designed, at least by the companies that sell them, to be carried by Americans (or other nationalities) that could be in danger in certain areas of the world simply because of their country of origin.

The CP's are actually manufactured by only a few sources, but are sold by many web sites and catalog mail order houses.

Most seem to be of good quality and will pass an inspection by someone not trained, or ill trained, in the art of passport inspection.

I had a conversation with a special agent of the Customs Department and asked him a couple of questions about CP's:

Me: "Are they legal?"

Customs: "If used for their intended purpose, we have no problem with them."

M: "Has anyone been caught trying to enter the United States with a CP?"

C: "Oh yes, a number of times. Tell your readers we are aware of what the documents look like and we do like to keep up on what countries still exist. You might say its part of the job."

M: "What about crossing into a third world country with a less educated border service?"

C: "I have heard of this situation occurring, but personally I wouldn't want to chance spending time in a third world jail."

M: "Are there any other uses for CP's you can share?"

C: "In many countries one must surrender one's passport to a hotel or innkeeper or even directly to the authorities. This procedure is designed to keep track of foreign nationals and in some extreme cases to prevent them from leaving the country."

I know of times in this situation when a CP has been substituted for a real passport, although again I would want to be very, very careful about the sophistication of the forces involved before attempting this.

Of course the obvious use of a CP is to establish an ID (with back up documents) in order to open a bank account or perform other cash-involved transactions. In any case I can think of this would be quite illegal.

The following is a letter directly from one of the largest and probably best suppliers of these types of documents.

Inside Address
123 Happy Go Lucky Lane
Ilove, HI 12345

Dear Mr. French:

Thank you for your recent request regarding International Drivers Permits, we comment as follows:

It is not necessary in most countries to produce your regular drivers license together with an international permit. As the International permit is normally issued only after one's regular license has been produced, the international license is acceptable on it's own. Most purchasers of the IDL's purchase a certificate of residence at the same time as their IDL which confirms that the holder resides in the county specified on the IDL, hence all bases are covered.

All camouflage passports are based on countries that no longer exist. If they were based on existing countries, they'd be forgeries and therefore illegal. Here's some info on camo passports for you:

Camouflage passports are replicas of passports from countries that no longer exist or countries that have changed their names. The countries generally were small, out of the way places and the average official would know almost nothing about them. These documents are approved by the U.S. State department as a means of protecting U.S. citizens from religious fundamentalists, anti-wealth zealots, hijackers, thieves and terrorists, unscrupulous merchants, angry mobs, kidnappers, and other dangerous groups. There have been many instances where holders of these documents have managed to escape danger simply because they were not carrying their regular first world passports.

We offer the very best camo passports available. Each passport comes with 2 ID documents and a drivers license. Passports and back up documents are available from the following countries:

British Honduras, Rhodesia, Burma, New Granada, Dutch Guiana, Netherlands East Indies, British West Indies, Republic of Zanzibar, Eastern Samoa, New Hebrides, British Guiana, Spanish Guinea, South Vietnam, and USSR.

$XXX buys you the passport of your choice, 2 pieces of back-up ID and a drivers License.

Trusting that the above is in order and looking forward to hearing from you.

Henry Morgan
Proprietor

The Freebooter
PO Box 489
St. Peter Port
Guernsey GY1 6BS, C.I.

www. Freebooter.com

The following page shows a camo passport, as well as a "drivers license" from :

Quester Press Ltd.
6-8 High Street
Bishops Waltham
Hampshire S032 !AB
UK
Fax 44-1489 890044

The documents are well made, feel and look like the real thing. Each one has an entry stamp or two and can be backed – up by a couple pieces of ancillary ID.

In my opinion they would pass to any untrained, and perhaps a few trained eyes.

Quester also has a newsletter and a couple of interesting reports.

Please fax, or write for the latest prices.

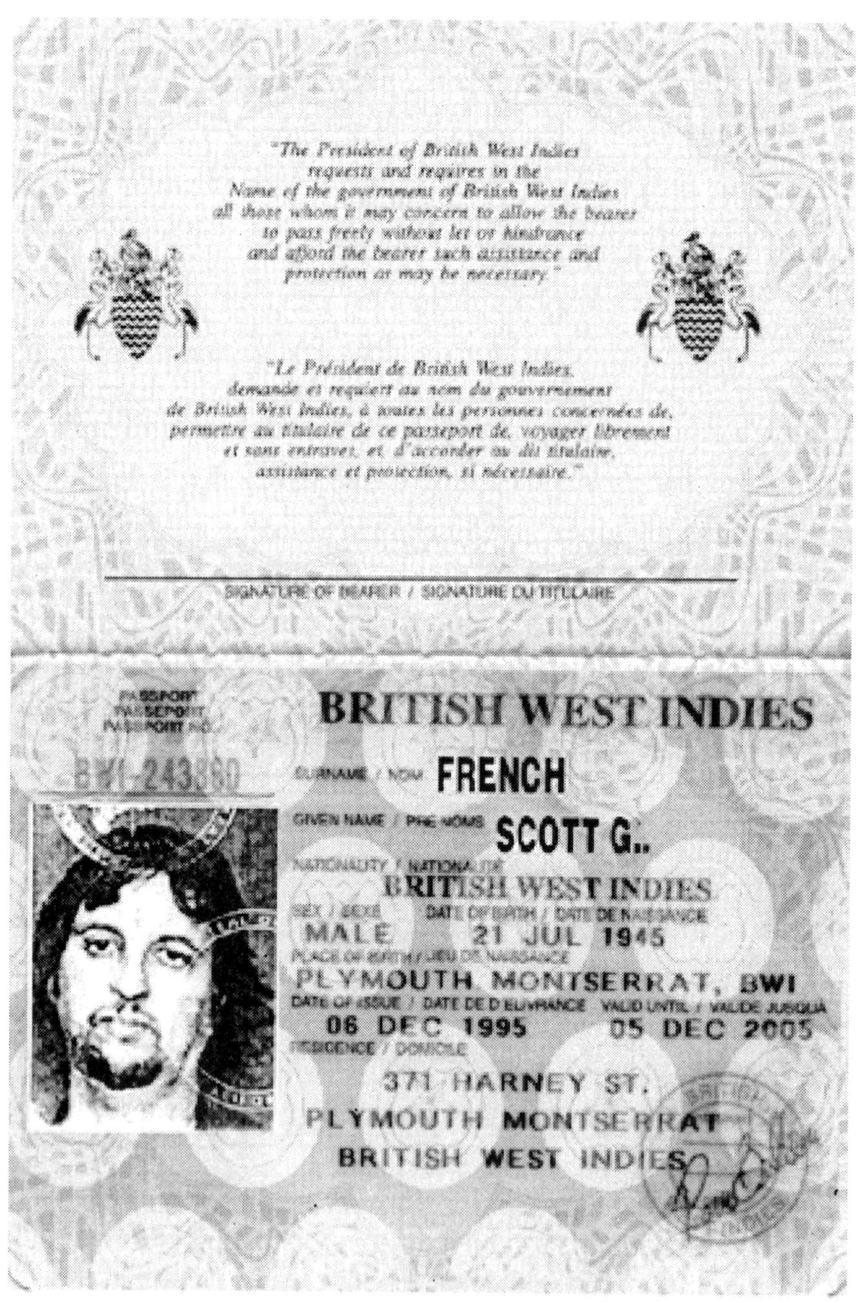
"The President of British West Indies
requests and requires in the
Name of the government of British West Indies
all those whom it may concern to allow the bearer
to pass freely without let or hindrance
and afford the bearer such assistance and
protection as may be necessary."
"Le Président de British West Indies
demande et requiert au nom du gouvernement
de British West Indies, à toutes les personnes concernées de,
permettre au titulaire de ce passeport de, voyager librement
et sans entraves, et, d'accorder au dit titulaire,
assistance et protection, si nécessaire."
SIGNATURE OF BEARER / SIGNATURE DU TITULAIRE
BRITISH WEST INDIES
SURNAME / NOM
FRENCH
GIVEN NAME / PRENOMS
SCOTT G.
NATIONALITY / NATIONALITE
BRITISH WEST INDIES
SEX / SEXE
MALE
DATE OF BIRTH / DATE DE NAISSANCE
21 JUL 1945
PLACE OF BIRTH / LIEU DE NAISSANCE
PLYMOUTH MONTSERRAT, BWI
DATE OF ISSUE / DATE DE DELIVRANCE
06 DEC 1995
VALID UNTIL / VALIDE JUSQUA
05 DEC 2005
RESIDENCE / DOMICILE
371 HARNEY ST.
PLYMOUTH MONTSERRAT
BRITISH WEST INDIES

NEW
GRANADA
NG-296427
SCOTT ENGLISH
21-07-1945
M
BLUE
1.83M
25-07-1996
24-07-2006
DRIVERS LICENSE
<<NG-427-ENGL>>

Catch Those Illegal

Real Americans are not the only group suffering the slings and arrows of "new and improved" (just like your laundry detergent) ID procedures.

After California governor Pete Wilson's plan to require every California citizen to carry a card proving they really are California citizens was defeated, the INS took up the ball and ran with it.

The "Green Card" (which has not been green for a number of years) has always been the primary ID for those of us that look like we might have entered the U.S. by climbing a fence rather than by traditional means, has just undergone a major overhaul to help prevent counterfeiting.

This step probably was necessary – anyone who has ever drifted into East Los Angeles and doesn't appear to be a caucasian cop could purchase a very realistic green card (and often driver's license) within a few minutes.

Same goes for any major Chinatown in the country.

A History Of The Green Card

What is known today as a "Green Card" came in a variety of different formats and colors during its history. We still refer to all versions as Green Cards for the same reason dismissal notices is called "pink slips." Yet the card's purpose of indicating a lawful permanent resident's authorization to live and work in the United States has remained constant. Alien Registration Act of 1940.

As a national defense measure, the Alien Registration Act of 1940 required for the first time in the nation's history that all aliens (non-U.S. citizens) within the United States register with the federal government at post offices. Their registration forms were forwarded to the Immigration and Naturalization Service (INS) for processing, after which a receipt card (Form AR-3) was mailed to each registrant as proof of compliance with the law.

The law did not discriminate between legal and illegal alien residents. All aliens had to register, and all received AR-3s. Post World War II – The First Green Card

As World War II ended and large-scale immigration to the United States resumed, alien registration ceased to take place at post offices and became part of regular immigration procedures at ports of entry.

The INS, based on the alien's admission status, issued different documents to serve as Alien Registration Receipt Cards.

For example, visitors received an I-94c, temporary foreign laborers received an I-100a, and legal permanent residents (LPRs) received an I-151. The small, green Form I-151 had immediate value in identifying its holder as an alien who was entitled to live and work indefinitely in the United States.

The Internal Security Act of 1950 – The Value of the Green Card Increases
Following passage of the Internal Security Act of 1950, new regulations issued by INS made the Alien Registration Receipt Card, Form I-151, even more valuable.

Effective April 17,1951, aliens holding AR-3 cards could replace them with a new Form I-151 (Green Card). However, only those with legal status could replace their AR-3. Aliens who could not prove their legal admission into the United States could not qualify for LPR status and were subject to prosecution for violating U.S. immigration laws. As a result, the Form I-151 card represented security to its holder.

It indicated the right to live and work in the United States permanently and instantly communicated that right to law enforcement officials.

Because of the card's cumbersome official title – Alien Registration Receipt Card, aliens, immigration attorneys, and enforcement officers came to refer to it by its color, calling it the "Green Card.

The Green Card changed color in the early 1950's, the status of being a Green Card holder became so desirable that counterfeit Form I-151s became a serious problem.

To combat document fraud, the INS issued 17 different re-designs of the Form I-151 between 1952 and its complete revision in 1977. In 1964, the color of the Green Card was changed to pale blue. After 1964, it became a dark blue.

Regardless of color, the Form I-151 still carried with it the benefits indicated by the term Green Card, and those who wanted, obtained, issued or inspected it continued to refer to it by that name.

During the mid-1970's, INS studied methods to produce a more counterfeit-resistant Green Card. The study resulted in centralized card production at the Immigration Card Facility in Texas.

This created standardization and accountability lacking with local card production. In addition, new materials and technologies were introduced to create a new machine verifiable Green Card.

The new Green Card, first issued in 1977, also had a new form number, I-551. The 1986 Immigration Reform and Control Act (IRCA). In 1986, the Immigration Reform and Control Act, for the first time, gave employers legal incentives for verifying employment documents.

However, the many and varied versions of the Green Card made this task daunting. To simplify the verification process for employers, as well as to further reduce the counterfeiting risk, INS once again created a new card version in 1989.

To further combat document fraud, effective March 20,1996, the old Form I-151 Green Cards issued prior to 1979, became obsolete. The Form I-551 Alien Registration Receipt Card became the only valid Green Card.

Despite these efforts, the anti-fraud technology utilized for the 1989 card version was quickly matched by counterfeiting technology, forcing INS to develop a more secure "Green Card. "

The Green Card became green again in order to thwart counterfeiters, INS switched to the high-tech Integrated Card Production System (ICPS).

Today's ICPS cards mark a significant achievement in the history of Green Card production. Although the card form number remains the same, Form I-551, the new card now contains many state-of-the-art security features that can be expanded, as necessary, to keep one step ahead of counterfeiters.

The card also features a name change from "Alien Registration Receipt Card" to "Permanent Resident Card."

One of the most secure documents in the federal government, the new Green Card can easily incorporate future technology to maintain its resistance to counterfeiting. As older versions of the Green Cards are taken out of circulation as they expire, the new card will gradually become the only valid Form I-551 in circulation.

Following is the text of an immigration and Naturalization Service fact sheet on the new "Green Card" that officials believe will curtail fraud and help employers comply with U.S. immigration law.

- The new card is a major milestone in combating document fraud. Produced by state-of-the-art technology, the card is more durable, more tamper-resistant, and more counterfeit-resistant
- In addition, the new Green Card has several visible high-tech security features that will assist employers in identifying valid cards more easily, thereby helping them comply with workplace immigration laws

- The new Permanent Resident Card is being produced by INS' new Integrated Card Production System (ICPS) machines, which enable INS to continuously expand security features to stay ahead of counterfeiters

- Made up of several different components, these one-of-a-kind machines perform a number of complex tasks in a single automated process

- These tasks range from digital printing, laser etching and encoding the optical stripe, to applying other visible and invisible security features and generating the card's mailing package

- By automatically producing a complete package ready for mailing, the ICPS will reduce manufacturing time and greatly increase the accuracy of information in the new cards

- The Green Card, previously named the Alien Registration Receipt Card, is now officially called the Permanent Resident Card. The card's form number, Form I-551, remains the same

- Unlike the previous laminated paper cards, the new Permanent Resident Card is a plastic document similar to a credit card. It has digital photograph, and fingerprint images which are an integral part of the card and, therefore, more tamper-resistant

- It features a hologram depicting the Statue of Liberty, the letters "USA" in large print, an outline of the United States and the INS seal

- On the reverse side of the card, there is an optical memory stripe – similar to CD-ROM disk technology – with an engraved version of the information contained on the front of the card, including the cardholder's photograph, name, signature, date of birth and alien registration number

- This laser-etched information cannot be erased or altered. In addition, this same information, along with the cardholder's fingerprint, is digitally encoded in the stripe and can only be read by INS personnel using a specially designed reader

- The new Green Card will cost approximately $10 per card to produce, which is comparable to the production cost of the older version

- The INS will issue only the new version of the Green Card. Individuals with approved applications for permanent resident status as well as those applying to renew expired cards will receive the new Green Card

- Holders of previous versions of the Green Card do not need to replace their cards. Cards issued since 1989 are valid for 10 years and will remain valid until the expiration date indicated on the face of the card, allowing gradual card replacement for the approximately 10 million current cardholders

- Form I-551 Green Cards that were issued from 1977 to 1989 and do not have an expiration date will remain valid until INS announces an official replacement program for these cards in the future

- A Green Card is obtained when an individual becomes a lawful permanent resident. The Green Card has a 10-year validity period, and cardholders must renew their cards when they expire

- To renew expired "Green Cards," cardholders must submit to their local INS office a completed Form I-90, along with a filing fee

- Distribution of the first new cards had been delayed for several months due to unforeseen quality control problems associated with the startup of this complex new technology. These manufacturing problem should have been fixed, and the cards are now being produced at two INS facilities

- Distribution of the first 50,000 new Green Cards to permanent residents began on April 21, 1998, as does a broad outreach effort to introduce the card and its features to employers and the general public

- Production of the new cards is underway at two locations; St. Albans, Vermont and Laguna Niguel, California. By the end of this calendar year, three more sites will be on-line, one in Lincoln, Nebraska and two more in Kentucky

This same system will be employed to produce Employment Authorization Documents (authorizes a nonimmigrant to work in the United States and is generally valid for one-year period) as well as Foreign Student Cards (issued to certain nonimmigrant students or exchange students under a pilot program).

- One should also note a few obscure other ID documents are still valid such as the Northern Mariana Islands Card, issued during a two-year period that ended July 1, 1990

The Service issued Northern Mariana Identification Cards to aliens who acquired U.S. citizenship when the Covenant to Establish a Commonwealth of the Northern Mariana Islands in Political Union with the United States became effective on November 3, 1986. These cards remain valid as evidence of U.S. citizenship.

Although INS no longer issues these cards, a U.S. citizen to whom a card was issued may file Form I-777, Application for Issuance or Replacement of Northern Mariana Card, to obtain replacement of a lost, stolen, or mutilated Northern Mariana Identification Card

- The law requires an employee to present to an employer documentation that establishes his or her identity and eligibility to work in the United States. This is necessary for completion of the Employment Eligibility Verification Form, Form I-9. The employee has the choice of which document(s) to present

After being hired, an employee who is a lawful permanent resident can present a Green Card to establish both identity and employment eligibility for the Form I-9. If the employer examines the card and believes it does not appear genuine, the employer may ask the employee to provide alternative documentation. The employer should show the employee the complete list of documents and ask whether they can present other acceptable documentation.

- The new Green Card incorporates several visible security features which employers can see when examining the card for employment verification purposes. These include the holograms and the optical memory stripe with the laser-etched engraving of the cardholder's information

4. For more information on the use of the new Green Card for employment eligibility verification, employers can contact the INS Office of Business Liaison or visit INS World Wide Web site at http://www.ins.usdoj.gov.

How to Steal Anyone's Identity

One of the most successful, virtually under prosecuted and lucrative crimes of the decade are known as identity theft. A determined crook can make $100,000 in a few weeks, leave almost no trail and suffer very little fear of arrest.

As one might expect, it's also one of the fastest growing crimes in the country. To be a trifle more exact, over 400,000 people were victimized by this particular crime during the past year.

Damn few people went to jail.

When a disabled telecommuter received her credit report from TRW it was seven pages long and had over 15 past due fraudulent accounts. There was also a judgment against her from an eviction that had taken place from an apartment.

Later, she also received notice that she had defaulted on a loan. When she went to file criminal charges against her identity thief, the local sheriff's department said that the case would probably never be looked at because there were only two detectives and "it was not as important as a murder."

TRW required that she proves to the 15 creditors herself that she had filed a criminal report by sending them notarized statements (at a cost of $10 each). None of the creditors prosecuted the thief...

Identity Theft: The Problem

Identity theft occurs when someone uses the identifying information of another person, name, Social Security Number, mother's maiden name, or other personal information, to commit fraud or engage in other unlawful activities.

For example, an identity thief may open a new credit card account under someone else's name. When the identity thief fails to pay the bills, the bad debt is reported on the victim's credit report.

Other common forms of identity theft include taking over an existing credit card account and making unauthorized charges on it (typically, the identity thief forestalls discovery by the victims by contacting the credit card issuer and changing the billing address on the account), taking out loans in another person's name, writing fraudulent checks using another person's name and/or account number; and using personal information to access, and transfer money out of, another person's bank or brokerage account.

Fraud Units: Overview

The Vice President of Associated Credit Bureaus, Inc., provided overview information on the fraud units of the three national credit bureaus – Equifax, Inc., Experian Corporation; and Trans Union Corporation. The overview information covered, for example, the year that the respective fraud unit was created and the year that a toll-free number was available to consumers.

According to this official, all of the fraud units have increased their staffing levels in recent years due to various reasons, including more referrals from the creditor community and a greater incidence of credit fraud. Also, this official commented that one national bureau does track some fraud statistics, but the other two national bureaus do not.

He added that, the three bureaus may be willing to consider the feasibility of systematically and consistently tracking various forms of fraud, including identity fraud, "if the value of such an effort outweighs the costs."

In extreme cases, the identity thief may completely take over his or her victim's identity – opening a bank account, getting multiple credit cards, buying a car, getting a home mortgage and even working under the victim's name.

Identity theft almost always involves a financial service institution in some way, as a lender, holder of a bank account, or credit card or debit card issuer, because, as the bank robber Willie Sutton observed, "that is where the money is."

Identity theft involving financial services institutions, is accomplished through a wide variety of means. Historically, identity thieves have been able to get the personal information they need to operate through simple, "low-tech" methods: intercepting orders of new checks in the mail, or rifling through the trash to get discarded bank account statements or pre-approved credit card offers.

Sometimes, identity thieves will try to trick others into giving up this information. As discussed in more detail below, one way in which identity thieves do this is by "pretexting," or calling on false pretenses, such as by telephoning banks and posing as the account holder. In other cases, the identity thief may contact the victim directly.

In a practice known as "skimming," identity thieves use computers to read and store the information encoded on the magnetic strip of an ATM or credit card when that card is inserted through either a specialized card reader or a legitimate payment mechanism (e.g., the card reader used to pay for gas at the pump in a gas station). Once stored, that information can be re-encoded onto any other card with a magnetic strip, instantly transforming a blank card into a machine-readable ATM or credit card identical to that of the victim.

In addition, the increased availability of information on the Internet can facilitate identity theft. For individuals who are victims of identity theft, the costs can be significant and long-lasting. Identity thieves can run up debts in the tens of thousands of dollars under their victims' names. Even where the individual consumer is not legally liable for these debts, the consequences to the consumer are often considerable.

The consumer's credit history is frequently scarred, and he or she typically must spend numerous hours sometimes over the course of months or even years contesting bills and straightening out credit reporting errors. In the interim, the consumer victim may be denied loans, mortgages, and employment; a bad credit report may even prevent him or her from something as simple as opening a new bank account at when other accounts are tainted and a new account is essential.

The government is finally getting around to passing laws to deal with the problem of ID theft, but the actual prosecution is still lagging a bit in the background as we will soon see...

The Identity Theft And Assumption Deterrence Act Of 1998

Recently, Congress passed the Identity Theft and Assumption Deterrence Act of 1998 ("Identity Theft Act" or "Act"). The Act addresses identity theft in two significant ways. First, the Act strengthens the criminal laws governing identity theft. Specifically, the Act amends 18 U.S.C. §1028 ("Fraud and related activity in connection with identification documents") to make it a federal crime to: knowingly transfer or use, without lawful authority, a means of identification of another person with the intent to commit, or to aid or abet, any unlawful activity that constitutes a violation of Federal law, or that constitutes a felony under any applicable State or local law.

Previously, 18 U.S.C. § 1028 addressed only the fraudulent creation, use, or transfer of identification documents, and not theft or criminal use of the underlying personal information. Thus, the Act criminalizes fraud in connection with unlawful theft and misuse of personal identifying information itself, regardless of whether it appears or is used in documents.

Furthermore, one who violates this prohibition and thereby obtains anything of value aggregating to $1000 or more during any one-year period, is subject to a fine and imprisonment of up 15 years.

These criminal provisions of the Act are enforced by the U.S. Department of Justice, working with investigatory agencies including the U.S. Secret Service, the Federal Bureau of Investigation, and the U.S. Postal Inspection Service.

The second way in which the Act addresses the problem of identity theft is by improving assistance to victims.

Particularly, the Act provides for a centralized complaint and consumer education service for victims of identity theft, and gives the responsibility of developing this service to the Federal Trade Commission. The Act directs that the Commission establishes procedures to log the receipt of complaints by victims of identity theft; and provide identity theft victims with informational materials; and refer complaints to applicable entities, including the major national consumer reporting agencies and law enforcement agencies.

Since its inception in 1865 the Secret Service has been involved in the investigation of counterfeit monetary instruments which affect the integrity and well being of this nation's financial and payment systems.

As a law enforcement bureau within the Department of the Treasury, the Secret Service has been concerned about the crimes which could occur with the evolution of payment systems from cash to plastic and electronic media.

The illegal use of personal identifiers and other related data often available through electronic media has led to a burgeoning phenomenon, often referred to, as identity fraud.

The Secret Service has investigative jurisdiction over credit card and other access device fraud, fraudulent identification, and financial fraud involving computer access. Recent trends in criminal activity have taught us that these crimes are often committed in conjunction with other fraud related activity as well as more violent crimes.

Just as the proliferation of counterfeit currency threatened the economy in 1865, weaknesses in the security of our system of payments could threaten the long term well being of our financial system. Acts of stealing or interfering with the use of personal identifiers such as (Social Security Numbers, credit cards or personal identifications) range from the simple to the complex.

Federal Agencies Responsibilities Regarding Identity Fraud

No One Federal agency has primary jurisdiction regarding identity fraud; rather, several have roles including:

- Secret Service
- FBI
- SSA
- IRS
- Postal Service

For our purposes let's postulate that two separate forms of Identity Assumer's (IA) exist – the first group would be the most common, the complete thief, one who takes over another's life, mostly likely for monetary gain.

The second type would be the partial IA, more than likely a person in the wrong place at the right time. Perhaps a gas station or convenience store clerk who, after seeing the piercing ray of blue light realized that damn credit number on the yellow slip still clutched in his fist was as good as gold.

Your author just happened to be personally acquainted (no I didn't do it and no I didn't turn them in – lot's of nine millimeters floating around) with a group of folks practicing one method of "partial ID theft."

This story was recently documented as the cops swooped in on a couple of warehouses in San Jose, California, where a group of Asians had bribed postal workers to divert credit cards from their intended receivers and pass them along to the group.

The workers were also briefed to pick out the easily identified follow-up letters which ask the recipient to call if the original card did not arrive.

The Partial Identity Assumers utilized the stolen cards (which were as yet not reported as stolen) by paying friends, friends of friends and newly found friends, a percentage to charge large items which could be easily resold, or in some cases returned to the store for cash.

They also specialized in mail order and Internet shopping using a variety of PMB's and a couple of real addresses rented for this purpose.

They were busted only because they had filled two huge warehouses to overflowing with TV's, VCR's, and other high ticket items and were having trouble reselling them fast enough.

In Houston, Texas, one enterprising IA applied for and received a credit bureau listing. Then he gained access to one of the top three credit bureaus where he downloaded approximately 500 credit reports. With this information, he committed identity fraud which resulted not only in financial losses to various banks, but also in aggravation suffered when the victims attempted to correct their own credit histories.

When convicted the bad guy was sentenced to 2 years probation and a $500 fine.

An example of a high end ID theft scheme wherein victim's identities were stolen and used by an organized group of individuals to purchase at least 9 vehicles and more than 15 homes in Richmond Virginia.

This case was brought to the attention of the Secret Service after a defendant, using the identity of someone else had attempted to obtain financing for purposes of purchasing a car.

The Secret Service (ed. note; neither the SS nor the FTC will become involved in a case unless they feel it represents a major, probably gang related, amount of money) contacted the true identity holder and was informed that he had neither applied for financing nor given permission for anyone else to do so, using his identifiers.

The investigation revealed that this defendant was part of a group of individuals who assumed the identities of numerous individuals in a successful attempt to apply for and receive home mortgages; home equity loans on the fraudulently purchased homes; and financing for automobiles.

Upon approval of financing for the vehicles, members of the group would purchase the vehicles using the stolen identifiers. The vehicles would then be re-registered in another state using counterfeit certificate of title documents to prove ownership.

This process yielded a fraudulently obtained, but genuine registration and certificate of title. The vehicles would then be sold under new title, and the profits either distributed among the group or applied to additional crimes.

In California a number of people have been victimized by someone walking into a high end (read "Porsche" here) car dealer, purchasing a $60K car by offering $8,000 in cash and "financing" the remainder.

The car would then be advertised at a discount, the loan "paid off" with the victim's high limit Amex card and then sold.

As one might expect the insurance industry has finally figured out how to make a profit on identity theft. The coverage offers consumers insurance protection for the cost of clearing their name and correcting their financial records if they are the victims of the growing crime of identity fraud.

The new policy reimburses policy holders for up to $15,000 in expenses they may incur as a result of becoming a victim of identity fraud. Expenses covered include legal expenses, loan re-application fees, telephone and certified mailing charges, notary expenses and lost wages for time taken from work to deal with the fraud.

While generally not liable for bad debts the criminal accumulates, the identity fraud victim is left with a damaged credit history that can take considerable time and money to restore. As one identity fraud victim recently commented, "It's not the amount of money that's never recovered. It's the amount of money wasted in coping with this.

The number of telephone calls to just one of the three main credit reporting agencies regarding questions or complaints about identity fraud grew to more than 1,500 per day – a 15 fold increase from 1992 to 1998. This growth may be explained by the incentive to criminals for this new crime.

Complete Identity Assumption still ranks as the hottest crime around – let's look at step-by-step identity theft through the eyes of a top notch Identity Assumer (IA).

One's first concern is to steal/assume an ID that is economically viable. It's an unwritten rule that if one becomes a person with bad credit, outstanding felony warrants, unpaid child support and is running a crack house to support himself, one deserves whatever karma accompanies the takeover.

The first step into the abyss is to isolate someone whose ID would be financially advantageous.

A number of tried and true ways exist to accomplish this task including:

Simply driving to the local mall, picking out the person with the nice slant nose turbo 911, running their plate (in most states) and getting their name and address (a bit more difficult now that DMV info is governed).

Going on-line, or to the local library and looking in one of many "award" journals. A good example is Who's Who, unlike most people's preconceived notions. WW prints many, many volumes from WW in America to WW in Plumbing. They make a living by including as many people as they can, in as many volumes as possible and then selling at least one copy to the recipient of the "honor" of being listed.

Most people will tell their innermost secrets to any "exclusive" directory

Again on-line or in person, choose a lawyer, doctor, professor – they'll all be listed in the AMA, ABA, *Journal of Very Rich Pediatricians*, whatever.
Besides a name one can usually also glean such interesting facts as where the person went to school, associations he belongs to, work phone numbers, advanced degrees, awards, possibly their addresses or at least partial addresses, along with a bunch of ancillary materials that can be of use in a pretext situation.

College yearbooks and alumni letters are a gold mine of who has made it and what they like to brag about.

Hint here is to choose a rather unique name, a good IA will not use John Smith, but rather Stephen Klausman, M.D.

So what does the IA need for a hostile, non-corporate takeover?

Full name
Address and phone number
Social Security Number
Birth date
Mother's maiden name

Would like, but not absolutely necessary:

Bank account info
Property records
Work history
Credit cards (and limits)

With luck the IA may have already gleaned some of these facts – if not they are fairly easy to obtain. The first step would be to utilize one of the many people finders on the net, checking for a home address and any other information available.

AnyWho.com is one of my favorites.

This search is free and works most of the time.

Next most IA's run what is known as a "credit header search" or "national locator search." The primary difference between the two being the first will cost about $8.00 for each of the three major credit bureaus, the latter $59.95 for the same information.

You choose.

There are literally thousands of private detectives and information brokers that will run these searches for anyone.

In most cases this will return the current address, last two addresses (or at least the last two that were reported by a similar searcher. Not always 100% accurate).

Often the target's Social Security number and possibly employment data.

Note this is NOT a credit report, the access of which is limited by the Fair Credit Reporting Act (which basically says you must being doing business with a person in order to pull their entire credit report) but simply a header report, information which is not governed by the same regulations.

If a company pulls one's full credit report, the person whose report is activated is automatically notified, leaving a paper trail of who purchased the information.

Header requests are not noted on the target's credit history nor is the target notified. EXCEPT IN THE STATE OF NEVADA which does have a law requiring header searches to be reported to the target.

This entire search process can be cut to the bone by employing an information broker who will supply not only the credit header info, but such other interesting data as credit card bills, phone records, asset information and so on.

As the following article from the FTC shows, the information broker business is going through a bit of turmoil at this point in time, but most are still operating, business as usual.

Most information brokers will deal with their client's on a completely anonymous basis, i.e., you send a money order and then call, or have them fax the local Mail Box USA store for the search results.

Your government is moving, albeit at a snail's pace, to curb some of the flow of information available on the net and/or through information brokers.

The following case has not been resolved, as of this writing, and the firm in question is still in business, taking requests for "private" information.

> The Federal Trade Commission recently announced that it had charged an "information broker" with illegally obtaining and selling consumers' private financial information.
>
> The case against Touch Tone Information, Inc. represents the first federal action against an information brokerage agency engaged in such practices. The Commission alleged that Touch Tone obtains consumers' information by "pretexting."

As the Commission testified at Congressional hearings last summer, pretexting is a term of art coined by the private investigation industry to describe the practice of getting personal information about others under false pretenses. The case, filed in federal court in Colorado, seeks an injunction and all illegally gained profits.

"Touch Tone's pretexting is a particularly pernicious invasion of consumers privacy – using deception to gain access to sensitive, private financial information," said Robert Pitofsky, Chairman of the FTC.

"This case should send a strong message to information brokers that the FTC will pursue firms that use false pretenses to profit at the expense of consumers privacy and also create opportunities for economic injury to consumers by, for example, making consumers more vulnerable to identify theft."

According to the Commission, the type of pretexting done by Touch Tone involves calling banks and using deceptive means to obtain a consumer's private financial information. Often the caller will impersonate the account holder by providing the account holder's name, address, date of birth and Social Security Number and then lie about the circumstances of the inquiry – e.g., by claiming to have forgotten their checkbook and asking about made-up deposits to the account. Information brokers often market pretexting services via the Internet to anyone willing to pay.

The FTC's complaint outlining the charges alleges that Touch Tone's practice of pretexting is a deceptive act in violation of the FTC Act. Pretexting is deceptive, the agency said, because it involves a material representation that is likely to be misleading.

After obtaining the target's credit header info (usually containing his SS Number) the IA will often run a creditor search.

At the moment the actual listing of creditors that anyone deals with is not privacy protected. In other words, if you have a Wells Fargo Visa card account with a $200 balance and a $10,000 limit, your payment history as well as the account number is not public record but the fact that you have that account is.

After running the creditor search, the IA will often return to his information broker and run a more comprehensive creditor search so he knows everywhere the target has an account and/or credit card, he does not to apply to the same institution for a "new" card or credit line, as well as to verify the target does, indeed, have A-1 credit.

A few shortcuts should also be mentioned:

Dumpster diving

What time do they pick up the garbage in your target's neighborhood?

5 AM?

Show up at 4 AM in a ratty pickup truck and empty Dr. Klausman's garbage in the back. This action will probably not initiate too many calls to 911.

Garbage is gold.

What can an IA dig out (no pun intended) over a several garbage collection period? Checks, check stubs, possibly virgin credit card promotional checks, credit card receipts, cell phone, mortgage info, work pay stubs, phone bills (including those to creditors), approved credit cards, approved second mortgages, on and on not to mention a complete "alive" credit history. Wallet or purse theft is coming back into vogue due the concentration of information in one area.

Some burglars go in only to recover names, numbers, files, passwords and financial information, leaving the tradition items in place.

Other possibilities include:

Rifling through co-worker's desk drawers (or purse).

Mail theft.

Soliciting info by employing phony job ads, internet deals and so on.

BIG ONE. Pull the entire credit report. This is, as noted, is illegal in most cases and does leave an audit trail, but some clever IA's form their own phony company ($25 for a business license, a few bucks for a phone number) called Acme Collections and then pull the entire reports without fear of discovery, as they will not be around when the consumer (if he ever does) questions the inquiry.

It's also very, easy to get a sleazy appliance store, used car dealer, whatever to pull a report or two for a few bucks incentive.

Privacy Journal has also pointed out "how automated credit bureaus freely accept an address change without confirming it or notifying the consumer who is the subject of the file.

An imposter can easily have a retail store enter a change of address for a consumer whose identity the imposter has misappropriated, and that is what thousands of credit fraud perpetrators are doing."

Other information retrieval possibilities include:

- Searching erased disks for any retrievable data

- Sending false messages on the Internet (spoofing) in an effort to collect private information. For example, posing as travel agents or other service providers, identity thieves can make off with one's credit card number once it has been entered to purchase a ticket or service

- Sending e-mail using someone else's computer or e-mail address

- Using various software programs such as "signals analysis" and "sniffer" programs to intercept financial data, passwords, addresses or other personal information being sent over networks

- Breaking into computer systems and gaining access to personal data. For example, names addresses and credit card or Social Insurance/Security numbers (SIN's/SSN's) located in the databases of governments, financial organizations, employers, creditors, and credit bureaus which can be downloaded by employees, former employees or external hackers

- "Shoulder surfing", watching touch tone phone entries on a pay phone normally transpires at a public place, such as an airport and can include magic codes including, but not limited to PIN's, check account verifiers, Social Security, etc. This procedure is sometimes aided with the a pair of small binoculars

- Mail theft works well in low income areas, or where one can bribe a mail drop (or postal mail worker) to remove the necessary documents

And of course, pretexting.

So what does the IA now know about Dr. Klausman?

Hopefully, his name, birth date, we know his Social Security number, his home address, his home telephone number, his work address, his work telephone, his two previous addresses and maybe even his previous employer, as well as to whom he owes money.

Now The IA simply needs to morph into his target.

How?

Well, see the IA simply needs a passable ID. The best example, of course would be a drivers license.

And yes, it is possible to get one in ah, a "close personal friend's" name, see the section on drivers licenses.

A passport will work in some cases (although people are much more comfortable with a drivers license which is easier to obtain and does not contain anywhere near the security features than they are a passport).

The real trick here is that while most bank, postal and even some private mail box personnel know what a drivers license looks like, especially one from their own state, damn few know what a state issued ID (non-driving) looks like.

Especially if it is from another state.

Most so-called (fake) "state ID's" are ridiculous copies designed to do nothing but separate uninformed web surfers from their hard earned money. However, there are a couple of exceptions that will pass in most situations, especially when backed up with ancillary ID.

See that chapter.

Please.

Let's break here and take a look at what your tax dollars say about living a lie – from the Federal Law Enforcement Training Center, Enforcement Operations Division, and I quote :

(Instruction for undercover agents) "In assuming an undercover role, the agent will have to display a high degree of dramatic skill. The undercover agent will actually adopt the characteristics, such as likes and dislikes, living standards, methods, attitude, psychology and other peculiarities which make up the nature of the criminal.

The success of the investigation and the life of the undercover agent may well depend on his overall acting abilities."

The good news (if you are an IA) is that this is overkill. Do your job right and nobody will be looking for you for at least 60-90 days.

And damn near nobody will remember you.

So now Doc Klausman needs a permanent domicile wherein he can receive mail and phone calls. Here's how that is usually accomplished –

In the old days one simply went out and rented an apartment. Still a viable solution. The complex probably will run your credit, ah, rather, Dr. Klausman's credit, but that's A OKAY.

So you need this place because that spiteful wife of yours wants you out, your company wants you to rent an apartment on this coast to deal with your ever - increasing territory.

Whatever…

Most writers in this field advise that one never actually move into the apartment, simply use it as a mail/phone drop.

Second choice is to rent what the post office lovingly now calls a private mail box, or PMB, from a willing participant in crime such as Mail Boxes Be Us.

- First problem herein is that many (but not all) credit bureaus have purchased a CD which flags all well-known mail drops. Be advised however, there still exists non-chain, private, private mail drops that do not show up on the standard credit checks as a PMB

Most are located in another business as a secondary cash flow. (Okay I use one run by a nice little old lady in the back of her second hand "junk" shop)

A number of answering services will also perform mail receiving services if you call and ask them for that specific service.

Yes you will show an ID and pay for a terminated phone number, but NO it will not show up on most credit checks, and you aren't really paying rent.
Are you?

As this is written the post office is attempting to force all "PMB's" to stop delivering mail that does not contain the tip-off phrase "PMB."

Reason, although they won't tell you this, is that they don't want the competition and are going deeper into the Private Mail Box business themselves.

The PO has lost the first two rounds of this battle due to hundreds of thousands of complaints and actually issued a statement to the effect they "really didn't mean they wouldn't deliver the mail, but, ah, they would like to see those three initials on every piece of mail going to a Boxes Be Us drop."

Pretty sure the government has thrown in the towel but pay attention.

- It also possible to obtain a phone number at this point by either contacting an answering service, paging company or voice mail provider and simply pay the fee. Most telephone companies will list you in their white pages for a very nominal fee

- In fact some, such as U.S. West don't even require a voice mail, they will issue the number, list it and bill you at any address you so desire

- Next viable solution is to pick up the local newspapers and look under the "share rentals" category in the classifieds. Make a couple of appointments, dress like an upscale local, point out you are an airline pilot/steward/flying doctor/financial consultant and will be spending only a few days a month in your rented room

Not only do you not have too many friends in the immediate area, your particular religion doesn't believe in throwing parties, you will pay your rent in advance and are, generally, a very tolerant person.

You probably have now just rented a permanent address and maybe even a phone without a credit check or even showing ID.

Most larger cities have temporary residences which are rented out for a 2-6 month period. Often located near institutions of higher learning these are usually moderately upscale apartment buildings whose owners find tax or personal benefit in temporary or sublet renting.

A call to one or more real estate agents, especially in an area of a transient or seasonal population will also provide interesting possibilities.

These latter two concepts will require a credit check. But what the heck, you've got great credit by this point.

When the IA fills out the rental application he knows it's going to a credit agency; if not one of the big three, a smaller version that deals with at least one of them.

Okay, technically Dr. K has great credit, the IA will probably get the rental which will automatically change his, your, credit address (as far as the bureaus are concerned) to a new address.

- BUT the IA does not want to run up too many flags at any particular agency, so it is perfectly smart and legit to ask which agency they are going to run this app through ('cause those assholes at, oh, well, one of them, have screwed the report up so badly you had to hire an attorney to straighten things out")
- They should volunteer this information, no problem. This fact is important in the off chance the IA want's to rent two or three more residences in near future

Once the IA has established an and phone number the idea is to *get credit!*

- Many IA's will file a change of address with the post office at this point in order to order checks and other monetary instruments

Imagine you suddenly need new credit, but have a respectful history. Where would you go?

The smart IA goes back to his friendly Internet and finds high rate, high fee card offers.

Please realize if a bank is offering a 7.9% Visa card, they're going to have a much more stringent credit qualification process than one that charges 18% or 20%.

The greedier the bank, the simpler the application process.

The idea is that all banks and credit granting organizations build in a loss factor to cover this type of fraud. It is not a big thing, as long as it stays within limits, so why rock the boat?

So five of the ten apps are going to slide through, no hang ups.

A few will call to make sure the phone number is valid as well to make some credit comment.

At this point our IA can pick up the phone, or call back and say, "You know, I've been having some credit problems, which credit bureau did you access?"

"That makes sense, I have been the victim of credit fraud and those SOB's don't want to investigate it."

Most bureaus will be happy to consider the fact their competitors are jerks and go from there.
What if you are missing one or more of the Crucial Identifiers?

Say the birth date?

Pretext.

Or maybe you are telephobic and like to spend money without cause.

This is how pretexting works. *Make yourself into someone the target would want to give information to!!*

So the IA calls up the target and says, "Hi, my name is Jeffery Springer and I'm with the National Plumber's Top Gun Award Committee and we're updating our list and I'd like to know whether are you are working at the National Plumbers College, have received the Pipe Dream Award three years in a row, your interests still lie with dissimilar metal welding and blah blah, blah."

Target goes, "oh yes."

"Where did you go to college? We've got a BS from CU and your masters from Stanford. Your birth date is July 14 1964."

Target responds, "right, all true, except my birth date is really June 16, and I've published a number of articles which should be of interest to your publication".

Once the IA has the birth date he, like any good salesman, uses the target's ego, "we're going include you in our new directory of *Cutting Edge Plumbers* in a couple of weeks.

I'll personally send you a check copy, just initial it if all is correct and fax it back to my attention. get it, simply initial it if everything is OK and send it back."

That will put the target at ease because everybody likes to be stroked and professional people are used to being asked these kind of questions.

Besides the sources I've covered there are various directories, like the National Faculty Directory which lists many prominent professors and includes much needed information, often including birth dates.

Specifically The National Faculty Directory is a huge set of three or four volumes that list the faculty member of every accredited college of higher learning in the United States and Canada. Generally the entry will have the persons full name, their birth date, their department, all of that kind of stuff and it's available in most libraries.

Whatever route the IA has trod he now has an ID, a n address whether it be a 6' x 6' box, or a shared roommate situation, or a real abode.

The IA will most likely now apply for credit. He wants to do it rapidly because all these applications go in at about the same time so he makes a stack of three credit card applications that clear through Experian, three that clear through Trans Union, and three through Equifax.

John Jay Klausman M.D., of course, uses his new address. The laws of the universe say because the address on the other bureaus might not have been changed yet but most of the others will probably actually go through because by the time they're processed, that new address will show up on the next credit bureau.

Doc is soon going to be the proud father of a fist full of plastic.

What a good IA does while waiting for things to progress is to jump on the Great American Bandwagon called Instant Credit.

A store like Needless Markup charges 22% on their in-house card because they will provide instant credit to almost anyone right on the spot.

The IA walks into a few Fast And Quick We Don't Deny Anybody Anything electronic, furniture and even jewelry stores.

Therein, he applies for their store cards. He gets them and then purchases his dream items with an eye towards which is the most easily resold. Point being, in a short period of time he will have amassed a massive ability to access money but he's not quite ready yet.

The next thing an IA will probably do is to open a bank account. Simply take in a good ID and lay a little money on the counter.

Of course the AI wants over-draft protection, just on the off chance a check should be written for more money than actually exists in the account.

Now comes the step known, just like those old magazine ads, as "get rich quick."

The IA has a bunch of "real" cards, department stores cards, hopefully an ATM card or two.

The IA will now go and max out these plastics out and turn them into cash as rapidly as possible. A key is that most credit cards come with convenience checks.

Fill out those free checks for as much as possible to move that money into another bank account.

For example, if a bank gives an AI a Visa card with an $10,000 limit, it looks bad if one goes to a bank five days in a row and takes a $300 cash advance out of an ATM or teller window. It looks better if you just write one of those "quick" checks for $3,000.

The issuing institution will process this check without any problem.

So over the next couple of weeks the thief writes convenience checks against the cash advance limit, or in some cases, the entire credit limit of the cards he's set up. The reason the AI does this concurrently is at the end of the month, all of those creditors are going to report to the bureau, the sudden influx of charges on those accounts.

If all of the sudden all of those accounts show up with a huge balance, that's going to set off a warning bell but by the time that happens, our buddy is long gone. So he writes the convenience checks, and runs them through.

Checks clear pretty quickly with electronic check clearing; by law within three business days the funds will actually have gone from the credit card company into one's account.

Cash is cash, VCR's can be turned into cash pretty easily.

About 60 days later the original ID holder will start getting phone calls. And he's not going to know a damn thing about it.

By the time he puts it all together, the IA has moved to another city and repeated the process. He may do three or four cities this same fashion.

If the IA has used different names, addresses and creditors, odds are the Feds will never really get involved.

The Secret Service, and to some degree the Federal Trade Commission will rarely give the time of day to any ID theft case unless the amounts are staggering and/or they suspect an organization/gang is behind the whole enchilada.

Some IA's will actually pay the minimum due on all invoices in order to extend the time on target, as well as maintain, or develop the original rating into more cards, more scams.

However the reason this scam works in the first place are that no one immediately grasps the problem. The first few notifications will often be written off as mistakes, by the time any law enforcement agency bothers to get involved a good IA has moved to another location.

One reason for the lack of enthusiasm on the part of law enforcement is that all credit issuers have a profit-loss bottom line that includes losses due to fraud and/or bounced checks. Their annual fees and "bounce fees" (often set at very high rates, up to something like $29.00), cover the company's losses, often making a profit in the deal.

According to some authorities, such as John Q. Newman, author of Identity Theft, the Cyber Crime of the Millennium. (a recommended read) credit card lending is the single most profitable item banks, and financial institutions do, but it's also vulnerable to being penetrated by fraud. So all they've simply done is increase the cost to us in terms of those fees to cover what they lose.

So many times the bank is not all that concerned because as long as their losses for the year don't exceed what they expect to lose, then they're not too concerned about it.

How To Protect Against Credit Identity Theft

It is impossible for a consumer to prevent all distribution of his or her personal identification and credit information, or to exercise meaningful control over all the possible uses of that information.

Nonetheless, one can take steps to reduce the risk of theft and misuse of his or her personal identification and credit information. For example:

- Do not routinely carry your Social Security card, your birth certificate, your passport or more than one or two credit cards. When you must carry some or all of these, take special precautions to reduce the risk of loss or theft

- Always take credit card, debit card and ATM receipts with you. Never throw them in a public trash container. Tear them up or shred them at home when you no longer need them

- Do not leave bill payment envelopes at your mailbox for the postal carrier to pick up. Install a lock on your mailbox if you live in an area where mail theft has occurred

- Tear up or shred unused pre-approved credit card solicitations and convenience checks

- Carefully review your credit card statements and utility bills (including cellular telephone bills) for unauthorized use as soon as you receive them. If you suspect unauthorized use, contact the provider's customer service and fraud departments immediately

- Order your credit report each year from each of the three major credit reporting agencies. Check each credit report carefully for accuracy and for indications of fraud, such as credit accounts that you did not open; applications for credit that you did not authorize; credit inquiries that you did not initiate; charges that you did not incur; and defaults and delinquencies that you did not cause. Check the identifying information in your credit report to be sure it is accurate (especially your name, address, and Social Security Number)

- Never give out your credit card, bank account or Social Security Number over the telephone unless you placed the call and you have a trusted business relationship with the business or organization

- Guard against overuse of your Social Security number. Release it only when necessary – for example, on tax forms and employment records, or for banking, stock and property transactions

- Never have your Social Security number printed on your checks. Do not allow a merchant to write your Social Security Number on your check

- If a business requests your Social Security number, ask to use an alternate number. Some businesses have systems to identify their customers that do not use Social Security Numbers. If the business does not have such an alternate system, ask to use an alternate identifier that you will remember (for example, a combination of the letters of your last name and numbers). You can lawfully refuse to give a private business your Social Security Number, but the business then can refuse to provide you service

- If a government agency asks for your Social Security number, a Privacy Act notice should accompany the request. This notice will explain whether your Social Security Number is required or merely requested; the use that will be made of your Social Security Number; and what will happen if you refuse to provide it

- If you do not receive your credit card statement on time (or if you do not receive a new or renewed credit card when you expect it), call the creditor to see whether a change of address request has been filed in your name, or if additional or replacement credit cards have been requested on your account. If either has happened, inform the creditor that you did not make the request and instruct the creditor not to honor it

- Call the post office to see whether a change of address request has been filed in your name. If this has happened, immediately notify the Postal Inspector

- If you shop on the Internet, use a secure browser which encrypts or scrambles purchase information, or place your order by telephone or mail

- Check your Social Security Earnings and Benefits statement once each year to make sure that someone else is not using your Social Security Number for employment. You can order this statement from the Social Security Administration

- Consider having your name removed from marketing lists. A first step is to write the Direct Marketing Association and ask that your name be removed from all lists they control

- The three major credit reporting agencies uses information from credit reports to develop lists of consumers who meet criteria specified by potential creditors. You can request that your credit information not be used for these purposes. Doing this will limit the number of pre-approved credit offers that you receive

- Credit card issuers often compile lists of marketing information about their cardholders based on their purchases. Under the law in some states, you can request your credit card issuers not to disclose to marketers of goods any marketing information that identifies you

- Consider not listing your residence telephone number in the telephone book, or if you really want privacy have it unlisted in someone else's name. Although the phone company may not agree with this policy they do not normally require ID to began an account

- If you do want a listed number consider listing just your name and residence telephone number. If you decide to list your name and telephone number, consider not listing your professional qualification or affiliation (for example, "Dr., Atty., or Ph.D.")

- Make a list of, or photocopy, all of your credit cards. For each card, include the account number, expiration date, credit limit and the telephone numbers of customer service and fraud departments. Keep this list in a safe place (not your wallet or purse) so that you can contact each creditor quickly if your cards are lost or stolen. Make a similar list for your bank accounts

- Cancel your unused credit cards so that their account numbers will not appear on your credit report. (If an identity thief obtains your credit report, the thief may use the account numbers to obtain credit in your name. To help avoid this problem, some credit reporting agencies "truncate" account numbers on credit reports)

- When creating passwords and PIN's (personal identification numbers) do not use any part of your Social Security Number, birth date, middle name, wife's name, child's name, pet's name, mother's maiden name, address, consecutive numbers, or anything that an IA could easily deduce or discover

- Memorize all your passwords and Pins; never write them in your wallet, purse or Rolodex

- When you order new checks, pick them up at the bank instead of having them mailed to your home

After

One must act quickly upon learning that he or she is the victim of credit identity theft. Acting quickly will help prevent the thief from making further use of the victim's credit identity, and make the process of restoring the victim's credit standing less burdensome.

- The victim should keep a log of the date, time and substance of all personal and telephone conversations regarding the theft. The log also should include the name; title and telephone number of each person to whom the victim speak. The victim should follow up each telephone call with a letter that confirms the conversation and any agreed-upon action. The victim should send all correspondence by certified mail, return receipt requested, and keep a copy of each letter and each return receipt

The following tips are offered to help a victim report and document the theft of his or her credit identity and to help the victim begin to rebuild his or her credit standing. Each case of credit identity theft involves unique facts and circumstances, and other than reporting the crime to the police, one victim will not necessarily take the same steps as other victims. If your credit identity has been stolen, you should review all of the following tips and choose those that are appropriate to your situation.

- Report the crime to the police immediately. Effective January 1, 1998, California Penal Code section 530.5 classified identity theft as a crime. Under legislation effective January 1, 1999, the crime of identity theft may be either a misdemeanor or a felony. Ask the police to issue a police report pursuant to Penal Code section 530.5 on the theft of your personal identification information

- Give the police as much information and documentation as possible. Creditors, banks, credit reporting agencies and insurance companies may require you to provide a police report to verify that you are a victim of the crime of identity theft

- Call the fraud units of the three major credit reporting agencies. Inform each credit reporting agency of the theft of your credit cards, account numbers or identifying information

- Request that a fraud alert be placed in your file. Ask how long the fraud alert will remain posted in your file

- Request that a victim's statement be added to your credit report – for example: "My identification has been used to apply for credit fraudulently. Call me at XXX to verify any application for credit."

- Some credit reporting agencies requires that you provide a copy of your telephone bill to verify your identity

- Request each credit reporting agency to remove all information that appears in your credit report as a result of the theft of your personal identification and credit information. It may take some time to have all of this erroneous information removed from each of your credit reports

- Ask each credit reporting agency to send you a copy of your corrected credit report. When you receive your corrected credit reports, verify that all of the erroneous information has been removed from each report, and that each report contains the fraud alert and victim's statement that you requested. It's a good idea to send a letter to each credit reporting agency every two to three months explaining that you are the victim of credit identity theft and asking that you be provided a free copy of your credit report. This will enable you to check your credit reports for new erroneous information, and for previously-deleted erroneous information that might have reappeared

Note the law now (post 1998) requires credit reporting agencies to block reporting of any information that a victim of identity theft alleges appears in his or her credit report as a result of the crime of identity theft. The victim must submit to the credit reporting agency a copy of a valid police report filed under Penal Code section 530.5.

- Call each of your credit card issuers to report that you are the victim of credit identity theft. Ask each credit card issuer to cancel your card and provide a replacement card with a new account number. Immediately follow up each telephone call with a letter that confirms the conversation and the action the credit card issuer has agreed to take

- Ask each credit card issuer about the status of your account. Ask if the card issuer has received a change of address request, or a request for additional or replacement credit cards. If you have not filed a change of address request or requested additional credit cards, instruct the card issuer not to honor these requests

Also, note that a consumer's liability for unauthorized use of a credit card cannot be more than $50.14 The consumer must notify the credit card issuer promptly upon learning of the unauthorized use. Most creditors will waive (forgive) the $50 if the consumer notifies the creditor within two days after learning of the unauthorized use.

- Call each credit card issuer or creditor that has opened a new account that you did not authorize or apply for. These accounts probably will be listed in your credit reports. Explain that you are the victim of credit identity theft, and ask each issuer and creditor to close the account immediately. Some credit card issuers and creditors may ask you to sign an affidavit, or to submit a copy of the police report on the theft of your personal identification information. Ask each issuer and creditor to inform each credit reporting agency that the account was opened fraudulently and has been closed

- If your bank account information or checks have been stolen, or if a fraudulent bank account has been opened using your identification information, notify the bank and the check verification companies

- Close your checking and savings accounts and obtain new account numbers

- Ask the bank to use a new unique identifier for your accounts. Do not use your mother's maiden name, since this information is available in public records

- Call the payees of any outstanding checks that you are not certain you wrote. The payee is the person or business to whom you wrote the check. Explain to each payee that you are the victim of identity theft and that you have closed your checking account for that reason. Ask each payee to waive any late payment or returned check fee. Then send each payee a replacement check drawn on your new account and stop payment on the check that it replaces. It's a good idea to enclose a note with each check explaining why you are sending a replacement check and reminding the payee that the payee has agreed to waive the late payment or returned check fee (if the payee has agreed to do so)

- Get a new ATM card and PIN. Do not use your old password or PIN

- Notify your gas, electric, water and trash utilities that you are the victim of identity theft, and alert them to the possibility that the thief may try to establish accounts using your identification information. Provide similar notice to your local, long distance and cellular telephone services

- Ask the utility and telephone services to use a new unique identifier for your accounts. Do not use your mother's maiden name, since this information is available in public records. If your long distance calling card or PIN has been stolen, cancel them and obtain a new account

- If you have lost your drivers license, or if you suspect that someone may be using your drivers license number, contact your local Department of Motor Vehicles office It is possible to obtain a new drivers license number under limited circumstances

- If your Social Security number has become associated with dishonored checks and bad credit, it is possible, in extreme cases, to obtain a new Social Security Number

Be prepared for banks and credit grantors to ask you to fill out fraud affidavits to be notarized or signed under penalty of perjury. You can ask to have the fees for notarizing documents waived or reduced.

- If you suspect that an identity thief has stolen your mail or has filed a change of address request in your name, notify the Postal Inspector

- If you have a passport, notify the passport office that the identity thief may apply for a new passport

Even after providing the necessary legal documents one may find that a credit agency fails to take the appropriate action.

Unfortunately at this point one might be wise to seen the assistance of an attorney.

One can also expect demands of payment for bills run up by the IA. Since the victim of credit identity theft did not incur the debts caused by the thief, the victim ordinarily should not pay any debt which is the result of the theft. If a debt collector demands that the victim pays such a debt, the victim should explain why he or she does not owe the debt, and should send the debt collector a follow-up letter.

If you receive notice of collection or legal action due to an identity theft one must, again consider employing a member of the legal profession.

Resources:

If you've been a victim of ID theft, you can file a complaint with the FTC by contacting the FTC's Consumer Response Center.

By Mail:

Consumer Response Center
Federal Trade Commission
600 Pennsylvania Ave, NW
Washington, DC 20580

On The Internet:

www.ftc.gov/ftc/complaint.htm

National Banks:

Office of the Comptroller of the Currency
Customer Assistance Group
3701 McKinney Street
Suite 3710
Houston, TX 77010

(800) 613-6743

State Member Banks of the Federal Reserve System
Consumer and Community Affairs
Board of Governors of the Federal Reserve System
20th & Constitution Avenue, NW
Washington, DC 20551
(202) 452-3693

Non-Member Federally Insured Banks
Federal Deposit Insurance Corporation
Compliance and Consumer Affairs
550 17th Street, NW
Washington, DC 20429
(800) 934-3342

State and Federally Chartered Savings Associations
Office of Thrift Supervision
Consumer Affairs Office
1700 G Street, NW
Washington, DC 20552
(800) 842-6929

Federal Credit Unions
National Credit Union Administration
1775 Duke Street
Alexandria, VA 22314
(703) 518-6330

Other types of financial service providers (finance and leasing companies/retailers/credit bureaus):

Consumer Response Center
Federal Trade Commission
600 Pennsylvania Avenue, NW.
Washington, DC 20580
(202) FTC-HELP (382-4357)
TDD: (202) 326-2502

Victim Advice And Assistance

Privacy Rights Clearinghouse
1717 Kettner Boulevard
Suite 105
San Diego, CA 92101
Web: http://www.privacyrights.org/

California Public Interest Research Group (CalPIRG)

11965 Venice Boulevard
Suite 408
Los Angeles, CA 90066
Tel: (310) 397-3404
Web: http://www.pirg.org/calpirg/

Center for Law in the Public Interest
10951 W. Pico Boulevard
Third Floor
Los Angeles, CA 90064

Advice regarding credit identity theft; representation in selected cases.

Credit Reporting Agencies

The following addresses and telephone numbers are accurate as of this writing but may be subject to change in the future.

Experian (formerly TRW)
To report fraud: (888) EXPERIAN [(888) 397-3742] (toll free number)
FAX: (800) 301-7196, or
Experian Consumer Fraud Assistance,
P.O. Box 1017, Allen, TX 75013
To request report: (888) EXPERIAN (888) 397-3742 or P.O. Box 2104, Allen, TX 75013
To dispute information: Call number in credit report or (888) EXPERIAN [(888) 397-3742] (toll free number)
To opt out of pre-approved offers and marketing lists: (888) 567-8688.

Equifax
To report fraud: (800) 525-6285
To request report: (800) 685-1111, or P.O. Box 740241, Atlanta, GA 30374
To dispute information:
Call number in credit report, or P.O. Box 105873, Atlanta, GA 30348
To opt out of pre-approved offers: (888) 567-8688 (toll free), or Equifax Options, P.O. Box 740123, Atlanta, GA 30374

Trans Union
To report fraud: (800) 680-7289
To request report: (800) 888-4213, or P.O. Box 390, Springfield, PA 19064
To dispute information: Call the number in the credit report, or use "investigative request form" that accompanies the report order form.
To opt out of pre-approved offers: (888) 567-8688, or P.O. Box 97328, Jackson, MS 39238

Direct Marketing Information

To remove your name and address from national marketers' mail and telephone solicitation lists:
Direct Marketing Association

MAIL PREFERENCE SERVICE
P.O. Box 9008
Farmingdale, NY 11735

Direct Marketing Association
TELEPHONE PREFERENCE SERVICE
P.O. Box 9014
Farmingdale, NY 11735

Social Security Administration
To order your Social Security Earnings and Benefits statement:
(800) 772-1203, or
Social Security Administration
Data Operations Center
P.O. Box 7004
Wilkes Barre, PA 18767

To report that your Social Security number is being used by another person to obtain credit or for employment purposes:

Call or visit your local Social Security Administration office.

U.S. Secret Service

The Secret Service has jurisdiction over financial fraud cases, but usually does not investigate individual cases unless the dollar amount is high, or the victim is one of many people victimized by the same perpetrator or a fraud ring. See the "Secret Service" listing under "United States Government" in the white pages of the telephone directory.

Check Verification Companies

To report that your checks have been stolen or that bank accounts have been opened in your name without your consent:

CheckRite (800) 766-2748

ChexSystems (800) 428-9623, (800) 328- 5121 (regarding closed checking accounts only)

Cross Check (707) 586-0551

Equifax (800) 437-5120

National Processing Company (800) 526-5380

SCAN (800) 262-7771

Telecheck (800) 366-2425, (800) 710-9898

VISA: Perspectives on Identity-Fraud

In one year, U.S. fraud losses of VISA member banks totaled $490 million or about 0.1% of billing transactions ($505 billion).

Fraudulent applications accounted for about 5% of fraud losses account takeovers accounted for about 6% of fraud losses.

To Catch a Thief

How are the major credit agencies fighting back against Identity Assumers, most of whom have used a database to procure some, if not all of their information?

By forming a database to catch the data thieves in the act.

Equifax is the first major credit agency to offer, "a revolutionary new product offering fast, cost-effective protection against fraud with nationwide coverage".

Although they are not as forthcoming with the exact working details of **Fraudscan**, one can pretty much read between the lines and see an artificial intelligence program that compares data from a number of sources to find anomalies.

According to Equifax, Fraudscan detects, validates, and verifies potentially fraudulent information automatically and simultaneously at the time of application. It composes consumer-provided information against multiple nationwide databases, and issues a flag when it finds known or suspected fraudulent information on an application. Among other things, Fraud Scan runs a complete name check, along with a comprehensive address and phone number search.

Consumer data is transformed into standard format and a full report is returned within seconds.

Sounds great right? Okay, but one should still remember that most credit bureaus only check credit header files which do not necessarily reflect the truth.

See the chapter on legends.

Fraudscan:

- Verifies applicant's identity based on name, address and phone number

- Issues a flag when an applicant's address is a mail-receiving service, prison, check-cashing site , etc.

- Reformats applicant information into standard format, saving time by eliminating manual data reformatting

- Notifies the user when a Social Security number has never been issued – was issued before the applicant's date of birth – was issued to a person reported deceased or was issued in just the last five years

- Flags drivers license formats that are not valid for the state indicated

- Issues a warning when an area code has-or is about to – change and returns the alternate area code

- Warns you when an applicant's phone number does not match their zip code – is associated with high-risk service, i.e. wireless phones and pagers, or is invalid

- Has no consumer disclosure requirement-flags are not part of a consumer's credit file and cannot be used as a basis for denying credit or employment

FraudScan is part of a growing family of innovative products and services that comprise the Equifax Total Solution – a strategic master plan for growth and control.

Hopefully by now, you the reader can pick out a number of databases FraudScan is using from Social Security Death Records, simple SS number sequences matches and area code-to-zip code matches.

All are public records.

Most of this would not stop a professional IA as he would be very careful to match the various numbers. If one is assuming someone else's ID the SS number will, of course, have been issued and during the correct time period.

Who this will catch are quick buck artists trying to pass checks, or even people attempting to build a new, secondary (or ancillary) ID.

See these chapters.

Another Equifax program called **Secure Authentication** (quoting here from the press release) "simplifies the sign-on process while verifying the user's identity in a simple, real-time process in a matter of seconds:

First, the user completes and submits an online application form.

Second, the Equifax Secure authentication engine then displays a multiple-choice questionnaire compiled from information managed by consumer and business information sources. These questions can include elements from the user's financial history.

Third, the user then completes and submits the multiple choice questionnaire form.

Fourth, the authentication engine conducts a series of functions with algorithms to compare responses in the interactive query, delivering a response to determine if the person is who they claim to be. If the engine can verify the user's identity, the user moves to the next step in the customer-defined application process. If the engine cannot verify identity, the user is directed to complete the identity verification process manually."

This particular comparison is not too different from those used by major banks, "this credit card can not be used until it is verified. Please call from your home phone."

Basically if your touch tone-in the correct mother's maiden name, billing zip code and possibly the last four digits of the owner's SS number the card will be approved.

If something goes awry, one still has a chance at convincing the nice clerk that whomever entered the data in the first place goofed.

This is easier than on might think as the main reason one is required to "call from his home number" is so the 800 line being called has a permanent record of where the call was made from.

Caller ID blocking DOES NOT block 800# ID.

Another Equifax entry into the anti-fraud field is called **Exchange 2000**.

Once again we'll delve into what their press release folks have to say about this program – "a comprehensive database-matching service that helps communication and utility providers prevent application fraud and recover unpaid balances.

Exchange 2000 helps validate application data and locate skip accounts by comparing new-applicant information with past-due and unpaid-final-bill data contributed by the member companies.

Using key components that include name, address, telephone number, drivers license and Social Security number, Exchange 2000 matches the information and delivers results in detailed reports.

Identifying fraud and location individuals who owe past-due and final-bill balances

Exchange 2000:

- Can provide new-applicant, past-due and unpaid-final bill matching services between member companies
- Identifies potentially erroneous Social Security numbers, helping reduce risk exposure
- Delivers current addresses and telephone numbers for unpaid accounts, complementing existing collection procedures and reducing administrative time and expenses
- Interfaces with other services, include **POSITIVE ID SM, Smart Letter SM** collection notices, revenue recovery models and outside collection agencies
- Generates detailed management reports for tracking collection activities, system effectiveness, aged uncollected accounts receivable and account payment profiles
- Ensures the confidentiality of all information, preserving consumer rights to privacy and fair information practices while protection customer relationships

Is Equifax Everywhere?

More Credit Bureau Fraud Fighting

Equifax has also announced a new offensive against fraud, which combats fraudulent cashing of payroll checks at supermarkets across the country.

PayCheck Accept reduces fraud by performing basic identification validation, monitoring prior check cashing experience and activity, validating Social Security numbers and comparing the check payee to identification information in the Equifax credit database.

Because supermarkets and other stores perform as one of the largest check authorization companies in the world for personal checks, Equifax developed PayCheck Accept, a unique solution to combat payroll check cashing fraud.

PayCheck Accept validates the identification of a person presenting a payroll check for cash by matching the name on the check with the Social Security number the consumer enters into a secure key pad at the supermarket customer service counter.

A successful validation is required only once by each consumer to facilitate future check cashing privileges, thereby enhancing the store's service to its customers.

Equifax Check Solutions provide the most comprehensive identification process, due to the unique availability of data from several Equifax proprietary databases.

Check Solutions maintains a database with positive check transactions by more than 120 million consumers. Additionally, the Equifax credit database contains information on approximately 200 million Americans, virtually every adult in the country.

I should point out Equifax is only checking their own files to verify the SS number *not* the Social Security Administration's.

Check Fraud

Check fraud is one of the largest challenges facing financial institutions. Technology has made it increasingly easy for criminals, either independently or in organized gangs, to create increasingly realistic counterfeit checks and false identification that can be used to defraud banks.

The scope of the problem can be shown by some recent statistics. According to the FBI's Financial Institution Fraud and Failure Report; 60 percent of all criminal referrals relate to check fraud. Further, a recent survey by the American Bankers Association found that 54 percent of community banks, 94 percent of mid-sized banks, and 88 percent of large banks sustained losses from check fraud.

In two years, the number of fraudulent checks submitted increased 136 percent, from 537,000 to 1,267,000. Over the same period, annual losses from those frauds increased to reach $815 million. That amounts to more than 12 times the amount banks lose annually because of bank robberies. Conservative estimates are that banks will lose $1 billion to check fraud in the next year; less optimistic experts believe losses may be double or triple that amount.

Thrifts, savings banks, and other financial institutions, retail merchants, government agencies, and large corporations are also victims of check fraud. A recent survey of more than 2,000 large U.S. corporations concluded that, on average, they lost approximately $360,000 a year to check fraud. The FBI estimates that if commercial banks and other institutions combined their check fraud losses, the total would be $12 billion to $15 billion annually.

To protect themselves and their customers from check fraud, banks need to become familiar with common check fraud schemes. The following section details a number of methods by which criminals extract money from financial institutions.

Significant Terms

Some technical terms relating to checks and drafts are worth defining:

- Customer – a person with an account at the bank

- Drawee – a party, typically a bank that is required to pay out the money when a check or draft is presented

- Drawer – a person writing a check. The drawer is typically a customer of the drawee

- MICR – (Magnetic Ink Character Recognition) – numbers at the bottom of a check, printed in magnetic ink that can be read by machines. The numbers usually are encoded with the name and address of the drawee bank, the account number, and the check number. The dollar amount is added to the MICR line during check processing

- Payee – a party entitled, by the creation of a draft or check, to receive funds from a drawee

Presentment – the delivery of a check or draft to the drawee or the drawer for payment.

Check Fraud Schemes

Fraud schemes involving checks take many forms checks may be, either as to the payee or the amount:

- Counterfeited
- Forged, either as to signature or endorsement
- Drawn on closed accounts
- Used in a variety of schemes

Check fraud criminals may be bank insiders, independent operators, or organized gangs. The methods they use to further check fraud include:

- Getting customer information from bank insiders
- Stealing bank statements and checks
- Working with dishonest employees of merchants who accept payments by check
- Rifling through trash for information about bank relationships

Descriptions of some common check fraud schemes follow, with information on what makes them successful, and how they can be avoided.

Altered Checks

Altered checks are a common fraud that occurs after a legitimate maker creates a valid check to pay a debt. A criminal then takes the good check and uses chemicals or other means to erase the amount or the name of the payee so that new information can be entered. The new information can be added by typewriter, in handwriting, or with a laser printer or check imprinter, whichever seems most appropriate to the check.

Example 1: A door-to-door salesman sells a set of encyclopedias for $69.99. The customer pays by check, writing $69.99 to the far right on the line for the amount in figures, and the words "sixty-nine and 99/100" to the right far on the amount in text line. The criminal uses the blank spaces on both lines to alter the check by adding "9" before the numbers line, and the words "Nine Hundred" before the text line. The $69.99 check is now a fraudulent check for $969.99, which the criminal cashes.

Example 2: A small company that provides service to several small clients is paid by checks payable to "Johnson Co." or "Johnson Company." Criminals steal a number of those payment checks and use a chemical solution to erase the word Co. or Company, then type in the word Cooper. They subsequently cash the checks using false identification.

Example 3: A criminal steals a wallet, with a check in it, from the glove compartment of a car. The criminal uses the signatures on identification in the wallet as a basis for forging the endorsement. Then, using the identification in the wallet – altered if necessary – the criminal cashes the check at the payee's bank.

Altered check schemes can be successful when customers are careless and banks fail to check payee identification properly.

To protect against such frauds, customers should:

- Avoid leaving large blank spaces in the number or amount lines on checks they write
- Report to their banks when checks payable to them are stolen

Banks should:

- Review checks to ensure that the handwriting or print styles are consistent and that there are no signs of erasure or alteration
- Compare the signatures on items and the appearance of the presenter with the signature and picture on identification

Counterfeit Checks

Counterfeit checks are presented based on fraudulent identification or are false checks drawn on valid accounts.

Example 1: A group of criminals open checking accounts, cash counterfeit checks, and file false tax returns using fraudulent drivers' licenses, social security cards, and other identification. They use information from individual and corporate garbage as the basis for producing the identification with computer technology.

Example 2: A bank insider identifies corporate accounts that maintain large balances, steals genuine corporate checks, counterfeits them, and returns the valid checks to the bank. The bank insider is associated with a group of criminals which distribute the counterfeit checks throughout the area and cashes them using fictitious accounts.

Counterfeit check schemes can be successful when criminals are skillful in their use of technology to create false documents or have access to information and supplies from bank insiders.

To protect against such frauds, customers should protect their personal information, including account records.

Banks should:

- Review customer identification thoroughly
- Maintain separation of functions so that no one person has account information and access to controlled supplies such as commercial check stock
- Use mailings and other methods to warn customers about check fraud and the need to protect their information

Identity Assumption

Identity assumption in check fraud occurs when criminals learn information about a bank customer, such as name, address, bank account number, account balance, Social Security number, home and work telephone numbers, or employer, and use the information to misrepresent themselves as the valid bank customer. These schemes may involve changing account information, creating fictitious transactions between unsuspecting parties, or preparing checks drawn on the valid account and that is presented using false identification.

See the chapter and ancillary materials concerning this phenomenon.

This fraud is made easier when organizations, such as state DMV's use Social Security numbers on identification documents In such states, because those numbers are more available, banks must be especially careful.

Example 1: A bank customer pays a bill in the normal course of business. An employee of the payee then copies the check and provides it to a partner in crime who contacts the bank and, using information from the check, pretends to be the account holder. The criminal tells the bank that he or she has moved and needs new checks sent to the new address as quickly as possible. When the bank complies, the forged checks are written against the customer's account.

Example 2: A gang member steals a statement for an account at Bank A and another steals a box of new checks for a different person's account at Bank B.

The gang then prepares the stolen checks to be payable to the valid account at Bank A.

Using fraudulent identification, one of the criminals then poses as the payee to cash the checks at drive-through windows at Bank A. Because the criminals know there is sufficient cash in the account to cover the check, they can safely ask for immediate cash.

Example 3: A criminal uses customer information, sometimes from a bank insider, to order checks from a check printer, or to create counterfeit checks, and to create false identification. The criminal then writes fraudulent checks and presents them for deposit into the customer's account, requesting part of the deposit back in cash. The cash-out from the transaction represents the proceeds of the crime.

Identity assumption schemes can be successful when a bank:

- Accepts account changes over the telephone
- Is not careful in requiring and reviewing identification presented for cash-out transactions
- Has no limit on the size of cash transactions, especially at temporary or remote locations such as drive-through windows
- To protect against such frauds, banks should:
- Insure that changes to accounts are secure, by requiring customers to request changes writing or in some other way that guarantees the identity of the customer
- Limit the size of cash transactions at temporary or remote locations to require individuals presenting large items to complete the transaction in a regular bank office

Train personnel, including all tellers, to:

- Check identification carefully, particularly in split/deposit transactions
- Require two forms of identification
- Record the identification information on the back of the item presented
- Inspect checks carefully to ensure that they are not counterfeit such checks are often printed on lower quality paper, which tends to feel slippery, or are produced using desktop publishing equipment, which smudges when rubbed with a moist finger

Closed Account Fraud

Closed account frauds are based on checks being written against closed accounts. This type of fraud generally relies upon the float time involved in interbank transactions.

Example 1: A fraud ring provides "role players" with business checks drawn on closed accounts at a bank. The "role players" then deposit the checks into a new account at a different bank through one or more ATMs operated by other banks. The float time between the ATM deposits and the checks drawn on the closed accounts reaching the issuing bank for payment allows the criminals to withdraw funds from the new account.

Closed account frauds can be successful when customers do not destroy checks from unused accounts or do not properly inform their banks about account status.

To protect against such frauds, customers should:

- Keep their banks informed about the status of accounts
- Actively close unneeded accounts rather than simply not using them
- Destroy checks for unused or closed accounts

Banks should:

- Place special holds on checks drawn on accounts that have been inactive for some time
- Advise customers to destroy checks from closed accounts and notify the bank when they intend to close an account

New Account Fraud

A significant amount of check fraud involves new accounts, both personal and corporate, opened by criminals with the express intent of defrauding the bank.

Example 1: A criminal opens a new account using false employment information and incorrect addresses and telephone numbers. After conducting some small transactions or otherwise gaining information on the bank's procedures for posting checks, and ATM transactions and the type of identification required to cash checks, the criminal deposits bogus or stolen checks into the account and makes substantial withdrawals before the bank realizes it has been victimized.

Example 2: A criminal opens a corporate account using a fictitious company name and soon deposits a large amount in counterfeit checks into the account. After inflating the account with the counterfeit checks over a short period, the criminal then asks the bank to prepare cashier's checks for a large proportion of the account balance. Because the cashier's checks are reliable, they are easily converted to cash.

New account frauds are successful when banks do not check carefully the identification presented by people opening new accounts.

To protect against such frauds, banks should thoroughly investigate information presented by a prospective customer to ensure that it is accurate and valid. Banks may do this by:

- Calling the new customer at work or at home
- Sending thank you notes to new customers, in envelopes marked to request return of improperly addressed items and promising payment, and then watching for returns
- Contacting banks listed on the application for information on the customer's prior banking history
- Visually inspecting the business
- Obtaining a federal tax return or state certificate of incorporation for new corporate account
- To ensure the businesses are legitimate considering whether the business is consistent with the account activity
- Asking for a copy of a utility bill sent to the customer's address

Fraud by Bank Insiders

Often, check frauds depend on information provided by bank insiders. In addition to schemes discussed elsewhere, which may involve access to information about one account or relationship, frauds based on insider knowledge are often broader because they are based on knowledge of the bank's operations and access to many accounts.

Example 1: A former bank employee obtains legitimate bank account numbers and uses the numbers with fictitious corporate names to order company payroll checks. He and several cohorts then use false identification to open bank accounts and cash the checks.

Fraud by insiders can be successful when customer account information is not kept secure and if insiders know when checks are read by automatic check processing equipment. Checks processed automatically, unlike those processed manually, are not checked for agreement of MICR information and account information.

To protect against such frauds, banks should:

- Check the backgrounds of its employees
- Maintain a separation of functions so that no one person has access to customer account information and customer check stock

Telemarketing Fraud

Telemarketing frauds are based on the creation of "demand drafts," rather than checks. A demand draft resembles a personal check but carries no signature. In place of a signature, it has a notice that the account holder has given permission to have money withdrawn from his or her checking account to pay bills for goods and services.

Example 1: The criminal calls a consumer and announces that the consumer has won a cash prize. The criminal explains that, to deposit the prize into the "winner's" account, he or she needs the account information. Once the consumer provides the account information, the criminal prepares demand drafts and withdraws funds from the account. (A common variant is for the criminal to offer the consumer something for sale, such as a magazine subscription, in order to get the necessary account information.)

Example 2: A representative of a criminal organization contacts potential credit card users and promises to arrange for them to get VISA or MasterCard credit cards. The representative asks for checking account information to issue the card and, when the information is provided, prepares demand drafts against the consumers' accounts.

Telemarketing frauds can be successful when customers reveal confidential account information.

To protect against such frauds, banks should:

- Warn customers about them, either through direct mail or advertising in the bank
- Check a customer's file when a demand draft is presented to see if he or she has provided
- Written authorization for the bank to pay those drafts

Check Fraud By Gangs

Some gangs have become actively involved in check fraud. These gangs typically go after corporate accounts and have received a measure of notoriety because of their successes and failures.

Example 1: Gangs have traveled throughout the country cashing counterfeit payroll checks obtained by gang members in targeted corporations or financial institutions. They use sophisticated counterfeiting techniques to capture the company's logo and a company executive's signature by scanning them and to prepare payroll checks using account information from a company check or a bank insider. They use the same information and techniques to prepare false identification for the people who will cash the checks.

If insider information is not available, such gangs sometimes call the targeted company's accounts receivable department, tell them that they have funds to wire into the company's account, and get the company's bank account number to accomplish the transfer. The deposit, of course, never materializes.

Such gangs move into a city or town around payday and cash the checks at local institutions which have check cashing agreements with the targeted corporation.

Example 2: A fictitious foreign company sends a letter to an individual or U.S. company claiming to have a large quantity of money that must be transferred out of the foreign home country immediately. The foreign company asks the targeted individual or company to help set up a bank account into which the money can be transferred. They offer a sizable commission, while asking for the target's checking account information. The foreign company's representative then uses the account information to withdraw money from the target's checking account using bank drafts.

Banks should remember that, although the individual or U.S. company acted negligently, the bank may be liable for honoring the fraudulent draft. To protect against such fraud banks should:

- Warn customers about such schemes
- Check on new employees' backgrounds
- Request proper identification from customers before cashing checks

Preventive Measures – General Internal Controls

Strong organizational controls can reduce the likelihood of check fraud. A sound organizational strategy should require the bank to:

- Monitor, classify, and analyze losses and potential losses to identify trends
- Report findings from monitoring activities to the audit, risk-management, and security divisions and senior management
- Ensure communication among departments about check fraud concerns
- Assess operating procedures regularly and implement changes

- Target check fraud awareness training to specific check fraud schemes – how they occur, and how to prevent them

Internal Controls That Can Help Prevent Check Fraud By Bank Insiders Include:

- Ensure that account changes, such as adding names or changing addresses and/or other information, are authorized by the customer in writing, or in a way that guarantees that the customer is requesting the change

- Establish special protections for dormant accounts, such as requiring extra approvals and mandatory holds, and maintain special security for signature cards

- Maintain permanent signature cards for each account and keep files and appropriate documentation for business accounts (e.g., a certificate of incorporation, recent federal tax return, etc.)

- Separate duties to ensure that no one person in the bank, acting alone, can commit check fraud

- Ensure that persons other than those who open accounts or prepare statements handle night depository, ATM, ACH, and mail deposits

- Ensure that customer complaints and discrepancy reconcilement's are directed to staff who are not account openers, tellers, or bookkeepers

- Check the backgrounds of new hires

Education And Training

Alert and well-trained front line personnel, managers, and operations personnel are essential to effective check fraud prevention programs. Before beginning their positions, new employees should be trained in bank procedures concerning:

- What is acceptable identification
- Opening new accounts
- Cashing checks and accepting deposits
- Detecting counterfeit checks
- Cash-back transactions
- Backroom operations

Effective training and education is important in preventing check fraud losses. Suggested training for specific bank positions follows.

Teller Training

Banks must emphasize to all tellers the importance of being alert to check fraud. One way to focus on preventing check fraud is to include a separate section on it in teller manuals. That section can emphasize typical check fraud schemes and warning signs.

Some common warning signs include:

- A check that does not have a MICR line at the bottom
- A routing code in the MICR line that does not match the address of the drawee bank
- MICR ink that looks shiny or that feels raised. Magnetic ink is dull and can be read by an electronic reader
- Printing produces characters that are flat on the paper
- A check on which the name and address of the drawee bank is typed rather than printed, or that includes spelling errors
- A personal check that has no perforated edge
- A check on which information shows indications of having been altered, eradicated, or erased
- A check drawn on a new account which has no (or a low) sequence number or a high dollar amount
- A signature that is irregular-looking or shaky, or shows gaps in odd spots
- A check printed on poor quality paper that feels slippery
- Check colors that smear when rubbed with a moist finger. (This suggests they were prepared on a color copier)
- Checks payable to a corporation that are presented for cashing by an individual
- Banks should require that checks payable to a corporation be deposited into the corporation account for later disbursal by corporate check
- Corporate or government checks which show numbers that do not match in print style or otherwise suggest that the amount may have been increased
- Checks presented at busy times by belligerent or distracting, fast-talking customers who try to bypass procedures
- Checks which have dollar amounts in numbers and in words that do not match

- Items that are marked "void" or "nonnegotiable," yet are presented for cash or deposit

Guidelines To Consider When Cashing Checks

Although this list is not exhaustive, it provides a useful starting point when someone presents a check for payment.

- Properly identify customers, either through personal knowledge or signature and other personal identification. If in doubt, refer the customer to an account representative
- Be careful when paying customers, especially new customers, split checks for deposit and cash
- Require two forms of identification and list them on the back of the check
- Carefully review the identification to ensure it is genuine.
- Be alert for individuals who try to distract you while you are reviewing his or her identification
- Be careful when accepting official checks drawn on another financial institution such items are sometimes counterfeit
- Refer all questionable transactions to a supervisor for a second opinion
- Be sure the customer's account is open and has a positive balance

Remember: A bank may delay cashing a check for a reasonable amount of time to verify that a signature is genuine and to make sure that it has properly identified the person presenting it. A short delay may cause a criminal to leave the bank without a forged or altered check rather than risk being arrested.

New Accounts Representative

A significant amount of check fraud begins at the new accounts desk. A new accounts representative should remember it is possible that a new customer may be intending to defraud the bank. Banks should monitor new accounts diligently and should reconcile any discrepancies, or problems they identify promptly. The few extra steps it takes to become familiar with a customer can prevent significant losses.

New accounts representatives should be alert to the following signs that an account may be fraudulent. Each of these situations is not necessarily a problem, but should signal to the new accounts representative that further information may be required.

The new accounts representative should be alert when a new customer provides:

- A telephone number or exchange that does not match the address or that been disconnected
-
- A home address that is outside the bank's geographic area that is a major highway, or that is not a street mailing address. Such addresses include ones that are identified by post office box, suite, or drawer identifiers

- No employer name or an employer with no telephone number. This includes new customers who identify themselves as self-employed

- No drivers license

- Identification with a birth date (particularly the year) that does not match the birth date on the new account application

- Information that is in any way insufficient, false, or suspicious

Guidelines To Consider When Opening Accounts

Although this list is not exhaustive, it provides some procedures a representative should consider applying when opening new accounts:

Request two forms of personal identification. Acceptable identification includes:

- Drivers license
- U.S. passport or alien registration card
- Certified copy of birth certificate
- Government, company, or student identification card
- Credit card

Request documents on corporate accounts. Such documentation may include copies of:

- State incorporation certificate
- Corporate resolution
- Recent corporate federal tax return
- List of major suppliers and customers, with their geographic locations

Require complete information. The new account card should show street address, date of birth, drivers license number, and Social Security number or tax identification number.

Verify information provided:

- Compare the date of birth on the application with that on the drivers' license, passport, or alien registration card

- Check employment by telephoning the employer identified on the application

- Look up the customer's name, address, and telephone number in the telephone directory

- Check the new customer's banking history. Contact the banks with which the customer reports having had prior relationships, if any, and ask for the customer's:

A. Type of account(s) and balances.
B. Listed address(es).
C. Taxpayer identification number.

Use the address provided. A nice way to do this is to write a thank you letter to the new customer using the street address provided. If the letter is returned, the bank knows to investigate the account.

Visually inspect business premises. Drive by the business address to see if it fits with the type of business reported.

New accounts representatives should refer all inconsistencies identified and any difficulties in the new account opening process to a supervisor.

Other Preventive Measures – Positive Pay

Positive pay allows a company and its bank to work together to detect check fraud by identifying items presented for payment that the company did not issue. In the usual case, the company electronically transmits the bank a list of all checks it issued on a particular day. The bank verifies checks received for payment against that list and pays only those on the list.

The bank rejects:

- Checks not on the company's list
- Checks that exceed a specific dollar amount
- Checks that carry dates long past (stale checks)

The bank investigates rejected checks to find out if the items are fraudulent or in error. The bank only pays exception items approved by the company.

Reverse Positive Pay

Reverse positive pay is similar to positive pay, but the process is reversed, with the company, not the bank, maintaining the list of checks issued. When checks are presented for payment and clear through the Federal Reserve System, the Federal Reserve prepares a file of the check's account numbers, serial numbers, and dollar amounts and sends the file to the bank.

In reverse positive pay, the bank sends that file to the company, where the company compares the information to its internal records. The company lets the bank know which checks match its internal information, and the bank pays those items.

The bank then researches the checks that do not match, corrects any misreads or encoding errors, and determines if any items are fraudulent. The bank pays only "true" exceptions that is, those that can be reconciled with the company's files.

Electronic Check Presentment

Electronic check presentment (ECP) is an electronic/paper method of expediting check collection. Participating banks exchange check payment information before physically presenting the checks for payment.

The depository bank captures payment information from the MICR line of incoming checks and immediately transmits the information electronically to the paying bank. Later, the depository bank sends the actual check according to its normal paper deadlines. During check posting, the paying bank identifies checks that should be returned and immediately notifies the depository bank.

ECP supporters believe that it speeds up processing, controls cost and reduces fraud by providing early notification of return items.

Data Sharing – Cooperation Between Check Manufacturers And Banks

Several years ago the American Bankers Association and the National Retail Federation sponsored an inter-industry task force known as the BankCheck Fraud Task Force to examine solutions to check fraud problems. The Task Force has developed a data sharing program for closed accounts. This program prevents people who have outstanding checks due to retailers from opening new accounts.

Participating financial institutions report all checking accounts closed for cause to a central database called **ChexSystems**. ChexSystems transmits the closed account information to the shared check authorization network (SCAN) database. Participating banks use the SCAN information before opening new accounts to spot repeat offenders. A participating bank also can use MICR information from a check presented with the applicant's drivers license number to check the SCAN file for any previous bad account activity.

Check Security Features

Check manufacturers help deter check fraud by making checks difficult to copy, alter, or counterfeit. Some useful security measures include:

Watermarks

Watermarks are made by applying different degrees of pressure during the paper manufacturing process. Most watermarks make subtle designs on the front and back of the checks. These marks are not easily visible and can only be seen when they are held up to light at a 45-degree angle. This offers protection from counterfeiting because copiers and scanners generally cannot accurately copy watermarks.

Copy Void Pantograph

Pantographs are patented designs in the background pattern of checks. When photocopied, the pattern changes and the word "VOID" appears, making the copy nonnegotiable.

Chemical Voids

Chemical voids involve treating check paper in a manner that is not detectable until eradicator chemicals contact the paper. When chemicals are applied, the treatment causes the word "VOID" to appear, making the item nonnegotiable. Checks treated with chemical voids can not be altered without detection.

High-Resolution Microprinting

High-resolution microprinting is very small printing, typically used for the signature line of a check or around the border in what appears to be a line or pattern to the naked eye. When magnified, the line or patter in contains a series of words that run together or become totally illegible if the check has been photocopied or scanned with a desktop scanner.

Three-dimensional Reflective Holostripe

A holostripe is a metallic stripe that contains one or more holograms, similar to those on credit cards. These items are difficult to forge, scan, or reproduce because they are produced by a sophisticated, laser-based etching process.

Security Inks

Security inks react with common eradication chemicals. These inks reduce a forger's ability to modify the printed dollar amount or alter the designated payee because when solvents are applied, a chemical reaction with the security ink distorts the appearance of the check. This makes such items very difficult to alter without detection.

Check Forgery – A Trick

The American Bankers Association has just published "a new weapon" in their ongoing war against check fraud.

Said weapon is the Check Fraud Prevention Manual, available at no cost to ABA members in order to help bankers understand the mechanics of check fraud.

One would guess this would be a handy reference material for those on both sides of the fraud game.

Much of the following is directly from the Federal Bureau of Investigation – via one Special Agent Slotter who works in the Financial Institution Fraud Unit at FBI Headquarters in Washington, DC.

I'll include other research from both sides of the river in order to balance things out.

Outsider fraud now accounts for more than 60 percent of all fraud against financial institutions.

The most prevalent problem in the industry, by far, centers on check fraud, but also involves other counterfeit negotiable instruments, such as traveler's checks, credit cards, certified bank checks, money orders, and currency.

More than 1.2 million worthless checks are accepted for payment every day.

The technological improvements that have fueled the growth in check fraud schemes have made it difficult for law enforcement to combat the problem.

With the prevalence of laser printers and advanced duplication systems, the production of quality counterfeit checks has become common place. In addition, Congress unwittingly aided the business of duplicating and counterfeiting checks.

By passing legislation in 1988, known as Regulation CC,6 Congress made detecting fraudulent checks even more difficult for financial institutions. This law requires banks to process checks within a 72-hour period and ostensibly provides customers with increased access to deposited funds.

While the regulation might have succeeded in making depositor's funds more accessible, it also made passing fraudulent checks easier by giving banks less time to confirm the legitimacy of these transactions.

Check Fraud Organizations

World wide, 80 billion checks exchange hands annually; 60 billion of those are written in the United States.

As anyone who has mailed a check to the mortgage company 3 days before payday can attest, Americans have become enamored with writing checks and taking advantage of the "float" period, the time during the check-clearing process.

Criminal elements within numerous immigrant groups in the United States have analyzed American banking, noting the system's deficiencies and the fact that it affords opportunities for fraud.

The Major Fraud Groups

The principal ethnic enterprises involved in illegal check fraud schemes include Nigerian, Asian (particularly Vietnamese), Russian, Armenian, and Mexican groups. The majority of the Vietnamese, Armenian, and Mexican organizations base their operations in California, especially in the Orange County, San Francisco, and Sacramento areas. However, they have networked their operations throughout the country, with a number of connections in Chicago, Houston, and Washington, DC.

Despite the lack of a rigid hierarchy, members typically fall into one of several roles; leader, check procurer, counterfeiter, information broker, or check passer.

Leaders

Leaders of an organization generally have an extensive criminal history and possess above-average intelligence.

Often, they have a degree in business and/or law. These individuals provide the overall direction of the group, as well as expertise in understanding American business and the banking system.

Check Procurers

Check procurers obtain authentic checks, usually by stealing them while employed within a financial institution. Group members then sell or negotiate the stolen checks as is, or they duplicate the checks for future use.

Counterfeiters

Counterfeiters duplicate corporate, and payroll checks, traveler's checks, credit cards, certified bank checks, money orders, currency, and other negotiable instruments, as well as personal identification. They usually are well-versed in the use of personal computers, especially in the field of desk top publishing.

Information Brokers

In formation brokers gathers personal and financial information on legitimate individuals. Using this credible information, associates open new bank accounts, pass counterfeit checks, and secure loans, which they fail to repay.

Check Passers

Check passers actually negotiate stolen and counterfeit checks through the banking system and collect the proceeds to distribute to the group. They often travel throughout the country, opening new accounts and transporting their illicit proceeds. Typically they negotiate only about 10 percent of a group's illicit checks; the group sells the rest of the checks to other individuals and organizations.

Check passers maintain little contact or status within the hierarchy and often are the only members whose ethnic backgrounds differ from the core group. Ethnic organizations tend to distrust anyone not of their own heritage, making it difficult for law enforcement to infiltrate them. Even though police frequently arrest check passers throughout the country, these street-level criminals generally possess little information concerning upper-echelon group members.

Types Of Check Fraud Schemes

The variety of check fraud schemes perpetrated throughout the country ranges from depositing single stolen checks to counterfeiting thousands of negotiable instruments and processing them through hundreds of bank accounts. Although it is impossible to summarize all of the check fraud schemes currently operating three schemes in particular – large-scale counterfeiting, identity assumption, and payroll check fraud – typify frauds being tracked by bank security officials and law enforcement authorities throughout the nation.

Check Alternation

New technologies give check fraud perpetrators a wide variety of schemes and devices for committing their crimes. Chemical techniques and computers provide the primary means by which criminals manipulate and counterfeit checks. Legitimate personal checks can be changed easily by chemical means.

Similarly, someone well-versed in manipulation techniques can modify corporate checks, traveler's checks, bank checks, and U.S. Government checks with minimal effort.

Chemical alteration is commonly referred to as "check washing." Check washers use a variety of acid-based chemical solutions to erase amount and payee information, while maintaining the integrity of the preprinted information. They then dry the check and inscribe a new payee and a significantly higher dollar amount before presenting it to a bank for payment.

One acid-based solution even allows criminals to revise a check and subsequently destroy the evidence. In this instance, the check washers must move quickly because the chemical solution causes the paper to disintegrate within 24 hours, leaving no supporting evidence of the transaction.

A Trick

Another interesting phenomenon has made its way into the check business during the past couple of years. Using old formulas published in magician's manuals (and at least one modern hacking magazine) a number of companies have started marketing pens loaded with an "ink" which totally disappears within 24 hours.

The better grade of the paper involved; the better they work. "Bank grade" paper is about the best subject one can employ.

I was testing one of these pens when a friend of mine accidentally used it to pay his rent check.

Landlord, bank and friend were all understandably upset when the check turned completely blank in about 16 hours.

Perforation

Almost all legitimate checks have at least one perforated edge; counterfeit checks are often smooth on all sides.

Federal Reserve Routing And Transit Number

The routing and transit fraction number in the top right hand corner (below the check number) should correspond to the electronically encoded number, known as the MICR, on the bottom center of the check. Fully 98 percent of all fraudulent checks has an incorrect Federal Reserve transit number.

Federal Reserve District And Office

The first three digits in the MICR line represent the state and district office to which the bank is assigned. On fraudulent checks, these numbers often do not correspond appropriately Serial Number Match.

The encoded check serial number on the bottom left should correspond exactly with the check number in the top right corner.

Check low numbered checks also indicate potential fraud; 90 percent of all check frauds involving insufficient funds are numbered somewhere between 101 and 200.

Check Tricks

Remember when a check is presented to a bank for payment it is routed to the Federal Reserve Bank District as noted by the routing number of the check then to the district office of the bank, then to the clearing house.

By law the check must be cashed within 72 hours.

If the check is a forgery and forger has modified first four (4) numbers (routing numbers) it will be routed incorrectly and then returned to the bank where it was deposited.

This provides the forger up to 2 weeks of slack in which to continue without too much chance of detection.

Government Checks

Government checks (including social security and welfare) also are also forged on a routine basis.

Government checks should not be considered that much more solvent than any other paper and many government documents suggest that anyone who cashes these checks performs a very careful inspection of the ID of the person presenting said check.

Identification of U.S. Government Checks

- Smooth on edges of all four (4) sides.
- Federal Reserve Code Number is 000.
- Under the amount is an explanation code why the check was issued.
- A Social Security number is to the left and an "A" means that it is an exact match of the identity of who the check is made out to.

Identification of Traveler Checks

There are several varieties of travelers checks available today. The most common is Visa, Barclays Bank, Citicorp and the most popular – American Express Travelers checks.

The bank routing numbers for these are coded "800".

A Test

American Express has a built in feature in its checks to test authenticate of the check paper. On the reverse of the American Express Travelers Check, there are two denomination blocks or ovals. If a person were to wet the tip of a finger with saliva and touch the left oval it should smear. But **ONLY** on the left. If it smears it is real. If the right one smears, it is a forgery.

Fraud Prevention

In order to prevent fraud, check-printing companies offer a variety of counterfeiting safeguards.

All such features make attempted alteration detectable in one way or another. Yet, the known systems are not foolproof and often prove cost-prohibitive to the purchaser. In response, financial institutions have begun to implement a type of biometric fingerprint identifier as a more cost-effective approach. In early 1995 Bank of America (BOA) in Las Vegas, Nevada, became the first financial institution to use fingerprinting technology to deter check fraud.

At BOA, when customers who were not account holders presented checks for payment, they must place an inkless fingerprint next to their endorsement. When bank officials identify an attempted fraud, the fingerprinting system provides law enforcement with evidence and background information never before attainable at the onset of an investigation.

This pilot project has garnered impressive results. BOA officials report that the biometric identification system nearly has eliminated check fraud schemes perpetrated by outsiders.

It also has reduced the bank's overall fraud by 40 percent. 11 BOA's success in Nevada has spurred the Arizona Bankers Association to lead a campaign with member financial institutions to implement a similar program. A core group of Arizona-based banks implemented this technology, and it has now spread to other states.

A number of financial institutions have expressed a desire to expand the program to new customer accounts, another hotbed for fraudulent checking activities. During this implementation process, the banks involved have become cognizant of the sociological and privacy concerns underlying such an identification system.

Some customers fear the improper use of identifying information. Bank officials stress, however, that no central database of fingerprint information will be maintained and that these records will be furnished to law enforcement only pursuant to suspected criminal conduct.

Conclusion

Checks can be either stolen, manipulated, or counterfeited. Illicitly obtained checks can be negotiated immediately, altered, or used for future counterfeiting. Generally speaking, only unsophisticated criminals acting alone will immediately negotiate stolen checks by forging the signature. Most organized groups steal checks as a prelude to more enterprising endeavors.

Bank security officials and law enforcement agencies concur that the problems associated with check fraud and counterfeit negotiable instruments have reached epidemic proportions.

As criminal organizations become more sophisticated in the devices they use, law enforcement also must become more creative and sophisticated in the techniques used in its investigations.

Check-printing companies offer a variety of counterfeiting safeguards, such as embossing, artificial watermarks, laid lines, chemical voiding features, warning bands, high-resolution printing, dual image numbering, and security number fonts.

Check Fraud Indicators

Here's a bit more of what the FBI teaches their financial investigators:

Investigators must remain alert to indicators that signal check fraud activity. They can identify such leading indicators by completing a comprehensive crime survey, which requires evaluating demographic information, analyzing crime reports, and collecting data from financial and business communities, civic groups, and other law enforcement agencies. By analyzing suspicious activity reports, which financial institutions submit to the Financial Crimes Enforcement Network of the U.S. Department of the Treasury, and other check fraud complaints, local law enforcement agencies can identify a variety of factors, such as the types of fraud schemes prevalent in the area and the identities of banks that seem prone to check fraud activity.

Frequent check fraud attacks against a particular bank may result from its location, inadequate internal controls, or marketing strategies that present opportunities to savvy check fraud artists. Some mutual fund companies, for example, regularly allow customers to open accounts by mail. A significant number of check fraud complaints from a particular geographic area may indicate the presence of an active, organized group that warrants law enforcement attention.

Maintaining contact with banks and regulators may help investigators identify weaknesses, develop controls, and prevent future losses. At the same time, analyzing the complaints received from of the victims – such as department stores, check cashing establishments, and grocery stores – may help law enforcement determine the modus operandi of the fraud artists and assist in developing investigative strategies.

Other types of criminal activity related to check fraud may serve as leading indicators. Counterfeit identification documents, theft of identification by pickpockets, credit card fraud, and structured cash transactions may point to organized check fraud operations.

Confidential informants with knowledge of underworld trafficking in stolen and counterfeit identification documents can help investigators identify check passers and others involved in organized check frauds. An organized group may include a counterfeiter, or printer, a distributor, one or more providers of false identification, and several "Smurf's," who open false bank accounts or visit check cashing establishments to negotiate fraudulent checks.

Organized pickpocket rings represent excellent sources of false identification. On the streets of New York, a stolen wallet complete with identification and credit cards, referred to as a "spread," has resale value. People buy spreads for a variety of uses, including welfare, check immigration, and tax frauds. Therefore, informants who are familiar with pickpockets in the community can become reliable sources of information about people who buy stolen wallets, helping investigators uncover those involved in check fraud.

Each agency must take precautions not only to protect its undercover operatives but also to avoid the embarrassment that results when one agency learns that it has arranged to buy counterfeit checks from the undercover agent of another agency.

One approach to catching forgers is to depend on the forensic laboratory compares latent fingerprints and handwriting on the check with known fingerprints and handwriting exemplars to determine if they can be identified as the subject's. The evidence gets presented to a grand jury, which returns an indictment, thereby initiating the judicial process. *In reality, such cases can prove extremely difficult to solve.*

In many instances, investigators cannot develop key elements needed to resolve them. The surveillance cameras may not work, or the witnesses cannot give a consistent description of the suspect. The check passer wears gloves or does not leave prints on the checks, or the prints do not match any known prints. The laboratory may be unable to match the handwriting on the check with the writing sample provided by the suspect. Such obstacles may arise after investigators have worked for weeks or months examining documents and interviewing victims and witnesses.

If the investigation proves successful and the suspect goes to trial, another year or more may pass before the trial and sentencing. Check fraud investigations generally take the same amount of time, regardless of the amount of the check. *An average of 2 years elapses between the opening of a traditional New York FBI check fraud case and its final disposition.* Professional check passers know how long these investigations take. They also are confident that, as long as they do not become too greedy and remain willing to move around so as not to saturate a particular area with bad checks, the chances of getting caught using traditional methods are minimal.

Moreover, under federal sentencing guidelines, individuals with no prior convictions who pass checks for less than $70,000 can expect to receive probation. This serves as an incentive for defendants to plead guilty to a single count but provides no motivation for them to cooperate with law enforcement.

Because of their intrusive nature, undercover operations must be carefully formulated and evaluated to ensure the safety of undercover officers, minimize civil liability, and guard against entrapping potential subjects. The typical undercover scenario begins with the arrest of a check passer who agrees to cooperate and introduce investigators to others involved in the fraud.

This scenario, when properly executed, produces extremely strong evidence against the subjects. It also helps the prosecutor to define the true nature of the fraud by demonstrating that multiple transactions and high losses would have occurred without the investigation. Investigators and prosecutors also can take advantage of stronger penalties to encourage subjects to cooperate, thereby supporting the expansion and continuation of the operation.

Law enforcement also can support innovative fraud prevention techniques, such as the ink-less fingerprinting campaigns that some financial institutions have launched. Banks in Nevada, Arizona, and Texas experienced remarkable reductions in check fraud losses after they began requiring that non customers provide ink less fingerprints when cashing checks at the teller line.

Although initial tests of this technique in New York and California more than 10 years earlier met with mixed results, modern innovations in automated fingerprint processing and aggressive marketing by financial institutions resulted in more recent loss reductions of between 43 and 59 percent.

Some banks require that corporate customers submit the fingerprints of employees who have access to company accounts. In one instance, this practice resulted in the apprehension of a fugitive who had been wanted for murder for almost 20 years.

Red Flags That May Signal Check Fraud

FBI investigations identified common techniques used by fraudulent check passers in New York:

- Customer attempts to open an account with a corporate check or other third-party check
- Customer tries to flatter, hurry, or confuse the teller to draw attention away from the transaction. Customer delays endorsing a check or producing identification during peak hours to frustrate the teller and hurry the transaction
- Customer presents for cash a low-numbered check drawn on a new account
- Customer offers foreign documentation (birth certificate, passport, visa) or non photo identification (Social Security card, credit card) in lieu of photo identification to open an account or cash a check
- Customer offers altered or damaged identification to open an account or cash a check
- Customer attempts to cash or convert several small checks into wire transfer, gold, or other tender
- Customer requests an exception to established rules to force the transaction

How To Forge A Check With A Home Computer

Is it possible to create check using home/small business computers that will pass through the banking system undected?

Oh, yes, not only possible but fairly easy and accomplished on a regular basis.

Most forgers start off with a business account as they tend, by nature, to contain more money.

The first step is to procure a legitimate check to use as a base. Some forgers procure refund checks from airlines by paying cash at the ticket counter and then not taking the flight.

Other possibilities include any scam that provides a refund or dividend check.

Use cutting edge equipment – the fastest CPU, the best scanner, software and printer that one can afford. Remember that actual typography is rated at about 2200 per square inch (if one were to examine a character through a magnifying glass the "solid" character would consist of 2200 very small dots per square inch of space).

Marginal printers will only reproduce 300 dots-per-inch (especially black and white).

Many forged checks have been passed with a 300 DPI resolution.

Now 600 DPI is more the norm; Hewlett Packer offers a very affordable 1200 DPI printer and other, more specialized companies, offer 2000+ DPI machines for about $5K.

Remember we are talking black and white here – color also demands a high DPI ratio or, better yet, a continuous tone printer that will duplicate Picassos prints so well they will (and have) been sold at major art auctions.

But, it comes down to who is going to be doing the examining; a bartender, a cop, an art expert?

Each level will pass scrutiny.

Each level can be aided by a good stock of ancillary ID, a pretty face and a nice story ("sorry militia man, is my first time in the glorious United States, so nice to be in the land of the freedom and away from the terrible demigods of those communists.")

Maybe that's over playing one's hand a bit, but it all helps.

Now let's get into the actual (hypothetical, of course) steps one might take in order to duplicate a valid check:

Using the best scanner available, scan the check into a PICT file.

Using the latest and best copy of PhotoShop (or other less powerful graphics programs, although PS is probably the best choice become of its versatility including the ability to layer graphics).

Most artists will not magnify the image and allowing one to clean up the edges of the characters, which may be a little fuzzy.

Other Paint commands, which allow parts of an image to be captured and moved, are key to this forgery (details omitted). I have seen people use a command to enhance a shading effect in the logo of the bank, which the scanner had blurred.

Remove the check number that is usually stamped in red in the upper right corner of the check.

The magnetic ink characters at the bottom of the check should be copied and enhanced if necessary. Some artists will remove and replace them entirely with characters from the same font family.

- Copy the image to two other files. On one copy the forger will want to delete the payee name, the dollar amount and anything else that is to be changed
- Take the other file and perform a mirror function, i.e., delete everything except for the elements lost in the above step

- Procure some "safety" check paper that appears as close to the original as possible. Oddly enough this is neither illegal, nor particularly restricted

- Transfer the files to a graphics layout program, usually PageMaker or Quark and match the shape and size of the original check

Print a number of the now blank checks. Note that the numbers at the bottom of the check are printed with magnetic ink. At least two mag ink printers are now sold for the Macintosh should one desire to duplicate the numbers so they will pass a machine read inspection

The printers are loess than $2K each or one can utilize a mag ink cartridge in certain "normal" printers. This addition requires each check to be printed twice, once for the regular ink characters, one for the mag characters.

A Trick

The lack of magnetic ink will normally not stop a check from clearing, it simply alerts a human to look at the number and copy it manually onto a strip that is affixed to the check.

- Next one needs to open the second file, in order to add payee and amounts. These should be done with a real check writer if the original utilized this feature although it is possible to use a dot matrix printer with a font that looks like the original and obtain satisfactory results

- Add the payee and amount in this fashion

- Forge the signature – most forgers accomplish this by placing the original check on an artist's light table and tracing over the name. It is also possible to accomplish this on any glass surface that is backlit. Some people find it is easier to turn the check upside down for the signing

- If the check number is written in red ink use a color ink jet printer or a simple, inexpensive numbering machine available from office supply houses to re-acquire the check number in red

- Use an Exato knife to trim the straight side(s) of the check and a perforation machine (inexpensive and available) to duplicate the original edge scheme

How To Read A Check

If one is going to forge checks, protect one's check's from forgery, capture forgers, or is just worried about a particular check clearing the bank one needs to know the basics of check hieroglyphics.

Transit Number Or "Clearing House Number"

A directory of all banks in the United States listed alphabetically by states, cities in states and by the bank number assigned by the American Bankers Association set up a standardized system of numbering listing banks

The fraction that appears on the face of a check after the name of the drawee bank is erroneously called the "clearing house number" by the general public. Its correct designation is "transit number" and it is a numerical code designation to aid in the identification and routing of the check after it has been cashed

$$\frac{90\text{– }123}{1210}$$

Prefix Number Of Cities And States

The first number in the numerator of the fraction, indicating the city, or state in which the drawee bank is located

Numbers 1 to 49 indicate certain cities, the populations of which warrant assigning them their own number. Those cities on the Pacific Coast which have their own numbers are:

San Francisco	11	Portland	24
Los Angeles	16	Spokane	28
Seattle	19	Tacoma	34

The first number might, on the other hand indicate the state in which the drawee bank is located if it is not in a city that has been assigned a number. The state numbers are assigned as follows

Eastern States	20 to 58
Central States	70 to 79
Western States	90 to 99
Southeastern States	60 to 69
Southwestern States	80 to 88
Alaska, Hawaii	59
Puerto Rico	59

The numbers of the Western States are:

California	90	Nevada	94
Arizona	91	New Mexico	95
Idaho	92	Oregon	96

Montana	93	Utah	97
Washington	98		

Bank Number

Second number in the denominator of the fraction. This is the number assigned by the American Bankers Association to each bank. This number and the City or State Prefix Number must match the name and location of the drawee bank.

Routing Symbol

Denotes only banks whose checks are collectible through a Federal Reserve Bank, Federal Reserve member banks, and U. S. Treasury checks have one. On the latter two the numerator is 000. Checks whose transit numbers are not in the form of a fraction are on banks that are not members of the Federal Reserve System. The denominator will always be a three or four digit number.

In three digit denominators the first digit indicates the Federal Reserve District in which the drawee bank is located. In four digit denominators the first two digits indicate the Federal Reserve District. The Federal District main offices are:

1. Boston
2. New York
3. Philadelphia
4. Cleveland
5. Richmond
6. Atlanta
7. Chicago
8. St. Louis
9. Minneapolis
10. Kansas City
11. Dallas
12 San Francisco

The second digit in three digit numbers and the third digit in four digit numbers designates the Federal Reserve Bank or branch that serves the area in which the drawee bank is located-1 main office, 2 to 5 branches alphabetically. Digits 6 to 9 are reserved for special collection arrangements.

The third digit in three digit numbers and the fourth in four digit numbers used to denote the time needed for the document to clear the Federal Reserve Board, but this is now a standard 3 days for almost all checks.

Bank Privacy

Some good news on the privacy front, the law that would have required banks to monitor all activity without regard to size and report anything some suit thought was "suspicious" has been withdrawn from consideration.

Bank regulators said they will withdraw the controversial "know your customer" rule after being overwhelmed by more than 140,000 complaints that the rule is a massive invasion of privacy.

In one week they received over 54,000 calls about the law.

Exactly 18 callers were for its implementation...

"The proposal should be promptly withdrawn," said John D. Hawke Jr., comptroller of the currency. He was sworn in last December just as the four federal banking agencies issued the proposal requiring banks to monitor their customers' accounts, keep customer profiles, and report "suspicious" activity to federal law enforcers.

The rule was intended to, yep you got it, "help catch drug lords and other criminals who launder their money through banks."

Mr. Hawke said it inadvertently undermined confidence in the banking system by violating the traditionally confidential relationship between banks and their customers.

"Law-abiding citizens will understandably be apprehensive that their banks will report any transactions that may be the least out of the ordinary," he said, and people may come to view banks as "an extension of the law enforcement apparatus."

Christie Sciacca, associate director of the Federal Deposit Insurance Corp., said most of the 135,000 people who wrote the agency about the rule oppose it as an invasion of privacy, and several bills have been introduced in Congress to overturn it.

"The FDIC is listening and has received the message loud and clear," she said. "It is obvious to us that the proposal cannot become final."

The Federal Reserve appeared the most reluctant to concede the proposal was a mistake. Richard A. Small, an assistant director at the Fed, said that many banks already routinely monitor their customers' activities. The "Know Your Customer" program "would be nothing more than formalizing existing procedures," he said.

One Fed official said the public uproar over the proposal was "unprecedented" and he acknowledged that it "raises privacy concerns that also pose a real danger of eroding customer confidence in the institution at which they bank."

The rare withdrawal of a regulation by the nation's powerful banking agencies was prompted by the heated opposition of organizations as diverse as the American Civil Liberties Union, the Eagle Forum, the Free Congress Foundation and the Consumers Union.

These groups set off alarms with their members and helped stir up the whirlwind of complaints.

The rule "assumes that every bank customer is guilty until proven innocent," said Gregory T. Nojeim, legislative counsel for the ACLU. "A fifth-grader establishing a savings account for her allowance will have to worry that a generous cash gift from her grandparents may bring federal agents to her door."

Now for the bad news – An agency that makes the IRS and the NSA look like your local PTA was formed some 20 odd years ago.

FinCen (Financial Center) employs hundreds of "agents" some of the best Cray Super computers and what appears to be an unlimited (and partially hidden budget).

Some bureaucratic genius conceived of FinCen as a way around the laws designed to protect citizens from those damned drug dealers who seem to lurk in every corner of every bank, post office, credit union and money changer in our country.

FinCen protects us by avoiding the federal regulations that forbid agencies from sharing financial information without a warrant.

See, any agency from the IRS to the DEA can input any information they have on you and any other agency can withdraw it.

But *nobody* actually exchanges illegal information...

Well your friends at FinCen have gone long past the "Get To Know Your Customer" law shouted down by concerned citizens.
FinCen now publishes a report of "suspicious activities" even they are under the CTR transfer limits.

Suspicious Activity Reporting System (SARS), created by the five federal financial supervisory agencies and the Financial Crimes Enforcement Network (FinCen), is two years old. SARS has processed approximately 150,000 reports of suspicious activity submitted by depository institutions. Those reports are available electronically, in their entirety, to the system's builders, to five federal law enforcement agencies (with two additional agencies about to be added to the list), 52 state and territorial law enforcement agencies, and 25 state bank regulators.

The development and operation of SARS are a special responsibility and a special challenge. SARS was designed to be the centerpiece of a new approach to using the Bank Secrecy Act (BSA) to fight financial crime, and involved an unparalleled attempt to build an explicit and continuous data flow about potentially serious activity among: depository institutions detecting that activity; five federal financial supervisory agencies (the Federal Reserve Board, Office of the Comptroller of the Currency, Federal Deposit Insurance Corporation, Office of Thrift Supervision, and National Credit Union Administration).

Conclusion, SARS has made a strong and effective beginning. A nationwide system is now in place for the filing and distribution of suspicious activity reports. Equally, if not more importantly, the banking community has made strong efforts to support SARS FinCen is also responsible for analyzing this information and providing the resulting intelligence to investigators, regulators, and the banking industry to provide an ability to understand patterns of suspicious activity – or at least activity thought by bank officials to be suspicious – so that government can alert banks to emerging patterns of white collar crime.

On a more fundamental level, SARS reflects the philosophy that suspicious transaction reporting is central to counter-money laundering policy, both in the United States and abroad. Officials at financial institutions are more likely than government officials to have a sense as to what transactions appear to lack commercial justification or otherwise cannot be explained as falling within the usual methods of legitimate commerce. Under those circumstances, simply relying on currency transaction reporting is neither adequate nor cost effective for either the institutions involved or the government.

Here's how it works – Bankers are paying closer attention to the facts when determining whether or not activity is suspicious. Moreover, the addition of a detailed narrative makes the data more valuable than it was when banks could only check a box on the CTR. This value is illustrated by the fact that it is now possible to summarize the sorts of conduct involved in the reports. In addition, SAR filings in this group can become extremely valuable for certain investigations. This fact has been confirmed in a number of situations involving tax evasion.

There are a large number of cases that have been detected and explained by the filing institutions which might be called "sloppy money laundering" – repeated attempts and relatively unsophisticated schemes to structure deposits or to use several persons to move currency into the same account. Analysts have identified approximately 4,200 reports that involve the ongoing movement of funds in an organized way through particular accounts. For example, a number of reports appear to be linked to subjects under investigation in connection with the use of Black Market Peso Exchange transactions.
Approximately 4,000 reports focus on bank activity other than currency deposits and withdrawals – most importantly, suspicious funds transfer (wire transfer) transactions. In fact, a significant number of reports marked as "wire fraud" probably involve money laundering. FinCen analysts believe that this last group of reports are likely to provide the most promising area for case development.

What Other Nefarious Activities Can Get You A Federal Jacket?

Structuring – Ninety-four currency deposits, mostly in amounts slightly under the currency transaction reporting threshold ($10,000) and totaling $637,000 were made over a two-year period by a customer who identified herself as a "housewife."

A deposit was made in $100 bills (just under the reporting threshold) by a man.

A deposit of $500,000 was made in sequentially numbered traveler's checks.

A deposit of approximately $300,000 in traveler's checks containing illegible payees and endorsers' signatures was received from a foreign bank. A deposit of four blank $500 postal money orders in consecutive numbers and $1,780 (in $10 dollar bills) was made into an account from which the customer immediately used the total deposited to buy a bank check.

A purchase of two cashiers' checks for $9,000 was made using currency. The transactions were conducted by a husband and wife on consecutive days. The checks made payable to the same payee.

A purchase of bank checks for amounts between $4,000 and $9,000 was made by a customer on three consecutive days using currency. There were also a number of cases in which it was felt the target returned too many food stamps to a particular store.

Unusual Account Activity

Large amounts of currency were deposited into an account, followed soon after by the presentment to the account for payment of several checks whose payees were foreign nationals and businesses transactions involving food stamps.

A customer deposited "boxes of food stamps" in amounts inconsistent with the size of his discount grocery business.

So – wire transfers, buying four post money orders (even though way under the CTR limit), paying off a loan in cash and other major crimes can get you a visit from a nice IRS or other Federal agent.

Check: More Fraud Fighting

The banks, the feds, the credit agencies are all fighting back, here's a state-of-the -art look at what check manufacturers are doing to combat paper hanging.

Remember that many schemes come along; few actually get implemented on a wide scale, usually due to cost or incomplete technology.

It's unclear exactly how much money is lost to counterfeit and altered checks, but most experts agree that check fraud represents a billion plus industry.

As an example National Cash Register Corporation (NCR) has announced that it's integrating an ultraviolet-based check-fraud prevention system into its line of check products.

UV Smart, as the system is known, uses ultraviolet ink to protect key areas of information on checks and requires special UV lights to scan checks and look for alterations at the time of verification.

Besides fighting check fraud, UV Smart could possibly convince financial institutions to make the transition to check imaging. This system allows banks to capture pertinent bits of information from checks, instead of entire checks.

The bits include those parts of the check-payee, courtesy amount-that is protected with UV ink. In theory the entire check than be recreated including the UV security features.

Files created utilizing the UV Smart-perfected technology require about 85 percent less storage space than traditional check image capture systems.

A number of banks have licensed the system and are testing it as we speak.

The system not only deters fraud but can leverage the technology for a variety of new customer services, including data mining of information from checks, and fast, inexpensive transmission of pertinent check information to commercial customers.

It is thought that the SmartScan system can offset some of the problems with the positive pay system by allowing banks and clearinghouses immediate information about the check and the payee, allowing them to match critical data before forking over the cash.

Another company, BANKDetect has developed a PC-based system called **RiskTracker** that can predict the likelihood of a check deposit not being honored by the paying bank. The system attacks the deposit side of check fraud, assessing the risk of each account receiving a fraudulent check deposit, based upon the transaction activity of that account.

Eastman Kodak, Co. offers **Digital Science Image** verification system (IVS) to combat check fraud.

The system, initially developed for credit cards, will place a compressed image of a check writer on the face of a check, in the form of a thumbnail size bar code, which is then decompressed and read at the point of deposit or point of sale, using a special scanner gun.

Storage, is no problem, since the compression technology can reduce an average picture from 15 kilobytes in size to about 57 bytes. A bank could store about 20 million photos on a 1.2 gigabyte hard drive, or about 10 million portraits on a compact disk.

Fraud Fighting Continues

One new deterrent, sold under the name **SafeChecks**, uses halftones, the groups of thousands of small dots commonly used to print photographs in newspapers and magazines. When viewed at reading distance, the dots blend together into a continuous image. While the dots are typically one size, halftones can also be composed of big dots interspersed with little ones. If the little dots are small enough, they fall below the resolution threshold of most copiers and scanners and cannot be accurately reproduced. Designers can use this feature to make patterns that will spell out the word VOID on copies that do not appear on the original.

The check paper also includes a watermark, an image formed by varying the thickness of the paper during its manufacture. These images become part of the paper and are difficult to reproduce, because they cannot be seen with reflective light the kind used by scanners and copiers to make reproductions. The check will feature a warning banner that tells the recipient to look for the watermark.

This system also includes some fluorescent ink that will appear only under ultraviolet light.

The counterfeiter who attempts to modify a legitimate SafeCheck will run into other problems. A special chemical coating on the paper reacts to ink radicators, so any attempt to change the payee or dollar amount brings out the word VOID in three languages.

Canon Corp., the leading manufacturer of color copiers and a producer of printers and scanners, quietly incorporated two anti-counterfeiting features into its business products. The copiers include a specially programmed microchip that recognizes the currencies of several countries, including the United States and Japan. If someone attempts to copy the currency, the copier will print a black sheet of paper instead.

An additional deterrent imprints the machine's serial number on every copy it produces. The number is encoded in "micro dots" that can be printed anywhere on the page. The serial number can be decoded only with special equipment which the company provides to the Secret Service and other federal agencies for tracing counterfeits to the copier on which they were made.

How to Fake, Fraud, or Misuse Credit Cards

The thing is, you see, perfect plastic has become a misnomer – what percentage of your credit card bill is actually incurred from *presenting* the card?

Most crimes that fall into what our friends in law enforcement call credit fraud takes place without the benefit of any tangible card. Order something by mail, phone or the internet and one only needs to have *the information* contained on the card - not the actual card itself.

Hence the concept of credit card fraud has expanded on a logarithmic basis. Go on the net, dive a dumpster, bribe a waiter and you are now the legit card holder.

It was tougher in the old days (you know, pre-net, pre Amazom.com) when a would-be criminal was actually required to produce a small plastic wafer in order to reinforce the purchase.

But not impossible by any means.

Notably, nearly one-fifth of all U.S. credit card losses occurs in sunny California, an amount close to the combined total for the other five identified problem areas worldwide: Florida, Texas, New York, Asia, and Great Britain combined.

Card Counterfeiting

Cards can actually be manufactured from PVC blanks. The equipment involved is obtainable on the open market. With a bit of research one can find many companies that offered units for making plastic company ID, security or membership cards.

These cards can be designed with a credit supplier's logo by the same computerized design technique I've covered elsewhere.

Magnetic strips are available, or can be duplicated by using cut down video tape. They can even be encoded if one purchases a strip reader/writer.

Holograms can actually be manufactured (see that chapter), purchased on the black market, or a substitute faux hologram lookalike can be pressed onto the card.

What does our favorite FBI agent say about this concept?

"To understand the complexity and nature of this fraud, it is important to review the methodology used by counterfeiters in their operations. Until recently, most counterfeit credit cards were manufactured using a silk screening process that duplicated the card logo and background onto a plain white plastic card. With improvements in technology, however, counterfeiting a credit card has become a multi-step process, often using desktop computer systems and peripherals, including embossers, laminators, and tipping foil, to produce a more realistic looking card, complete with a hologram and fully encoded magnetic strip. Most of the supplies used to manufacture counterfeit bank cards, including the white plastic cards and Visa/MasterCard holograms (the Visa dove and the MasterCard interlocking globes), are smuggled into the United States from the Far East.

The magnetic strips and holograms used to counterfeit bank cards represent a distinct sub-market within the criminal community. Currently, there are 87 firms worldwide legally approved to manufacture cards with holograms for members of Visa and MasterCard, and only two companies, De La Rue (Great Britain) and American Bank Note Holographics (New York) authorized to manufacture actual card holograms.

Credit card companies started using holograms in 1981 as a safeguard against fraud; since then, however, large-scale hologram counterfeiting operations have developed in Taiwan, Hong Kong, and China. A separate market emerged for holograms, which usually sell for between $5 and $15, depending on their quality.

Smugglers bring holograms into the United States and Canada regularly. During one month, the Canadian Combined Forces Special Enforcement Unit and Combined Forces Asian Investigation Unit arrested members of a Chinese syndicate that produced approximately 300,000 counterfeit holograms, of which 250,000 already had been distributed. Based on the quantity delivered and using an estimated loss of $3,000 per card, Visa and MasterCard anticipated losses approaching $750 million caused by this group alone.

Often, the key to quickly identifying a counterfeit card lies in an examination of the hologram. On legitimate cards, the hologram is actually embedded in the plastic upon manufacture; counterfeit credit cards commonly contain a hologram decal purchased from an illegal distributor. These holograms are affixed to the top of the card, rather than embedded in the card, and can be seen or felt to rise slightly above the card face.

Counterfeiters sell magnetic strips for credit cards piecemeal. The strips contain names, account numbers, credit limits, and other identifying information for legitimate or contrived Visa/MasterCard card holders. Using a computer system, source materials, and peripheral equipment, a counterfeiter can compile a fraudulent bank card with relative ease."

How Good Are These Home Made Units?

As with most things in life, the outcome will vary in direct proportion to the amount of effort and money applied to the problem.

Most card counterfeiters utilize stolen (but real) numbers and real names on the card. This means, once accepted by a human clerk, even if the card won't swipe, it will show "approved" when the number is manually punched into the terminal.

A few years ago a gentleman I knew on a vague basis gave me full blown cards his organization had run off in the names Donald Duck, Mickey Mouse and Donald Trump.

They looked fine.

Some people have successfully modified existing credit cards by heating the area of the PVC that contains the name and account number with the use of an iron or soldering gun until the material becomes malleable. Then they re-press a new name and number set into the card.

This process works better on some cards then on others, and one must remember to demagnetize or re-encode the magnetic strip.

Credit Cards And Account Identification

A credit card or the numbers thereupon can reveal significant facts about the owner:

The first step is to learn to recognize which numbers relate to which cards:

Wells Fargo:
Name
MM/YY - MM/YY
4024 0071 XXX (X) XXX (X)

If the card begins with 4024 - 0071 it is a Wells Fargo issued credit card. If the marker between the dates (usually '-') is '*' it is a gold card.

If the "I" is followed by a 'C' mark it upward to a classic card.

No "I", but a "P" means a premier card.

American Express
37XN NXXXXX XXXXX
MM/Y1 THRU MM/Y2 Y1
Name AX

First two digits are always 37. If the N's are between 80-89 it is a gold card. If the N's equal 37 it's a platinum. First date is when owner got the card, second is expiration.

AMEX also has a four digit security number (non embossed) above the final card number group. This is used (rarely) to authenticate the card in mail order transactions).

More often they will simply ask for your billing zip code.

MasterCard
MasterCard
5XXX XXXX XXXX XXXX
XXXX AAA DD-MM-YY MM/YY
Name
First digit is always a 5.

VISA
VISA Name of Bank
4XXX XXX(X) XXX(X) XXX(X)=
MM/YY MM/YY*VISA

First digits are always 4333 or 4444.

A Trick to Identify Credit Cards

Have a credit card number, but don't know the bank of issuance? Try calling First Data Merchant Service's toll free number.

When the computer answers, choose option 5, then enter the first six digits of the credit card number, then hit the * key. The First Data number is 800/326-7991.

Credit Card Number Procurement

While credit card numbers are still stolen by crooks digging through restaurant dump bins, or keeping a copy of a gas receipt a new breed of number theft has pretty much left these simple schemes in the dust.

The internet IRC Channels (chat rooms) are nearly the perfect place for criminals to congregate, a sanctuary for those who want to trade or sell credit card numbers they've stolen on the Internet.

"Carders" are traders, their product being credit card information and/or complete financial identities.

There are a whole slew of chat rooms where any time, day or night, where someone, is attempting to trade a stolen card number or two for a "shell" – illegal access to a computer on the Internet.

Although a majority of the audience seem to fall into the under 18 crowd and may simply be offering (or buying) a single card, there are also instances of hundreds, even thousands of numbers for sale in a single batch. These are usually offered by suppliers who are able to steal thousands of credit card numbers from Web sites or other sources.

Getting them is not as hard as one might think; a number of reports recently have highlighted security vulnerabilities at e-commerce sites.

Theft methods include the use of packet sniffers (which steal data from the web intended for someone else) database cracking, or pretexting the user out of their card details by the use of fake web sites which offer amazing deals on products, or services.

The next step involves using a stolen number to purchase something – often something that can be sold easily. This leaves both a digital trail that must be covered and often involves contact with the real world in the form of a delivery person.

Carders will often order items delivered to a "drop" – perhaps a mail drop secured with fake ID or a nearby abandoned house, an office building or even a church where they can intercept the package after it's delivered.

Large operations will actually rent out a small office or storefront, usually paying cash and getting to know the Fed Ex delivery man very well over the next 30 days before they vanish.

Because of this problem the U.S. Postal Inspection Service has implemented the Express Mail Label Profiling Program to identify packages likely to contain contraband. The profile flags suspicious packages based on mail quantity, delivery frequency, destination, label and packaging material characteristics, etc.

The profile was developed initially to identify packages containing drugs. Postal inspectors in the drug unit forward profiles to the credit card fraud unit if they believe that non-drug criminal activity is occurring.

Through this program, postal inspectors can trace the illicit mail to both its source and its destination, thus identifying members of the fraud rings.

Another scheme I have personally seen utilized is to order a very expensive piece of merchandise to a particular point – perhaps even the CC owner's real address, and then just happen to be outside getting in the car, or working on the lawn when the UPS truck shows up.

Just a little bit of surveillance and the goods are signed for by the person who ordered them.

Delivered as promised.

On the Internet finding a place to ship purloined goods is all part of the trading process. ("I have virgin cc and need a drop"). "Virgins" are freshly stolen cards that have not yet been used illegally, worth much more than "used" cards.

Here's how it works: A thief posts a claim that he has a "bunch of fresh cards," and then to prove it, he posts a sample card, including billing addresses, phone number, etc., into the open chat room.

The circling sharks will immediately sense the blood and home in the wounded body. It's not unusual to see someone else place a post that the card has been maxed out within a few minutes of the original notification.

Although the actual theft of materials is a crime, the posting itself is still a gray area. To further complicate things, law enforcement must have some information delivered by an outside person in order to wander into a chat room.

Read snitch.

The FBI admits they do not have the manpower to police the multitude of rooms on a regular basis.

Even when Visa or MasterCard does receive a report that rarely ends the problem. Cards are actually issued by member banks, so each one must be contacted separately and told to cancel the card.

A batch of 2,000 numbers could involve hundreds of banks.

Advance Payment Schemes

Federal consumer credit regulations require credit card issuers to credit a customer's account as soon as payment is received, i.e., before the payment instrument has cleared the bank. While this regulation is intended to protect consumers, it also creates what a member of the California Bankers Association calls a "window of opportunity for fraud."

The scheme is simple. Using a counterfeit or stolen credit card, the group either makes an advance payment on the card or overpays an existing balance using a bogus check. Because the account is credited upon receipt of payment, cash advances immediately can be drawn against the bank card before the payment check has cleared. In the past criminal organizations have realized profits in excess of $1 million within a relatively short period of time utilizing this method.

How To Detect Fraudulent Credit Cards

A few things that should arouse suspicion during a physical credit card transaction include:

- No, or non-3-D hologram
- Card appears to peeling in layers
- Card is expired
- Card is not signed
- Name does match that of other ID materials
- Signature does match with other ID
- Card shows evidence of alternation or poor manufacturing

Technological Deterrents

To combat the problem of fraud, credit card manufacturers plan to employ a series of security features, most of which are designed to enhance customer identification and authorization requirements. Due to the shortcomings of holograms as a fraud deterrent, credit card manufacturers currently are modifying magnetic strip coding to include a number of additional personal identifiers, such as customer photographs, fingerprints, and personal histories. Photographs on the face of credit cards have been used by financial institutions for the past 25 years, but their value as a true fraud deterrent has been questioned because such photos can be altered easily. Eastman Kodak, Xerox, Gemplus and other companies have developed systems to digitally encode a customer's photo within the magnetic strip, enabling verification through specialized processing terminals at the point of sale.

The next generation of credit card technology involves the so-called Smart Cards, which will feature computer chip technology in lieu of holograms. Specifically, each card will contain a microprocessor memory chip, as well as data encoded on the magnetic strip. In addition to providing extra security benefits, the chip will allow customers to authorize off-line transactions, store prepaid values, and conduct secure transactions from remote locations. The chip will store more personal information about the cardholder than that currently available through the magnetic strip and will require the customer to verify the personal identification number (PIN) encoded on the microchip.

A Trick Source

Anyone who is interested in the latest methods bad people use to defraud banks, credit card companies how to trace any particular check or credit card to the bank that issued it (as well as the as phone numbers in order to verify any details about the document in question) might wish to purchase one or more books from The Fraud and Theft Information Bureau (POB 400, Boynton Beach, FL 33425).

These publications are designed for bank officers, large merchants, mail order houses and security folk.

Titles include BIN Number Directory of All Visa and MasterCard Issuing Banks ($5075.00, Directory of Mail Drop Addresses and Zip Codes ($605.50), Directory of all Prison and Jail Addresses and Zip Codes ($1515.00), As well as various guides or those who accept credit cards and checks.

My personal favorite would be The Top 100 Credit Card Crimes and How To Stop Them.

One publication, Best Articles From 100 Fraud & Theft Newsletter Issues (only $199.95!) claims, "subscribers paid $1500 for this inside information on how the FBI, Secret Service, police, attorneys general, DA's, US postal Service work with businesses to identify credit card thieves and counterfeiters. How to detect and halt losses from stolen and counterfeit credit cards, bad checks, theft by computer, shoplifting.

Case histories, including indictments and prosecutions, organized crime, new developments, fraudulent mail order, telemarketing and other companies."

Interesting reading for serious security officers or serious criminals.

Although they seem a trifle expensive, one should note the ones priced above $1,000 seem to include postage.

The $200 and under variety do not.

New Lives For New Livers

The new, true and updated story of fake, phony and otherwise "novelty" identification cards.

As follows:

If one does a key word search on the ol' world wide web, one will come up with as many as 25 sites offering "drivers licenses, SS cards, credit cards and other forms of "realistic, just like real government ID cards!"

Many sites include color samples one can down load. Most of these sites have pages of very authentic appearing DL's from every state and Canadian providence a few toss in foreign examples for those hard to please world travelers.

How can this be legal you, being an erudite reader, ask?

I answer, it ain't.

A couple of the sites actually state "illegal area, get us before the government shuts us down AGAIN!"

Others are operated from another country, usually Canada or England. These providers make the applicant write "novelty" on the application and "will not ship if you use the word "license'".

They point out that customs will let the packages go through if they contain only "novelty" items.

This is, unfortunately, primarily bullshit.

After ordering a number of said novelty items I can pretty much detail the concept...

- Many simply do not fill the orders at all

Screw you jack.

- The ones that do supply anything either make it so obviously not a government issued ID that bartenders in Shanghai will call their friends over and point at you with rude gestures, or stamp something to the effect of "NOT A GOVERNMENT DOCUMENT" in large red letters across the front

- Some firms combine the two techniques and ship a bullshit card that resembles nothing in nature and then stamp it, just so there is no confusion on the matter

- None of the products are even similar to the online samples

One company stamps "go kart license" across their ugly card. Although we are trying to keep up to date on this matter, and will do the same for you, AS OF THIS WRITING I KNOW OF ONE, ONLY ONE SITE THAT SELLS ANYTHING EVEN VAGUELY WORTH BUYING!

A number of years ago a gentleman I know produced and sold nice ID cards that had the state name across the top in red and included, on the reverse, a statement to the effect of, "all information on this card is true and accurate per original application."

Excellent double talk.

He eventually did include the wording, "not a government document," or something to that effect.

He still spent 6 months in the gray rock hotel, courtesy of the federal government for selling the cards...

A number of the sites out now seem to have copied his 20 year old concept right down to the red ink and state name.

I wish the providers well.

Several sites sell a CD ROM that lets the buyer start life over again with real government documents, a foolproof plan.

This concept is ripped off from the book Paper Trip (Eden Press) and is 20+ years old.

Things have changed over the years (see the letter from Barry Reid) due to such new fangled inventions as the social security death index. If anyone has an interest in this concept, I recommend the latest version of the Paper Trip series from Eden or Paladin.

A few other sites hype an interactive CD that gives one all the insights on the ID game. This disc is offered, apparently word-for-word, from several suppliers and ranges in price from $20-$50.

So far no one has filled our order for this item and the first supplier, "Underground Software" cashed a number of checks, closed down their web site and no longer return messages.

Templates for making your own, real drivers licenses (CD based, needs a color printer) in the same price range don't seem to get delivered on a regular basis either.

I should point out that no ink jet printer will "create" a drivers license, no matter how great the $20 template turns out to be. It is possible to fake a DL or other card by utilizing a digital camera, good computer, Adobe PhotoShop, a continuous tone printer and a talented graphic artist.

The latter is a non-dot oriented device that actually influences and mixes the colors as they actually go on the page. CT printers are now used to create upper end artist's prints.

In fact, for those of you old enough to remember, or, for that matter have any interest, Graham Nash of Crosby, Stills, N and Young owns a CT printer for hire.

Said printers are currently priced above $100K. Even if one could produce the graphics file and convince a continuos printer owner to run what appeared to be government ID cards there is still the problem of holograms, background UV lighting and the dreaded mag stripe.

Although some of the new "photo quality" prints currently close to this quality for a couple hundred bucks.

Not even counting the smart cards used by N.J. (soon by other states as well) which contain an embedded chip.

NONE of the sites currently available supplies these minor add-ons despite sales pitches to the contrary with the exception of the ID Shop (see article).

So what's the story on most web offers?

- Who buys phony ID's? And the answer is, "what are teenagers trying to get into bars?" Who would you postulate is going to listen to their complaints?

- Why are the suppliers in another country? Because no FBI, Postal Inspector or local DA gives a shit if they bilk some stupid American What Being Trying To Buy An Illegal Product In The First Place

- None of the current suppliers will send a sample card without a purchase. Gee, why would that be...

- Almost all "providers" refuse to take credit cards. Can you say the word "charge back?"

- Most are not even registered companies and demand one make out the money order to "Mr. Ted Kazinski, Unabomber", or some such

Obviously I'm not trying to get kids into bars (damn few children shell out for this particular publication) nor am I including this information for nefarious purposes, but many of my readers do have a need to know in this area.

What Can One Do, What Can One Do?

One can take my advice, check out the ID Shop web site and stop there, or one can also access a brand new, really cool web site that is doing a running commentary (reader supplied feedback) on the entire "novelty" ID situation. Go to http://pages.eidosnet.co.uk/fakeidman/.

Used with permission.

Fake ID Sites

Recommended Sites

For a site to be Recommended it must be:

- Long Established
- Not a Rip-Off!!
- Swift Delivery
- Accept Credit Cards
- Generate few complaints to me

Site	Cards	Certificates	Holograms U/V	Samples	Price	Credit Cards/Secure	Comments	Your Views
Sadbros	Y	Y	Y / Y	All- Good	£5 ($8)	Y / Y	Long established. Very good cards with latest designs. Cheap - very good quality.	Views
Belvine	Y	N	Y /Y	Some - Average	£5 ($8)	Y / Y	Long established. Good cards. Cheap - good quality.	Views

Reliable Sites

These are long-established sites where you can be pretty certain that you will receive your fake ids. This does not mean however that you will like what you get. Check out the VIEWS for each company.

Site	Cards	Certificates	Holograms/ U/V	Samples	Price	Credit Cards/Secure	Comments	Your Views
NoveltyID.com	Y	Y	Y / Y	Y - All	$40-65	N	Nice site. Good samples. Reasonable prices.	Views
TheIDShop	Y	N	N / ?	Y - All	$60	N	Nice site but samples not clear	Views
Eastcom	Y	N	Y / N	Y - All	$90	N	Shut Down ?	Views
Xotic.com (Eastcoast)	Y	N	? / ?	Y - All	$28	N	Novelty only as all cards state "Go-Kart license"	Views
Photoidcards	Y	N	Y / N	Y - All	$69	N		Views
Free ID Templates	N/A	N	N	Y - 2	Nil	N/A	Some free templates for download.	
IDNow	Y	N	? / ?	1	$100	N	Calif. only	Views
EYIC	Y	N	N / N	Y - All	£10 / $20	N	Plastic European Cards	
UltimateID	Y	N	? / Y	Y - All	$65	Y		Views
Id-cards.com	Y	N	? / ?	Y - All	$50	N		Views

New/Questionable Sites

These are either sites which are new or ones where I have never received any feedback - good or bad. If you order from one of these sites, let me know what you think.

Site	Cards	Certs.	Holograms/ U/V	Samples	Price	Credit Cards/Secure	Comments	Your Views
NoveltyID4U	Y	N	? / ?	Y - All	$15	N		Any views?
ID CARDZ	?	N	? / ?	N	295SEK ($36)	N	Site in Swedish. Seems to have usual features but no samples.	
FakeID.Net	Y	Y	Y / Y	Some	$10 per month + $10 per card template.	N	Template based - make your own cards. Membership scheme.	Views
Id Software	Y	N	? / ?	N	$10	N	Software based. Home card printing. Very little information.	
IDSolution	Y	N	Y / Y	Y - All	$150	N	Suspicious.	Views
Fakeidzone	Y	N	n/a	None	$20-50	N	Novelty Ids	
The IDStore	Y	N	Y / N	Some	$35	N	.	Views
Idzone	Y	?	? / ?	None	$50	?	Suspicious	
Espionage-store.com	Y	N	? / ?	None	$20	N	Looks Interesting	Views
Dupps Studio	Y	N	? / ?	None	$125	N	E-mail Only	
phonyID.com	Y	N	Y / ?	1	$225	N	Any views?	
The Idstore	Y	Y	Y / ?	Some	$35	N	Any views?	

Known Rip-Offs & Scam Sites

These are the sites which no matter how good they look, will take your money and send you nothing. These guys know that you are unlikely to complain because of the nature of fake identification. I have received tons of e-mails complaining about these sites. Please do not send any more unless you have new information etc.

Site	Comments	Your Views
Promaster	The Original Rip-Off!	Views
PhotoID	Related to Promaster	Views
Real ID	Suspicious. Anyone got any news?	Views
Statelicence	Another guise of IDS?	.
Anarchy Underground		Views
Fake-ID.org	Suspicious. Related to IDS?	Views
noveltyfakeids.com		Views

Other Cool Sites

SecretKnowledge.com	Great site for ID, Lockpicking, Scams, Cannabis Growing, Bugging etc
Morphiss Press	Books on how to get a new ID, passport, birth certificate etc. Anyone bought? Any good?
Cafe Covert	Cool Site covering every conceivable "dodgy" subject!
Coolcards.com	Novelty Card Design Site
Mailbox ID	$24.95 Book on ID, Birth Certificates etc - anyone bought?
Shedding Skin	Cool Hacking etc Links page
Nic-Inc.com	Various novelty cards, badges and other equipment
Mo Man's Sitel	Cool Hacking Site - many topics covered
driverslicenseguide.com	The official site for the bartenders guide.
prestigious-images.com	Transcripts, Social Security Cards, GreenCards etc

Real Good Fake ID

Okay so you've read the results of my research about purchasing ID cards on the web, or rather the *scams* that pass for purchasing ID cards on the web.

Is there any actual source I can recommend?

Yes.

There is one group that actually does a hell of a job producing ID cards. I have met the proprietors, examined the product, looked into their manufacturing systems and they *are* the best around.

Note these are legal ID's, i.e., The ID Shop does not sell items that exactly duplicate drivers licenses, nor that even employ the words, "drivers license."

Nobody in their right mind does.

What they do is produce a line of ID cards that are as good, or better than most state ID cards (as well as a number of more generic ID's).

Please note these are not little green cards that say "bounty hunter" and you type in your name and then laminate the card – these are real ID cards made on machines that cost far more than the Polaroid ID card cameras I've shown.

Let's back up a hair, here.

TheIDshop.com. began producing quality ID's over two years ago. Since that time they have added refined their product and now offer items that just cannot be found anywhere else.

For instance, they provide two completely different types of ID made with two completely different processes. As follows:

3M Process Novelty ID

- Printed on High-Quality 3M film (these are laminated ID's)
- 3M ID's take a week to make once we receive your order.
- Super sharp templates
- Highly durable
- Great low cost ID
- Rated the best value for the money by John Q. Newman

But the really good stuff is their PVC option:

The ID Shop is the first Id web site to ever offer PVC plastic ID's. These ID's are the highest quality novelty ID's around. They also come with many added security options such as holograms.

PVC Plastic Novelty ID:

- Printed on PVC Plastic
- All new templates designed
- We make the PVC ID's the same day we receive them, while the 3M ID's take about a week and a half to process.
- Holograms available
- 20 times more durable
- Different backs on ID's
- Sharper Quality ID's

One can order a real hologram on the PVC card for an additional $20. Note this is a real hologram, not just a glow-paint paste-on.

Why don't suppliers make this option available? Here's what the ID Shop folks had to say when I asked them that very question.

"We only offer one hologram at this time because the cost for one design is in excess of $20,000 (that is the minimum cost, a more realistic figure is $70,000).

The design we offer is a REAL hologram.

It has a continuous pattern of three objects: a lock, a key and the words "secure." These objects are printed all over the front of the ID. For an additional $20, we highly suggest the hologram option."

I also inquired about the possibility of a magnetic strip on the reverse of the card, "they are not all that important. A state can only read the state they are in, assuming that can even read the strip which most people cannot."

Let me regress for a second; I have yet to find a realistic ID for sale on the web except for the ID Shop examples.

And I did look.

Talk about a waste of money.

Here's the ID Shop's opinion of their competitors, mind you I'm reprinting this because I *agree* with it.

During the initial planning stages of The ID Shop, our founders spent countless hours analyzing the ID market. Several important discoveries were made about our competitors:

97% are frauds/scams.

Many utilize misleading or false advertisements.

Many contain alleged customer testimonies.

Many produce poor quality products.

In response to these conditions, we modeled The ID Shop around customer satisfaction and quality service. Our door is always open, and we encourage everyone to consider any and all competitors before making a decision. We will happily respond to all incoming e-mail within 48 hours.

Images on this web site are identical to the finished products, except for necessary web security devices/features. The words "SAMPLE" do not appear on the ID's this is only used for web-security. We do not promote or endorse any deceptive or misleading advertisements.

Instead of filling our pages with claims of satisfaction, which could be easily fabricated, we have opted to streamline our site for the benefit of you, the customer.

Finally, in light of the poor quality of our competitor's products, we have located the highest quality staff and purchased top-of-the-line production equipment for our merchandise."

Poly Vinyl Chloride (PVC) ID's are much easier to accept as most states are now using this process for their drivers licenses and state ID cards. They also incorporate a number of features both in manufacturing as well as appearance that gives credence to their very existence.

"Every ID Shop on a PVC card has been completely redesigned, making them look even better then before. We have created brand new templates front and BACK for all of the new PVC ID's. The 3M processed ID's have all the same back but the new PVC cards ID's have different backs. These ID's are ten times more durable; meaning you will never have to buy another ID ever again. The best reason for ordering a new PVC Plastic ID is that we are able to print a hologram on them for an additional $20. (We can ONLY print a hologram on the new PVC Plastic ID's)."

The ID Shop also offers other ID products including student cards and company badges.

The ID Shop is the only company to offer fully digital ID's complete with rich 32-Bit continuous tone color and new PVC Plastic Cards.

Check out their web site: www.theidshop.com.

Good stuff.

Roll Your Own

It is possible, in fact actually quite easy to create a completely fraudulent ID on a home computer. Although I still maintain one should obtain the best equipment one's budget can suffer, some people have shown a passable ID can be created with a total equipment investment of about $500.

My first recommendation is to use a Mac. Please no letters from die hard Windows fans; Mac's were designed to be graphic machines and still represent the best benchmark for most graphic functions.

In my opinion.

I actually maintain a Pentium unit for research and normal chores and an upper end Mac for graphic design and layout jobs.

Many professional graphic artists still operate in a Mac environment.

ID's that lend themselves to home duplication include student ID, Press Passes, State ID's and even drivers licenses.

Remember the key is the more dots-per-inch one prints the better quality the ID will appear. Continuous Tone Printers (super expensive) are the best, typography (usually figured at 2400 DPI) is second and then we come to high density lasers also see the chapter on check forgery) a 1200-2000 DPI laser does a very good job of small photo and seal reproduction.

A top notch photo style ink-jet will also suffice.

Software should include:

- A PostScript package for the printer which allows many graphic programs to function correctly
- A good graphic program such as Adobe PhotoShop
- If possible, a type program such as Illustrator

Here's a hard and fast course in ID creation:

Scan, into PhotoShop the "template" or background of a real ID card. Also scan larger than life as reducing the size has the effect of sharpening the image.

NOTE

Avoid the $30-$50 "programs" circling around the net that claim to be do-it–yourself ID manufacturing programs. We purchased a couple as test cases and, well, they all sucked.

The worst of the lot was from "Best Fake ID's.com", who promised "easy to use" templates of every state ID.

In reality all they did was scan in every page of the copyrighted Drivers License Manual I've covered elsewhere.

The "templates" still had the word SAMPLE stamped across them and used the same photos, numbers and details as the examples in the book.

Take the $50 and buy a good steak.

Scan into PhotoShop a recent photograph of the person for whom the ID is intended. Do this at a larger size than the final photo will appear on the card. Once the image is brought into PhotoShop it can then be adjusted to the necessary size.

One of the advantages of PhotoShop is that this process can be layered; i.e., each layer can contain separate elements that are adjusted to achieve the correct look before be combined into the final output.

Text can be inserted via PhotoShop, and tweaked to some degree, and then "blurred" in order to look a touch worn.

The caveat here are that programs like Illustrator actually allow a more comprehensive menu for type tweaking.

If one has access to such a program, create the type therein (EPS format) and copy into a PhotoShop layer for a final makeover.

A couple of tips:

- Keep each separate piece in it's own PS layer until it is time to finally place them on the master template

- If possible, work from film (slide or negative) when entering the data as this format provides the best detail

Logos, "stamps" and other markings are scanned into a PS logo, the size and look adjusted, depending on where other elements are scheduled to run (photo across logo, for instance) the layers can be pushed under, their colors brightened or dulled, etc. to make the final master appear correct.

Remember you are not adding mag stripes, or holograms with your printer, but these can be added later as shown.

Best Equipment For Fake ID Production

According to *Mac Addict Magazine*, who did a study on exactly which combination of hardware would fill the bill for do-it -yourself ID's, the following units represent the best choices per budget and performance:

Scanner:

Astra 2400S Umax Technologies scanner (around $400) and with a transparency scanner coupled to a Epson Photo 700 and Photo EX six color inkjet printer. The EX prints larger documents, both are a trifle slow but units produce works of wonder.

ScanMaker X6EL from Microtek does a good job with colors for about $250. Attached to an Epson America ($550) fast and performance just below par with professional units.

Trick For Homemade ID Finishing Touches

Holograms:

- Make your own per our instructions, hard, medium hard or quick and easy
- Go on the net, order from some company that knocks-off Levi's for a living in Hong Kong and sells fairly authentic holos
- Purchase ready made examples from companies like NIC – sure it don't look like the MasterCharge logo, most are sort of a pale green eagle or other "official" looking gram (but they often do work)
- Mag stripe available, can be created from video tape, readers and writers very available thru computer magazines. Most DL formats simply list the owner's basics in obtaining digital formats

Anti-Trick

A hologram should be an integral part of the card. One should not be able to peel it off with a fingernail.

The preceding section is a rough guide for ID artists and calls for the use of a couple of expensive, and somewhat difficult to use programs.

I can muddle through most Adobe applications including PhotoShop and PageMaker, but there are not pick-up-and-use concepts.

I tend to utilize a Mac, which was originally designed with the idea of graphics in mind and can grasp enough of the two Adobe programs to make an idea work.

Usually.

I like the layering aspect and numerous options that PhotoShop allow, by the same token, I can easily get lost in the detail forest.

The other option is to employ someone who can utilize these programs on a professional basis.

Someone one trusts completely.

IntelligenceHere.com employs a couple of different graphic artists, one who has, ah, how to put this delicately?

GA number 1 has come across the opportunity to work in this field before, as well as one who is just a "straight" GA.

The latter refused to work with the concept of a fake ID, although he did explain my questions on a hypothetical basis. The former contributed much of the following page.

He actually prefers the simplicity of programs such as CorelDraw over the more complicated PhotoShop/PageMaker combinations and feels that anyone with "artistic abilities" can re-create, fake or re-draw most objects with a PC and CorelDraw.

As he says, "you don't have to work in layers and you can import scans directly into the file or use as a trace and re-draw."

There are several ways to accomplish a successful duplication of any original. Here I have demonstrated the easiest ways to use CorelDraw without having to jump into a deep learning curve."

My little sidebar is that the following technique will also work on ID's, checks, stationary, wedding photos, whatever.

Scan in the original with the settings that allow you the best image from which to work.

Scan a second time and set the image choices to drop out the background, allowing you to retrieve the seals/symbols.

Match fonts and use the original as a sizing guild. TIP: you may have to use different fonts, within a word, stretch or condense copy to make a match.

To get the "stamped" image, type the letters individually. Copy and assign one a lighter color. Size one set slightly smaller and place each letter over the larger letter, choose both overlaying letters and blend them, one at a time.. For SAMPLE that runs over the photo, use the transparent option.

Use the Node option to reduce the background from the seal and remove the circle for the seals that overlays the photo. Or, redraw and fill in. This will allow the background to come through the seal as in the original. For the darker seal, match a circle size, use the transparent option and fill with a darker color and place over the seal. Group the object.

Use the original to draw lines and place created objects. Scan in a photo or insert photo at time of lamination if required. Corel gives you options to place an object to front/back, so you can place the sample and seals over the photo.

Using the seal you redrew or created, reduce to match size of those in the background. NOTE: you will have to reduce the line thickness as you reduce the image. Once this is in proportion, copy it to make one string of the background. Then copy the full line until there is enough to cover the background (this allows for exact placement and adjustment). You may choose to place this on a layer since it is time consuming for screen refresh. Now draw boxes and corners to cover the overspill of the background. Fill with white and remove the outline. Group. (You can't use the box and node curve edit because the inside will remaining square cornered.) FINAL: place all elements together. Output to a color printer or a professional "Firey Print". (This is a step up from copying and a step down from actual printing. However, you may not want to take this outside your privacy.)

Holograms

One of the primary security devices for any type of endorsed identifier from a drivers license to a whisky bottle label has become the hologram. This feature is attractive, "easy" to validate and difficult to imitate.

Or so modern thinking goes...

The hologram produces a 3-deminsonal figure when viewed under normal lighting conditions – nothing else does. Hence it is used to make a VISA card a VISA card and a California drivers license, well, a California drivers license.

Is it really a secure form of ID?

Portions of the following chapter are reprinted and/or edited with permission of several of the top hologram experts, scientists and engineers in the world.

Thank you to Mr. McGrew of New Light Industries, used with his permission. Steve McGrew President New Light Industries, Ltd. http://www.iea.com/~nli stevem@iea.com.

Also thank you to Dr. Geoge Kalligeros who teaches amateur holograms to high school students and teachers making their first holograms. Look at his web page for further information. http://members.aol.com/gakall/holopg.html.

Parts are derived from my own research.

What Is A Hologram?

It is a light wave interference pattern recorded on photographic film (or other suitable surface) that can produce a 3-dimensional image when illuminated properly.

How Is A Hologram Made?

A laser beam is split into two beams – the reference beam is spread by a lens or curved mirror and aimed directly at the film plate

The object beam is spread and aimed at the object. The object reflects some of the light on the holographic film-plate. The two beams interact forming an interference pattern on the film. This is the hologram. Laser light is needed because it is made of coherent waves (of same wavelength and phase).

The principle of holography was discovered in Britain by Dennis Gabor in 1948. He was awarded the Nobel price for this discovery in the early 70's.

How Is A Hologram Viewed?

When the hologram is illuminated from the original direction of the reference beam, a 3-dimensional image of the object appears where the object was originally. Some holograms must be viewed with laser or monochromatic (single color) light, and others with white light.

What Are The Main Types Of Holograms?

- Transmission Holograms: Viewable with laser light. They are made with both beams approaching the film from the SAME side
- Reflection (White Light) Holograms: Viewable with white lights from a suitable source such as spotlight, flashlight, the sun, etc. They are made with the two beams approaching the holographic film from OPPOSITE sides
- Multiple channel holograms: Two or more images are visible from different angles. There are different types of multiple channel holograms:
- Simple ones with 2, 3, or a few images each viewed from a different angle
- Multiplex: a large number of "flat" pictures of a subject viewed from different angles are combined into a single, 3-dimensional image of the object
- Rainbow holograms: The same image appears in a different color when viewed from different angles
- Real Image Holograms. These are usually reflection holograms made from a transmission original. The image dramatically projects IN FRONT OF THE PLATE toward the viewer. Most holograms in holography museums are of this type. The procedure for making them is quite elaborate and demands precise control of angles
- Mass-produced holograms
- Embossed: made by stamping on foiled backed Mylar film using a metal master (most common method)
- Polymer: made from light sensitive plastic. The Polaroid Corporation mass produces holograms by this method

- Dichromate's: very vivid holograms on jewelry, watches, etc. They are recorded on a light sensitive coating of gel that contains dichromate

The problem of hologram counterfeiting includes these aspects:

- The incentive for counterfeiters

- Methods, cost, and countermeasures for hologram counterfeiting

If a hologram is the key feature used to judge the validity of an identification card or a product, then the counterfeiter's incentive is directly related to the profits he can make by counterfeiting the hologram. A single example will suffice to show that the financial rewards to a hologram counterfeiter can be enormous on the level of tens to hundreds of millions of dollars.

A drivers license is for all practical purposes the American national ID card. There are several million people in and out of the country who would like to have a California drivers license as fraudulent evidence of U.S. citizenship. Without going into the politics and philosophy of that situation, we can still estimate the financial incentive a potential counterfeiter will have to duplicate the hologram on a drivers license, if holograms are the key security feature on a drivers license.

A good counterfeit drivers license can be worth $500 to $1500. At last count there were over a million illegal aliens in the Unites States. That means there is a potential market in excess of $500 million for counterfeit drivers' licenses.

Clearly, there is a large incentive for potential hologram counterfeiters. This incentive is easily enough to overcome even major technical challenges.

Methods For Hologram Counterfeiting

The current methods of hologram mastering and embossing were developed in 1980 in a garage in Santa Clara, California on a budget of roughly $9,000. The methods have been widely published, and there are hundreds of individuals and companies all over the world capable of duplicating the methods. There are however much simpler methods available for the counterfeiter.

Mechanical Copying

The simplest method for duplicating an embossed hologram is to use the hologram itself as a mold for producing an embossing die. This is accomplished by removing any adhesive or other coatings from the embossed surface of the hologram, silvering the clean embossed surface, and electroforming a metal such as nickel onto the silver. The electroform is then directly usable as a die for embossing into aluminized polyester or PVC. Counterfeits made this way can be so perfect that no expert will be able to distinguish them from the original hologram.

Contact Printing

Almost as simple as mechanical copying is the method of contact printing. In this case, a copy hologram is made by laying a photoresist coated plate in close contact to the original hologram and illuminating the original hologram through the photoresist plate. Diffracted and undiffracted light is reflected from the original hologram and a nearly identical copy is formed on the photoresist plate.

The photoresist plate is then silvered and electroplated with nickel; and the nickel plate is used as an embossing die. Counterfeits made by contact printing are similar enough to the original to pass even a close inspection, though with the right tools an expert may be able to detect them.

Two Step Copying

The image in a hologram is optically equivalent to the object from which it was made. It is relatively easy to make a good copy of a hologram by illuminating the hologram with laser light and recording a second hologram of the reconstructed light, then illuminating the second hologram and recording a third hologram using the real image of the first hologram. Counterfeits made by this method are very good. Though an expert with the right tools can detect them, these counterfeits will pass a close inspection by a non-expert.

Re-Mastering

The technology for making holograms from flat artwork or from solid models is widely known. A hologram made by one manufacturer can be approximately replicated by a counterfeiter by simply recreating the artwork, then making a hologram from the artwork.

Counterfeits made by re-mastering are rather easily detected upon close inspection if the artwork is sufficiently complicated or detailed.

However, it is very rare that security holograms are subjected to close inspection in actual use.

In some cases it is possible for a counterfeiter to acquire commercially available holograms which roughly resemble a security hologram. These simulations will almost never pass even a cursory inspection. However, it is a fact that even crude hologram simulations have been successfully used by counterfeiters.

Too often, a clerk will only look to see if there is a hologram on a card, and will not look to see what image is in the hologram!

Cost And Effectiveness Of Counterfeit Holograms

	Effectiveness	Lab Cost	Time	Product Cost
Mechanical Copying	5	$2,500	5 days	$.05
Contact Printing	4.5	$15,00 0	7 days	$.05
Two-Step Copying	4	$20,00 0	10 days	$.05
Re-Mastering	3	$25,00 0	20 days	$.05
Simulation	1	$ 0	0 days	$.25

Effectiveness And Cost Of Hologram Counterfeiting

The above shows New Light Industries estimates of the cost and effectiveness of hologram counterfeiting by the methods discussed above.

Effectiveness is on a scale of 1 to 5, with 5 being essentially a perfect copy. Lab cost is the cost of setting up enough equipment to do a good job of counterfeiting. Time is the number of days required to make a counterfeit embossing master from an original embossed hologram.

Product Cost is the cost of each embossed counterfeit hologram once the counterfeit embossing master has been made.

Effectiveness And Cost Of Hologram Counterfeiting

One interesting feature of the above figures that it indicates the easiest counterfeiting methods may produce the best counterfeits.

Characteristics That Make Holograms Counterfitable

It is important to examine the characteristics that make holograms easily counterfeitable. Holograms without these characteristics will be much more difficult to counterfeit:

- Non-variable holographic information: i.e., no information in the hologram which depends uniquely upon the content of the document it protects

- Accessibility of the embossed surface of the hologram to use as an electroforming mold

- Presence of a non-diffusely reflected portion of the illumination light, substantially stronger than the diffracted portion
- Unaltered polarization of the diffracted and reflected light from the hologram
- Ability of the hologram to be reconstructed using standard laser wavelengths
- No non-holographic information imposed on the light reflected from the hologram
- No large-angle, short wavelength "covert" image features in the hologram – a reasonably uncomplicated image
- Poor cooperation or communications between legitimate hologram manufacturers
- An uneducated or unobservant user base – verification performed by humans

A Secure Holographic I.D. Card

This card uses a hologram which is hot stamped in a pattern consisting of an array of very small dots. Over the hot stamping is applied a coating which bonds to the substrate between the dots.

Before the hologram is applied, the substrate is printed with variable information. The hologram itself is a stereogram of a well known human face.

Mechanical copying is effectively prevented because if an attempt is made to delaminate the coating from the substrate, the hologram is left as a large number of isolated dots which are useless as the basis for making an embossing die.

Differential adhesion between the hologram dots and the coating to the substrate will make it extremely difficult to remove the coating and the dots together as a single unit, in order to transfer the image to another card.

Contact copying is effectively prevented because the information printed on the substrate will be recorded in the contact copy. If an attempt is made to make a two-step copy of the hologram, the same problem arises: the variable printed information is recorded at the same time.

A photograph cannot be mistaken for a stereogram because the photograph lacks three dimensionality. As is well known in the security printing industry, a human face is very difficult to counterfeit without detection, so re-mastering the stereogram using a look-alike will be risky.

Any good look-alike of a famous person would be rather easy for the authorities to trace.

Re-mastering is made considerably more difficult by the fact that the hologram itself is a stereogram. Aside from the greater complexity of producing stereograms, the use of a well-known human subject will greatly complicate the counterfeiter's task.

Re-mastering and simulation are unlikely to be effective because human beings are exceptionally good at recognizing human faces and noticing small differences between them.

Conclusion

Simple hologram counterfeiting methods and some actual counterfeiting examples have been described, and a new holographic security device has been covered which should be fairly immune to the counterfeiting techniques which are effective on most holograms used in security applications today.

It is important to point out however, that the security of an identification card is based in turn on the security of all of the steps leading from the manufacturer to the user of the card. The steps form a chain, and no chain is any stronger than its weakest link.

There is no evidence to date that any of the manufacturers of security holograms keep accurate records of the number of holograms that are made or shipped, nor that there are accurate records of the number of holograms that are used or rejected by the card manufacturers.

There is no serial numbering on holograms. There is no formal association of security hologram manufacturers through which one manufacturer can avoid unintentionally counterfeiting another manufacturer's holograms.

There are several ways to make holograms which can be effective anti-counterfeiting devices, but at this point, there exists no standard method to prevent counterfeiting.

It is, indeed possible to make your own holograms. The “common” practice uses special plates and chemicals usually Russian in nature (check out www.3deep.com/products.html).

The procedure is exacting and requires some skill and knowledge of chemistry to accomplish – and have all one’s fingers still visible at the end.

Rather than use 20 pages to reiterate information that is available let me suggest that anyone who is serious about hologram manufacturing first check out the sample below, from Mr. George Kalligeros and then, if one is still interested pull up both Mr. Kalligeros and Mr. Steve McGrew’s (Northern Lights) web site mentioned at the beginning of this chapter.

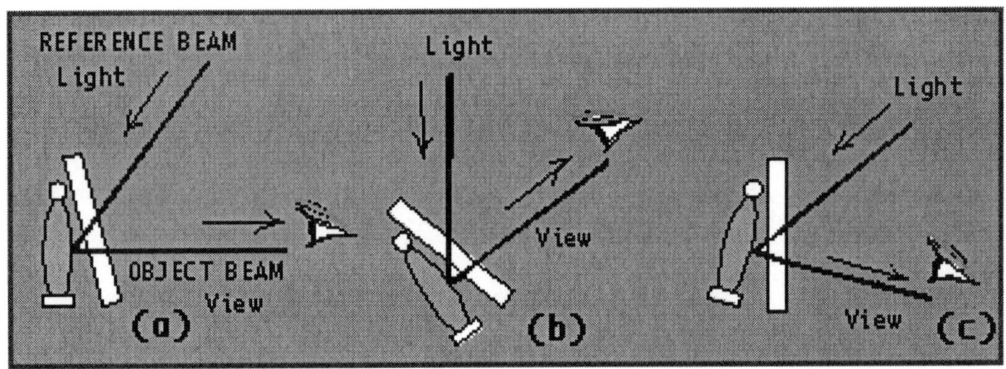

"Note: The viewing direction, should be approximately the opposite of the direction of the reflected light from the object when the hologram was made. (See diagram 5). To express it a little differently, the angle between the line of sight towards the image and the line of illumination is the same as the angle between the reference beam and the object beam. Diagram (a) shows the original positioning of the plate and the object for exposure and the directions of the two light beams. It also shows how the plate should be illuminated by a spotlight and how it should be viewed to see the image where the object WAS. When the plate is rotated, the lines of illumination and viewing rotate also."

Laser Holography A Major Trick

A gentleman by the name of Frank DeFreitas Email: frank@holoworld.com, web site http://www.holoworld.com/holo/diode.html

Maintains a site detailing his ongoing experiments to create holos using inexpensive supplies (such as an $8.00 laser diode pointer).

"My current magical journey of making holograms with a $7.99 laser pointer."

His pages do not exactly instruct one on how to make said hologram; but they do provide some interesting concepts as well as detail kits, supplies and courses Mr. DeFreitas recommends or sells.

"Up until just a few months ago, you needed an expensive laser to make holograms. Not any more. I'm creating holograms using a $7.99 laser pointer. This section of my web site will keep you up to date on my progress as I experiment with and develop, more advanced creative techniques such as color control and mixing, animation and simple stereograms utilizing the pointer as light source."

"My current experiments revolve around taking laser pointer holography a step further – into making multi-color holograms and other moderately-advanced techniques, such as animation and simple stereograms – and putting it all together into one inexpensive, easy-to-use system. There is a lot of room for experimentation and discovery, and it is a most exciting time once again in holography. My beginning goal is not to create any breath-taking content, or to get the brightest hologram (that will come later). Right now, I'm more concerned with getting the process to work and then work to improve image quality."

This gentleman really puts some effort into his work and details exactly how various lasers, plates, chemicals, etc. work as well as where to procure them.

"So, there you have it folks – an 8 x 10 single-beam reflection hologram with 8-inches of depth using a $7.99 laser pointer. And yes, I know I'm asking you to believe quite a lot. I would find it hard to believe myself, to tell you the truth. This has come a long way since the dim, little "frosty the snowman" hologram.

Although not designed for identification purposes Frank is a gold mine of hologram information.

How to Make State Seals and Holograms

A Trick – State Seals and Holograms

Besides the make-your -own concept for holograms there are a couple of other options:

- Some realistic holograms, including those that duplicate major credit card manufacturers are manufactured in other countries (read Hong Kong here) and sold on the web. Trick is to know your supplier as many, many web based ID suppliers are completely bogus
- NIC Law Enforcement Supply, 500 Flournoy Lucas Road, Bldg. 3, Shreveport, LA 71135 sells several "exclusive hologram type laminates" which arrive in the form of press on foil. One has an official looking eagle with the words "security seal" surrounding the bird; the others resemble law enforcement badges with various logos
- They give off a green glow and do resemble holograms
- The also sell peel-off hologram "security stickers" that, if removed, reveal the word "VOID" where the sticker was, much like the real thing

This very same company fills in the void created by the need for embossed state seals. As I have mentioned, many documents, including birth certificate copies, require an embossed seal. In the bad old days one had to bribe an unscrupulous die maker, or simply order a seal of "your design" which happened to coincide with a government state seal and hope for the best.

NIC sells all 50 state seals (dies and embossing press) as well as blank metallic seals which can be embossed at one's leisure.

Very nicely done, very reasonably priced.

Adds that personal touch to any ID card.

How to Make the World's Simplest ID

In the 1800's one "proved" one's identity when meeting someone by producing a calling card.

In the 1900's this small piece of card board evolved into the business card. A true business card not only provides all the necessary contact information but establishes the holder's identity.

Business cards traditionally made by hiring a graphic artist for the design and then having a printer run off a batch. Many printers demand (ed) runs of at least 500-1,000 before accepting a business card job.

Technology has moved to the point where a couple of much easier options exist, especially for "limited runs."

- Several $40 software programs allow even the graphically challenged to design and print their own cards in any quantity desired. Including the quantity of one
- Many copier centers have the ability to produce a small run, which includes on the spot design
- Large shopping malls and some airports feature a machine which allows one to input the necessary data and, using one of their stock designs, print a few cards instantly

A Small Trick

If one does not wish to utilize one's actual phone number, nor wish the person who answers to say they have never heard of Acme Collections, People Tracking and Used Car Sales, is to find a phone number that is constantly "busied out" in your particular area code.

This can be accomplished by running a war dialer program, reading the magazine *2600*, perusing local computer bulletin boards or just dialing numbers within a prefix until such a number is discovered.

These numbers are, among other things, maintained by local telco's for testing purposes and are often located in the lower end of the prefix (555-1234, etc.). The fact that one ever answers makes it a trifle difficult for card recipients to verify your information.

Letterheads, stationary and other "business ID" can be scanned into a computer, tweaked and reproduced or simply handed over to a quick printer/copier for a quick run.

Remember if you are scanning into a graphic program (such as PhotoShop) it's best to enter it larger than life and then shrink to size allowing better definition.

Legends and a Life of Their Own

Many years ago Barry Reid (Eden Press, Paper Trip, etc.) was discussing the rapidly increasing (remember this was years ago) amount of paper work the government was requiring every year just to prove you are who you are.

My feeling was one of creeping horror – more and more proof, more and more explanations for anyone who felt the urge to disappear or change for a period.

Barry's take was exactly the opposite, "no Scott, the more paper they want to see, the quicker they get tired of looking at what you have and assume you're A-1."

An interesting thought, and one I have come to agree with, although with the recent addition of smart cards, chips, and embedded fingerprints there is a tradeoff in progress.

With the publication of the Social Security Death Number database, various search engines that will flag any SS number issued within the last five years, the IRS releasing more information, it has gotten much harder to create a new person.

Well, of course, one could have a baby, but that's not what I'm speaking of, exactly.

If one birthed an ID a number of years ago – using the correct SS series, got a drivers license (probably based at a PMB before the databases were complied) bought into some of those "secured" credit cards, accepted a few pre-approved card offers, bought some stereo equipment, maybe a car AND PAID THE BILLS ON TIME.

Man be a citizen – at least as far as the credit bureaus are concerned.

Somebody runs a credit header, or even credit report on Citizen X, and guess what? He's a good guy, on-time bill payer, low profile, perfect citizen.

Really clever people (and no I didn't) may have even gotten a passport before the regulations tightened up.

This nonentity, whom the credit bureaus like, well, probably more than they like you, is called a legend.

The legend can buy a car, move to another country, open and close bank accounts, open offshore accounts and pretty much live its life like it wants to.

Even if the legend owner loves the U.S., has a credit with the IRS, has been cited for bravery by the DEA, what he has created is worth a bunch (what's a bunch? $100,000+) to the guy who just ran out with the banks total cash supply, sold his 200 K's of coke, or milked the pyramid scheme for all it's worth.

Legends are around, but they are rare, and not usually advertised in the local paper.

Starting a legend today is tough, which is why People-On-The-Run usually assume an ID, rather than attempt to create one.

A Trick

Once a person has established credit with any of the big three agencies and pays his bills on time for a few months he will begin to receive "pre-approved" credit card offers.

These names come from the credit agencies, or in some cases banks, who sell the "new" seem-to-be-paying customers to high interest credit card companies.

Credit bureaus often do not usually ask nor verify income – just payment history. Each large credit compiler has a department that rates their customers and decides whom to sell the new fish to.

It has been recorded that some people run up a decent bank and credit history, take every pre-approved card possible (although it's smarter to wait for the limits to go up prior to signing), apply for some on their own, borrow heavily, pay a while and then declare bankruptcy.

In fact, to quote Geoffrey Planer, a North Carolina bankruptcy lawyer, "you can't paper North Carolina with pre-approved cards and then complain about people filing bankruptcy."

As a final note, you do realize that "pre-approved" *does not*, by no means actually mean you are pre-approved for any type of credit. It simply means one's name was on the "good-hit sucker list."

After all, terms like pre-approved and pre-qualified are the reasons we have attorneys.

Fraud, ID's and You

This special section looks at the question of fraudulent ID's from a slightly different perspective than the regular chapters. Rather than discussing issues of fraud surrounding an individual identification document, this section considers fraud as a whole. Specifically, here we will address two areas: one, the purposes for which a person might seek to obtain a fraudulent ID; and two, the methods by which such ID's may be obtained.

Purposes Of Fraud

A person may choose to create a fraudulent identification document for him- or herself – and thus establish a new "pseudo-identity" – for a multitude of reasons. Some of the most common includes the following:

- Persons with bad credit histories who wish to reestablish credit. For anyone with a bankruptcy or other demerits on their credit record, obtaining new identification and creating a brand-new credit report are often an easy method to "starting over" with clean credit

- Persons who have obtained money through illegal means and are trying to hide the money in a bank account set up under a false name. This includes those involved in business scams, those who work under the table, and those who have purposely cheated on their income taxes. Counterfeit ID's are the key to establishing such new accounts

- Persons who are experiencing difficult personal or emotional problems. A person undergoing crisis may simply need to "check out" of their normal reality for a while

- Persons who have broken the law and are attempting to avoid arrest

- Persons who are in the United States illegally. Illegal immigrants will often attempt to obtain false ID documentation for two reasons: for themselves, an appropriate ID can provide the opportunity to obtain work in this country; for their children, a falsely obtained birth certificate brings with it all the rights and privileges of U.S. citizenship

- Persons who, for personal or political beliefs, wish to remain anonymous from the federal government. Theories abound as to the illicit activities of the government in denying basic freedoms to citizens, especially with regard to the rights to privacy and protection against unlawful search and seizure. For those who subscribe to these theories, or are even slightly convinced that they might be true, establishing a false identity via fraudulent ID's is an effective form of defense

Types Of Fraudulent ID's

Once an individual has decided to seek out false identification, he or she has three options of how to proceed. He or she may *doctor* an already existing document; they may *forge* an authentic-looking copy; or they may *illegally obtain* an actual, valid ID. Here are the three methods in detail:

- A *doctored* ID is one whose appearance has been changed in some way to include information that the bearer wishes to present. The most common example of this is the fake ID used by many high school students, on which their date of birth has been changed so that they appear to be of legal drinking age.

  Doctoring an ID already in one's possession is the simplest of all methods of ID fraud. However, it also leads to the least authentic-looking documents, and thus is most likely to be tagged as a fraud.

- A *counterfeit* ID is a fraudulent ID that has been created from scratch to resemble its valid counterpart. Counterfeiting takes more time and effort than doctoring; however, if it is done well, a counterfeit ID can be virtually indistinguishable from a real one, and thus is less likely to be tagged for fraud

  Producing counterfeit ID's is big business in this country. This is no surprise, given the huge number of identification documents floating out there and the powers that accrue to persons holding those documents. Professional counterfeiters are very successful in flooding the market with ID's that bear little if any difference from those that are officially issued.

- *Illegally obtaining* a valid ID is the most time-consuming but ultimately the most foolproof method of all. Procuring an actual ID, such as a driver's license, under a false name takes a great deal of preparation in terms of gathering together the appropriate documents necessary for the application. In many cases, doctoring or counterfeiting of earlier documents may be necessary

  However, once a valid ID is obtained, it provides a powerful tool in establishing a new identity. The ID can now be used to open accounts, gain employment, and obtain other forms of ID – anything that a *real* ID can do (since, technically speaking, this *is* a real that is, officially issued, ID).

For anyone seeking to create a lifelong, stable new identity, illegally obtaining a valid ID is the safest way to go.

How to Tell if an ID is Real

Because of the complexity of identification documents, from driver's licenses to military and immigrant cards, one would think there might be a comprehensive guide that would include all the various security features.

Many, many years ago my child, a gentleman (Keith Doerge) formed a company called Drivers License Guide Company in Redwood City, California and began publishing a yearly guide to virtually every ID in America plus some surrounding nations.

The first books we provided in a loose leaf binder, each one serial numbered and sold only to government agencies, licensed private investigators or law enforcement personnel.

And they made you prove it.

Each yearly Manual set the purchaser back a cool $150.00 and was worth every penny. I've still got a number of mine and enjoy perusing them.

The U.S. Identification Manual addressed everything, from state ID's, Air Traveler's Cards to CIA ID.

Great stuff.

A couple of years ago the company decided the market lay elsewhere, and changed both their publishing and marketing policy.

Still published by:

Drivers License Guide Company
1492 Oddstad Ave.
Redwood City, CA 94063

The new and sort of improved model is published every February, is thinner by 500% than the old model, non-loose-leaf BUT sold to anyone who will pay the (approximately) $20.00 fee.

This is a great, great book that allows cops, bank personnel, bartenders and other ID verifiers to quickly check out most of the common ID varieties (drivers license, state ID, military, some credit cards, etc.) in about 5 seconds.

Not only does the book list the major security features (holograms, shadowing, etc.) it provides instant check digit schemes for many ID's.

Every ID is presented in full color with security features visible.

This book is a must for:

- Anyone who has to validate an ID
- Anyone who wants to see how close a fake ID come to the real thing
- Anyone who is even considering manufacturing an ID

Island Hopping – How to Stash Your Money or Your Life Offshore

Sooner or later anyone who is researching alternative forms of ID, banking laws, the IRS and other hobby-oriented topics will come across a number of people who suggest one move one's savings and perhaps trading accounts, etc., to a bank in a country which does not give up one's financial profile to the first attorney or even federal agent who gives them a call requesting "private" information.

The most famous of these concepts is/was no doubt the great Swiss numbered account where one accessed, deposited and transferred funds with only a code number.

This concept was actually started during the Nazi area to protect hidden assets.

No name was required on the account itself.

Things have changed with regards to our friends the Swiss; very few, if any banking institutions offer pure numbered accounts anymore and one should know the Swiss have been cooperating on a regular basis with such agencies as the IRS, with the caveat that they felt the money on deposit came from a criminal activity.

If so, say bye-bye money.

Because I am not one of the world's main experts on the subject of moving money I have consulted a few whom I believe fall into that category, and their expertise will be incorporated into this chapter.

Before we get into that, let me express a few opinions I have gathered from studying this phenomenon for a number of years.

First and foremost is that once funds are in an offshore bank (in a well regulated country) they are pretty much gone from the grasp of anyone in this country. Divorce settlement? Lawsuit loss? Skip with the business partner's money?

Once the money tracker, be him federal or private, discover the calls to the bank in the Bahamas on a phone bill he simply writes it off and looks for more accessible funds.

Even Canada can be a bitch from which to eleviate funds.

Bank privacy laws in most of the "approved" countries prevent verifying the very existence of an account, much less paying any money to some foreigner who just happens to have a subpoena.

I have worked with a couple of the very best money hunters in the country, and even they give up when the offshore transfer order is unveiled.

So it does work for some people; don't bother taking your $10K nest egg and calling Panama. These accounts are designed for people with *money*. The banks are not in it for the sheer fun of talking to Americans, and the transfer charges will soon eat up a small deposit, assuming the bank would even bother with such a small amount in the first place.

It's also difficult to write a check for the transmission repair to the local gas station from the Second Bank of the Caymans.

And if you violate certain programs designed to flag possible offenders the IRS will become your best friend and possibly live-in guest.

However, there are times when offshore makes sense, even if you haven't won the state lottery in the previous month.

Besides the numbered or hidden account it is also possible to procure an offshore credit card (Visa, MasterCard) or an offshore ATM card which will allow one to withdraw funds anywhere in the world with a minimum of record keeping.

Many of these accounts are set up by third parties, or people, for monetary consideration. I am going provide some sources but simply can't recommend any particular group that I have not personally used.

Handing money over to someone one has never actually met, just because their web site is sooo cool, it has to remain your decision.

One can also hire consultants, usually attorneys of some sort, in the target country to smooth things over.

Again for a fee.

Finally, one can contact the bank directly in many cases and establish an account or ATM card without paying $500-$5,000 to a middleman.

I'm going to list a number of these banks that will consider doing business individuals.

Much as within the U.S., many will want a secured deposit for a credit card or a service fee for an ATM card.

If one has enough reason to take offshore monetary precautions, these are minor hassles.

But choosing the right country as well as a trustworthy bank cannot be over-stressed.

An experienced and reputable lawyer (contradiction in terms?) can smooth this process like oil on water.

There are some very good overseas investments that are also not reported to, well, to various federal agencies, such as Swiss annuities, but this is a personal choice.

I do not, read my lips, suggest anyone violate American banking laws unless you are prepared to take the risk of spending your golden years a Federal penitentiary, or, at the minimum, lose your investments.

But, it is not necessarily illegal to bank offshore!!

There is nothing illegal about moving money into another bank or investment. The problem arises when one moves assets into accounts offshore and does not declare their existence to the tax authorities.

That *is* illegal. Americans are required to pay taxes on income no matter where it comes from.

The primary reason for money moving is to protect one's assets into a legal entity which will protect them from attack by frivolous litigation, seizing from government, attack from an estranged spouse and so on.

Please note the following is informational, but also pretty much an ad for a certain offshore establishing agency. *Again, I cannot personally recommend or un-recommend these folks, I haven't used them.*

However this will provide a look at the costs and considerations involved in this type of transaction.

At Piazza Financial Services LTD (A certified Agent of The Finor Organization) web site we believe in providing value for money for our clients. Furthermore, when providing our services, our focus is on building the quality and value of relationships with our clients over an extended period of time. Basic asset protection structures start as low as U.S. $2,500 for an average family, with annual costs as low as U.S. $1,800. Of course this cost rises with the complexity involved, but rarely exceeds U.S. $30,000 initial cost.

What Is The Minimum Amount I Should Start With?

That depends on your reasons for going offshore. If it is for asset protection you should be considering how much you are risking by not going offshore, namely, lawyers fees, time, loss of assets etc. If it is for tax reasons you should be looking at the annual costs against how much tax you can save (i.e. $18,000 is 30% of $60,000).

Are there any other advantages to going offshore ?

The best place to start is to contact U.S. at support@piazza-financial-services.co.uk.

Now Read This Please

The following is used by permission from John Bull who runs Privacy World. These guys have been around a long time and have a good reputation in the overall scheme of things.

The following article is compiled by one David Johnson, a consultant specializing in privacy, security and investigative matters. It is used by permission of the author.

This originally appeared via privacy@privacyworld.com. A firm specializing in setting up Western European Bank accounts, ATM and credit cards.

What The IRS And Other Tax Authorities Don't Want You To Know.

By David Johnson

When you have something to hide, the simple rule of thumb is do – it offshore. After all, if you are reading this your goal is to keep your financial business to yourself. The purpose of this article is to give an introductory inside look at banking and investing overseas, using fiscal tax shelters (havens) to reduce or eliminate taxes, and foremost, to provide confidentiality in personal and business matters, period.

For various reasons, offshore banking has been tagged as "unsafe," "risky," "illegal" or "for the wealthy," let's separate the facts from the bull!

First off, one must understand that it is normal for those that know little or nothing about something (besides what they hear from other even less knowledgeable people) to be afraid and suspicious about it. Misinformed financial planners, attorneys and accountants may know economics and the law in the United States or their country of residence, but few know about handling business outside their domicile.

Let's tackle these misconceptions one at a time.

Legality

There isn't and probably never be a law restricting the sending of funds outside the U.S.A. How do I know? Simple. As a country dependent on International trade (billions of dollars a year and counting) the American economy would be destroyed.

How? Since all U.S. global trade is transacted in U.S. dollars, there would be no exports or imports, due to the fact that the United States would not be able to buy and sell goods.

Make sense? If you wanted to, you could move or transfer some or all of your money out of your bank or credit union to anywhere in the world, legally.

The IRS and U.S. banks disseminate negative propaganda dealing with offshore banking, making it seem unsafe or some type of criminal act.

Why? Banks just want to keep your money in their institutions to use for their own profitable purposes.

Did you know that most U.S. banks themselves accept deposits from people overseas and often invest in foreign stocks and hold accounts with foreign banks?

It's true! As far as the IRS is concerned, they obviously want your money in U.S. banks where they can tax every dollar you earn in interest, and keep track of how many liquid assets you have and where they are.

The confusion with tax legalities is sometimes due to lack of knowledge. In the U.S. tax evasion is a crime, tax avoidance is not. As you know, there are zillions of laws on the books in every country. Without a doubt what is legal in one place may be against the law elsewhere.

For example tax evasion is not a crime in jurisdictions where there is no income tax. Thus, in most cases (except those with significant political and/or business weight), countries that are not allies usually don't assist other nations in enforcing laws that are not laws in their countries. Further, a country has no legal right to conduct an investigation in a foreign country without consent of the respective government.

In reality, a country has every right to deny any other nation permission to make examinations in their territory. Therefore, it is difficult if not impossible for authorities in the U.S. or elsewhere to obtain financial transaction records of tax evaders in many foreign-based institutions (outside of those located in areas that have some type of cooperation treaties).

Strict banking secrecy laws also contribute to this difficulty. Most tax havens impose lengthy prison terms and/or hefty fines for violations of a client's secrecy.

INTER-FIPOL (The International Fiscal Police) is the tax crime equivalent of INTERPOL (The International Police Organization), which is a network of law enforcement authorities in numerous countries which exchange information on criminals. Many evaders are opening accounts in fictitious names and using mail forwarding and pick up drops for privacy.

Practicality

Movie-makers and recent international scandals, such as BCCI and Iran-Contra, have contributed to negative views about offshore banking. Contrary to popular belief, rich criminals and corrupt government officials make up a small segment of the total number of customers at any given offshore institution.

Now more than ever the average American blue collar worker and businessman are using offshore banking as a way to reduce taxes (through legal avoidance). Many accounts may be opened for the same amount required in the U.S. (about $100) or less. In some cases, there is no minimum opening deposit at all. Further, the interest rates are usually substantially higher than in the U.S. (since federal law sets limits on the amount of interest a bank can pay you).

But by far the reason most people turn to offshore banks is their confidentiality.

One might ask, "if these banks are so good, why don't they advertise in the U.S.?" The answer is simple.

They are prohibited! Federal law restricts offshore banks from advertising their services in U.S. magazines and newspapers, unless they agree to the same restrictions that govern FDIC. Institutions (such as interest limitation).

Why? To keep the competition down. Opening an account with these banks is as simple as writing a formal letter to the institution, and requesting information about their various services and the appropriate application forms, and returning them to the bank. It really is that easy! Most banks never really have to see you in person.

Safety

All offshore banks are regulated in one form or another, like their U.S. counterparts, but minus the limiting federal laws. Less restrictive regulations abroad allow foreign banks more freedom in locating the best investments worldwide. Allowing them to pass on and share their profits with their customers. They usually only allow a liquidity factor (insurance) of about 10% of public deposits.

Many offshore banks are self-insured; meaning they have at least one dollar in cash to cover every dollar on deposit this translates to 100% plus insurance. Also, the majority of the worlds largest and strongest banks (as far as assets go) are overseas, not in the United States. Call your local library's business and finance or commercial department and ask the librarian to look up these details.

Internal Revenue Service (IRS)

Treasury form 90. 22-1 (report of foreign bank and financial accounts) must by law, be completed and returned to the IRS by June 30th. Each year if you possess a foreign account *Everybody surely files!*
For a copy of the form, call the IRS at (800) 829-1040, or check your phone directory for the number of your nearest forms distribution center.

U.S. Customs

The U.S. Department of Treasury's Currency and Foreign Transactions Reporting Act details which monetary instruments (checks, money orders etc.) must, by law be reported to the federal government. A copy of an illustrated circular, which explains the act in full, is available for the cost of $5 from Worldwide Consultants, 242 West Pratt Blvd., Suite 971, Chicago, IL 60645 U.S.A

What Doesn't Have To Be Reported

Here are two categories of instruments that one is not required to report. If you make out a personal check or money order to an offshore bank, you don't have to report it. And if you have a check or money order payable to you, you may restrictively endorse it (i.e. pay to the order of ABC bank), and you do not have to report that either.

Tax Evasion

If you deposit your paycheck in a U.S. bank, chances are you've already paid income taxes on it. So you have no further obligations, since taxes were deducted before the money even hit your hand.

With a savings or brokerage account, at the end of the year when you get your annual statement, you simply add the total amount of interest or profit earned on your income, and pay taxes on the grand total.

The same is only true offshore if the country the bank is located in imposes a withholding tax. Since I'm on the subject of taxes, did you know that the United States and the Philippines are the only two nations in the world that tax income earned outside of their countries?

Below are a few examples of ways some individuals have cheated the taxman. Neither the author nor the published of this book endorses any illegal act, and, in fact, we both suggest you check the very latest laws and regulations before doing anything even mildly unsavory.

A lawyer received payment by personal check from a client and deposited it in his offshore account. Since the deposit didn't appear on his business records, the chances are it would never be found out (even if he was audited).

One couple sold a valuable antique and had the buyer send then payment directly to their offshore bank account. Later the couple used the money to tour Europe and the Caribbean.

Another example is the savings and loan bank customer who enticed his "unscrupulous" banker to electronically transfer a large sum of cash offshore without reporting the transaction to the IRS. The customer then borrowed the money back from the offshore bank. Since loan proceeds are not taxable, no taxes were paid.

These types of schemes are no longer used by the rich with extra money to hide, but by average Americans who don't like to pay taxes on every cent they earn.

How Hidden Assets Are Found

Having conducted investigations in the U.S. and abroad, I am familiar with the various techniques which may be used to locate leads to funds being kept offshore.

Here are a few:

- Checking passports (and travel agents) for evidence of visits to "high profile" destinations such as: Switzerland, Cayman Islands, The Bahamas, Isle of Man, Netherlands Antilles, and other known banking and tax havens. Travel to these types of areas will surely throw up a red flag, giving investigators a place to start looking for your assets

- Examining telephone (home, business and hotel), fax and mobile (cellular) phone records to identify undisclosed business connections and contacts

- Reviewing credit card statements to determine whom you do business with, where you travel (domestic & foreign), and what products and services you use. These records leave a paper trail a mile long

- Using a mail cover in order to compile a list of parties that you have a relationship with by recording the return addresses on your incoming mail

- Looking into banking transactions. All withdrawals of $3000 or more must be reported by your bank to the federal government, whether made by cash, check or electronic transfer. Keep your transactions under $3000

- Checking private courier's logs (UPS, DHL, Federal Express, Airborne Express etc.) for delivery of special or important letters and packages. Examining telex records of your company or business to locate areas of foreign activity

The following input is from Arnold Cornez, JD, Consulting Editor for *The Offshore Journal* –

Is A Trust The Best Entity?

Well, it depends upon the all the facts. Alternative structures include: offshore asset protection trust (APT: grantor or non-grantor), private family foundation, etc.

What Are The Risks That The Assets Will Be Confiscated By The Foreign Government?

This is obviously a political risk to a large degree.

Which Havens Are The "Best" In Terms Of Stability?

Low risk in the better, politically stable jurisdictions. The Bahamas are one of the oldest democracies in the Americas. Columbus first landed in the Bahamas in 1492. Their banks must keep one dollar of reserves for each dollar on deposit

The British dependent territories of the British Virgin Islands (BVI), Turks and Caicos and The Caymans have their banking audited by the Bank of England.

Can The Trust Invest In The U.S. As An Individual Would – In Stocks, Bonds And Mutual Funds? How Is It Taxed?

The trust can invest anywhere in the world, over 100 bourses, buying high quality stocks not qualified for sale in the U.S. because the issuers don't care to go through the rigorous and costly SEC qualification. It's not necessary for them.

What Is The Range Of Assets For Which This Makes Sense?

High Net Worth (HNW) persons – more than $500,000 in liquid assets for professional portfolio management.

Depends upon all the "bells and whistles" required for a total structure. There is a first-year setup fee, annual performance fees, second year annual fees, extraordinary fees, etc.

What Kind Of Lawyer Is Best Suited For This? Should The Lawyer Practice In The Client's State?

Most U.S. lawyers don't know enough to help and are reluctant to suggest going offshore to avoid malpractice. You don't need a lawyer. There are very qualified CPAs, financial planners, etc. who know much more than most attorneys on the subject. This is an issue of offshore and local (onshore) lawyers are for local activities. To the extent that assets go offshore, a local lawyer is not necessary. The offshore issues can be treated independently of the domestic issues to the extent that a portion of the estate is earmarked to go offshore independently of the domestic (onshore) estate planning.

From a privacy stand point, one might not want to disclose their offshore activities to their onshore lawyer.

More in my book: "The Offshore Money Book," a Comprehensive Guide for Reluctant Americans. International Publishing Company, ISBN: 0-9422641- Arnold L. Cornez, JD

Actual Credit Cards

It is extremely difficult to obtain a true "credit card" from an offshore bank until you have established credit in that foreign jurisdiction or with that bank from whom you are seeking a credit card.

Most offshore card programs are secured International Visa cards backed by savings on deposit as security or a debit card program where you carry a surplus (interest free in the Visa account). The credit line varies and can be around 67% of the amount on deposit in the secured program.

The savings earn interest program, then creates an offshore income reporting issue. The deposit is backed by either a savings account or a CD.

Debit (ATM) Cards

Because debit cards simply subtract funds from monies already in stock, there is no credit involved. As one might suspect this makes debit cards a bit easier to obtain.

Many of the banks on my list will be happy to help one set up an ATM account Clearing is done, much as in the U.S. through major organizations such as Cirrus, MasterCard and SWITCH.

These cards are simply used in the same manner as one would use the local First Bank of Cleveland ATM card.

If one is attempting to get a combination credit/ATM card, such as those common in the states, expect a security deposit to required by the bank somewhere in the area of 1.5 - 3 times the card limit.

As in the U.S., one could reasonably expect this to be waived if one had a *major* account with the bank in question.

As I mentioned one can go through a service that will set up this service for one for a fee, or one can attempt to do it on one's own.

If a fee-based (legitimate) organization does the sherpa work, the banks will be a bit more open to the concept.

The question of whether its beneficial is more difficult – I'm sure we all have our own views on that. It certainly adds an extra layer of privacy which is something that many people strive for without being law breakers. Where offshore asset protection measures have been put in place it can provide a convenient method of providing access to offshore assets without taking them onshore. I suppose its all a matter of motives.

If I can assist anybody further please contact me.

Martin Katz, Trinity International
Isle of Man Tel +44 1624 629615
Fax +44 1624 626976
www.enterprise.net/trinity

Remember it is NOT illegal to have an offshore bank account if you are a U.S. citizen or resident. However, if you have an offshore bank account and do NOT report the account that is a criminal act, i.e. not reporting the account. Of course, if you report the account, then you lose your anonymity and privacy. What good does it do to have an offshore account without anonymity?

The above information was provided by *The Offshore Journal* a monthly email news digest about current events in the world of offshore tax havens and international finance. *The Offshore Journal* was founded by Arnold L. Cornez, JD. Sponsored by Research Press, Inc. publisher of *The Jacobs Report on Asset Protection Strategies, Offshore Tax Strategies and The Off Shore Journal* by Arnold Cornez, JD Copyright, 1998 all rights reserved. Research Press, Inc. Box 8194 Prairie Village, KS 66208. Email: rpi@rpifs.com, web site: http://www.rpifs.com/ofshore/osfaq.html

Loop Hole?

Editor's note: I cannot recommend (nor not recommend) Privacy World, or any other offshore group that sets up accounts or cards for Americans. I simply have not used them.

If I were in the process of accomplishing any of the above actions I would want to see some verifiable accounts, successful customers I might contact, check out other web sites and, basically, perform the same operations as if I were buying a used car from someone in England.

The nice folks at Privacy World feel the way around many of these minor little IRS annoyances is as follows:

While having an offshore Bank account IS a U.S. reporting requirement, having an offshore ATM CARD in an anonymous name with any amount of money is NOT a reporting requirement under our understanding of current U.S. laws. If the ATM Card is not an account, you do NOT have to report it, get it?

Naturally, you should check this out with a knowledgeable lawyer if your are in the states. Since 65% of our customers are from OUTSIDE the states nearly *everyone* can now take advantage of this exciting opportunity, including our American friends and customers.

Privacy World can offer you an ATM card in ANY name with ANY picture ID that clearly shows a picture and a signature. I repeat ANY picture ID and absolutely NO notarizations required! For instance, a camouflage passport, an International Driver License, a health card, a Company ID card can be used to get a truly anonymous ATM Card.

How much would you pay for an anonymous, judgment proof ATM card from which you can draw unlimited amounts of cash anywhere in the world, 24 HOURS A DAY?

Imagine this situation: Your kid is going to college in New York (or anywhere else in the world). You want her to have ready access to cash for emergencies. You give her a plastic ATM card that enables her to withdraw up to the local equivalent of U.S. $20,000 (you set the amount anywhere from $1,000 to infinity).

The card can be used anywhere in the world to access the cash, in any Automatic Teller Machine. No identity cards need be shown. No one aside from yourself can find out where the money is, or how much is in the account backing this card.

If the card is lost or stolen, no one else can use it because it can be activated only by a secret PIN code. The bank does not know the true identity of the owner of the funds. If the funds are not used, they can be transferred anywhere in the world. You can raise or lower the amount in the account at any time. The offer makes it easy to supply a dependent, friend, relative anywhere in the world with a weekly, monthly or annual allowance.

You can give your ATM card to an employee you send abroad to cover his expenses. It is a plastic "smart" card where the person setting it up decides how much money to "back" the card with, and whether or not to replenish the funds.

If your creditor wants the money in the form of a check, gold bullion, shares of stock or bonds delivered at any bank anywhere in the world, he can arrange for the transfer without your knowing about the destination of the funds once you authorize the transfer of the bearer share corporation to his control.

Final Example: You are moving to (or already living in) a country full of grasping, corrupt public officials who can be relied upon to tax, confiscate seize and freeze everything in sight. There are also kidnappers, and others around who might cause you trouble if they knew you had access to large sums of cash. You want to be able to access a few hundred dollars in cash spending money every few days in a low profile way.

Once you get your anonymous "ATM card" and for the rest of your life you have access to cash anywhere in your home country or abroad quite anonymously.

You go up to an automatic teller machine, insert the card, press buttons asking for the screen to print out in your language and spew out the cash you want. You identify yourself only by PIN number. No signature or identity documents are ever required for cash withdrawals.

After paying the fees for setting your ATM card up, you can make the transfer of funds to a major international bank in a first class offshore banking center. If anything goes wrong or the application is refused, your set up fee will be refunded in full, immediately.

To get this truly anonymous ATM card all we require is any picture ID sent to U.S. along with the application form. This option is U.S. $500. You can expect your totally anonymous card to be processed in 14 working days and we can start to proceed with clear fax copies or by attached JPEG email (ID with application form) once your payment has been received.

Details: How An Offshore ATM Card Works

We supply you with an application for your ATM card. Only the name from your camouflage passport, or other ID need appears on the card. Your signature is never required for ATM cash withdrawals. The bank does not know your true name or identity. You can use a ready made ID for instant access.

Alternatively you may choose any name (not already in use at that bank) for you by purchasing an Int'l DL or camouflage passport direct from U.S. Just email and ask for details. The cost for the anonymous ATM card is just $500 and is less than others charge just for setting up a corporation or inferior asset protection plan.

Privacy yes, Crime No! Important Note: This ATM card may not be used for laundering money or to further any activity defined as criminal at the site of the bank account. If in doubt, ask us!

You may use a "pen name" in dealing with U.S. It would be a bad idea, but, you can if you wish, make deposits to your card direct and in person at any of the branches of any international bank. You could even arrange to make check or wire transfer withdrawals in person, but this would compromise your anonymity. Details will be supplied upon establishing an account.

Withdrawal limits: In most countries, there is a limit of approximately $500 per card use. But, there is no daily limit, and no limit on how many times you can use the card to withdraw cash. Some countries and some ATM machines may have different rules. Generally speaking, you can empty out your account at any time. We suggest a minimum opening balance of $1,000 but is not required to avoid charges, and we recommend that except for emergencies, the balance be kept at more than the absolute minimum.

Do you want an anonymous ATM card? You pay us, Third World Trading Corporation, at the address below, $500 for providing you with full details, and an application. We will e-mail or fax you the application. You simply fill out the application and return to our fax or email address. We are not a party to your transactions, monetary or otherwise. After the introduction is made, you are all set and ready to go in 14 days or less.

In about 3 weeks, you will receive your ATM card. If the anonymous feature of the ATM card is of no use to you, we suggest you let us know. We can make cheaper setup arrangements for a simple offshore account to a named and identified individual who merely wants a regular Visa, MasterCard or other credit card or directly to the account of your corporation that we can easily set up for you as well. With your card you receive detailed instructions on this subject.

Annual Charges: Just as with most credit cards, and corporations, there are annual charges more fully explained in the "Introduction" letter. You will be able to withdraw cash anonymously, up to certain limits, out of a wall anywhere in the world where the ATM system is operative. Presently there are tens of thousands of locations accessible all over the world, with new ones opening every day. You can immediately withdraw up to $3,000. Only $100 is required (after opening) to maintain your ATM Account in good standing. You just put the card in any Automatic Teller Machine at any bank & enter your pin number to take out cash. Each time you use the ATM you will incur bank charges around U.S. $5 per transaction.

But, we have found you come out far ahead because charges and exchange rate spreads are much greater on cashing traveler's checks or changing cash into local currency. In a few countries you will be able to use your "Anonymous ATM card" as a charge card. Only a person who has the ATM CARD and who knows the PIN code can make withdrawals.

The ATM card is linked to the U.S. Dollar and rises and falls at it does.

"The best anonymous privacy tool yet at thousands of dollars cheaper than inferior other products, " says, Dr. Seymour Samson.

While there can be direct access to the bank by fax, mail instructions, phone or otherwise, we strongly recommend that (for anonymity) all such activity is transacted in private. i.e., pgp email or by phone calls from a public telephone booth with a special code word the customer set's up directly with the bank.

Tax Status: You must get a local opinion in your home country as we are not tax lawyers. However, in most countries, the arrangement described here is a tax neutral, non-reportable event much like keeping cash savings in your mattress. As the "ATM card is not "owned " by you, it is not reportable in countries that require an annual balance sheet to be filed.

As it pays no interest, it is not reportable in those countries requiring an annual disclosure of offshore income. You are responsible for complying with your own local rules and regulations.

To Re-capitulate:

- Use ANY picture ID to open
- No ID required to access funds in cash
- No Signature required to access your funds in cash
- Only U.S. $100 to maintain account in good standing without bank charges
- 24 Hour Instant access worldwide to your CASH funds
- Your name unknown to bank, not linked to card
- Deposit & Withdrawals in Anonymity
- Double Protection of Bank Secrecy plus true anonymity
- Chose your own name or use your existing picture ID
- Set your own cash balance after opening deposit of $1,000
- Totally Anonymous & Transferable
- Protected by bank secrecy laws
- No reporting requirements that we know of
- Wire transfers or checks into and out of ATM account
- Card can be replaced if lost or stolen
- Carry in your wallet like an ordinary card

Originally supplied to several clients for $1,500.

Personally used and recommended by Dr. Seymour Samson and Dr. Julian Potts. Total Set-up Cost: $500. Comes with complete instructions and all particulars. To open remit funds for U.S.D $500 which includes the setups fee's and our introduction fee. [Ask us about your preferred method of transferring funds. E-mail privacy@privacyworld.com

Third World Trading Corp.
Attn: Privacy World
PO Box 87-3892
Panama, Republic of Panama

Offshore Scams

You Can't Know Too Much About Scams!

By Arnold L. Cornez, JD The Global Group Limited
arnie@bahamas.net.bs, www.global.bs used with permission.

Email and the Internet have opened new flood gates for scam artists, hucksters and checkered people. As a Contributing Editor of *OFFSHORE*, an e-Journal (a monthly, on the Net, for info, email to rpi@sky.net). I have seen the rebirth of most scams bedecked in new covers – pyramid schemes, Ponzi schemes, chain letters and just plain vanilla consumer rip-offs.

Before we get started you should know that almost weekly, I am asked for my opinion on so and so's book and theories, such and such an investment program, this or that person or company, etc. But, I'm afraid to answer these questions in open forum, lawsuits for defamation (liable or slander) in this overly-litigious U.S. society terrify me. So, I candidly tell my readers just that. I do, however, answer such inquiries for clients, but then only on a very confidential, for your eyes only

The purpose of this article, then, is not to name names as if we were the "Offshore Consumer Report", but rather to give readers a basic understanding of what I consider some of the most common Offshore scams. Here is my basic list:

Here is a list of avenues which are considered dangerous for you to pursue:

- Advance Fee Scams
- Bank Debenture Trading Scams
- Common Law Business Organizations
- Constitutional Trusts
- Contractual Business Organization
- Defective Trusts
- Dominion of Melchizedek
- Employee leasing company programs structured offshore
- Income deferment

- Income reductions through so called personal employment contracts
- Kingdom of Enen Kio
- Latvian banks
- The "New Utopia" tax haven investment
- The Nigerian Fraud
- Offers to create a new credit profile
- The Omega Program
- Passport Swindles
- Personally Owned Offshore Banks in Obscure Tax Havens
- Prime Bank Guarantees
- Principality of New Utopia
- Profit diversion schemes
- Pure Trusts
- Self-liquidating loans
- Strategies that rest upon resignation by a U.S. person after problems arise
- Tax Protest Schemes
- Unrealistic returns on investments

Some that I find particularly offensive are:

Buy A Private Offshore Bank Scam

In my view, spending $25 – $70 thousand on an offshore private bank is foolhardy for MOST people. For all but the astute and educated financier, they seldom make a useful business vehicle.

The promoters of offshore bank schemes claim they offer two primary advantages: the first is privacy, and the second is the ability of the offshore bank to accumulate (undistributed) profits without those profits being subject to U.S. tax via its U.S. shareholders (an exception to the traditional for profit corporation which is still taxed on accumulated but undistributed earnings).

Many buyers have been convinced by promoters that they need a private bank for marshaling assets for various ventures or pooling funds for investing. But, quite frankly that is hogwash. There are better and much less expensive vehicles for doing the same thing.

In most cases the sale of private banks to ordinary offshore investors is a consumer rip-off. Some hucksters are buying so called "banking licenses" in obscure and untested jurisdictions in bulk for around $2,500 each and then selling them to unsuspecting offshore newbies for upwards of $70,000. Many of the South Pacific tax havens – .a major source of private banking "licenses" – are close to being insolvent. A fact that few promoters discuss with their clients. These jurisdictions stay "afloat" only because of generous financial support from other nations such as New Zealand and Australia. When they eventually do go bankrupt, where will that leave Mr. and Mrs. Offshore newbie and their private South Pacific tax haven bank?

Another problem with these licenses is that they may not be assignable or transferable without the consent of the tax haven – a minor fact often overlooked and not disclosed by the promoters who sell to unsuspecting customers. In many situations the promoter sells it and says "Good Bye!" to the customer leaving the buyers to fend for themselves.

Operating an offshore bank so as to qualify for the special status offered under both Canadian and U.S. tax laws means actually operating a banking institution, this is not a learn as you go endeavor. If someone wants to sell you an offshore bank ask him this: who will run it?

The Cookie Cutter Trusts Scam:

In contrast to the claims of various multilevel marketing (MLM) schemes that mass market "off-the-shelf" or "boiler plate" offshore trusts, there is no such thing as a good "one-size-fits-all" trust agreement. Yes they appear to be inexpensive, but, in my opinion they amount to nothing more than scratch paper.

An offshore trust (APT) must be customized for you and your family. The IRS and Revenue Canada have imposed so many reporting requirements on the APT that to be tax compliant, you could spend hours just preparing the necessary forms. With these disclosure forms there is no longer any privacy with the APT. It is only good for asset protection.

And, contrary to what you may hear at that MLM "business briefing" or on that telephone "conference call" with the "Betty Crocker" of cookie cutter trusts herself, used alone, a trust does not provide any avenue for legal tax avoidance.

While we are on the topic of trusts, avoid the "grass roots" activists. You will know these folks by the terms they throw around, such as: pure trust, constitutional trust, sovereign citizenship, etc. Even if they have a constitutional leg to stand on, all that getting involved with them will get you is a file at the IRS or Revenue Canada labeled " Tax Protester; audit often."

Fast Wealth For Little Investment Scam:

"Unbelievable Rates of Return" usually aren't believable. You know the old saw, if it sounds too-good-to-be-true, then it probably is. Don't let down your normal, protective safe-guards for the allure and romance of offshore investing. There is nothing magic about going offshore. High returns come with high risks. Claims of impossible returns mean the likely loss of your investment.

Avoid anything to do with prime bank notes or guarantees, the "world's top 100 banks ", the roll program. etc. These all have the get-rich-quick allure, but, they are usually "Catch 22" programs designed to rip you off. Yes there may be Prime Bank Notes but if there are, they are for the $100 million dollar crowd. That lets me out – how about you?

The Nigeria Scam:

(Ed. note: for God's sake don't have anything to do with Nigeria; don't even accept paid phone calls from that particular Hole-In-The -Wall Gang hang out.)

Nigeria is one of the least respected business communities worldwide. Don't do any business with Nigeria. Don't even answer that first fax to share in "secret" misplaced governmental money. The scam has been around longer than Rip van Winkle and continues to lure the suckers who are driven by greed to letting down their safeguards.

Okay, the next section is written and used by permission by one Arnold L. Cornez, JD, an international financial consultant and principal associate of the Nassau based The Global Group Limited. His critically acclaimed book The Offshore Money Book is available from www.bahamas.net and you may contact Mr. Cornez at his Menlo Park, California office or mail at **offshore@offshore-net.com**.

I have his book, I highly recommend it as the best of next i.e. Mr. C concentrates on one particular area and updates many other long standing authors such as Dr. Hill.

If you are serious about moving money buy this book and read it, and read it, and read it...

You may want to consultant his firm for specifics.

What To Do If You've Been Scammed

If you've been conned by a scamster, you can file complaints with the following, all of whom offer free information and assistance:

Your state attorney general; you'll find the address and telephone number in your phone book.

The Federal Trade Commission, Telemarketing Fraud, Room 200, 6th St. and Pennsylvania Ave. NW, Washington, D.C. 20580. For a booklet that lists your Rights, call the FTC at 202-326-2222.

The National Fraud Information Center, a private nonprofit organization, has a form you can fill out and submit online for telemarketing and Internet consumer problems.

Check out **Call for Action**, a Washington, D.C.-based network of consumer hotlines: 301-537-8260. Call for Action has consumer counselors who can help route your complaint through the proper channels.

Scott's List

From my own research I can tell you there are a number of reputable offshore banks that will (or do so at the time of this writing) consider anyone for an offshore account.

Some will provide checking, some credit cards, some ATM. It's up to you to find what is best for your particular situation.

Some will demand a U.S. Bank reference along with a photo ID; some will not bother with this. Others will accept any "valid" ID...

Personally I feel this last problem is not a problem unless you are stashing millions of ill-gotten gains.

A few may require a personal visit with ID, some will perform certain services without the necessity of a meet.

These banks have been in business for some time and have a reputation for honesty. Do remember the laws and the various governments are subject to change.

The Bahamas is a nice place to start – 700 Islands littered about 7,000 miles of free sea. Only 20 or so islands are inhabited, and they are but a short flight from Miami.

They speak the Queen's English, are great places to visit and have a solid reputation as a tax haven.

The Bahamas is a Commonwealth and is independent.

The main island is called New Province and is where more that half of the population resides. It is also the main tourist attraction offering many night clubs, casinos, restaurants and duty free shopping.

First National Bank of Boston
Box N 3930. Corner Charlottt and Shirly STs. Nassau. Bahamas
Fax 242 328 2750.
Telex 20 272. Telex 20189.

Glacia Trading Ltd.
Box N 3029.
Fax 242 323 7918.

Gonet Bank and Trust Ltd.
Box N 4837.
Fax 242 323 7986.

Hong Kong and Shanghai Banking Corp Ltd.
Box N 4917.
Fax 242 5622.
Telex 242 5622.
Telex 20289.

Seattle First National Bank.
Box N 9100, Nassau., Bahamas.
Telex 20 158

Suisse Security Bank and Trust
Box N 4801., Nassau., Bahamas
Fax 242 356 4281.

Sumitomo Bank of California
Box N 9100., Nassau., Bahamas
Tel 242 393 7411.

Barclays Bank
Bay St. Tel 242 256 8000 Harbour Bay
Palmdale Tel 242 322 1231 Thompson Blvd

Barclays Bank
Governors Harbor
Facilities as follows. Checking Accounts, Savings Accounts, Personal Loans, Business Loans, Overdraft Facilities, Call Deposits, Foreign Currency Accounts and International Payment Service.

Other good options are the Turks and Caicos Islands:

Bank of Nova Scotia
Town Centre Mall., Box 15., Providencials., Turks and Caicos Islands
Fax 809 94 64755.

First National Bank Ltd.
Box 58., Providencials.

Fax 809 94 64061.

Turks and Caicos Banking Co.
Box 123 Grand Turk., Turks and Caicos Islands
Fax 809 94 62365.

Next come the companies that specialize in setting up offshore accounts for a fee inlcude:

International Company Services T.C.I. Ltd.
Box 107 Oceanic Hose Ducke St., Grand Turk and Caicos Islands
Fax 809 94 62504.

Grand Turk Int Trust Ltd.
Hibiscus Sq Pond St., Box 156 Grand Turk
Fax 809 94 62774.

Logerg Corporate Services.
Chancery Court Leeward Hwy. Box 209, Providencials., Turks and Caicos Islands
Fax 809 94 64410.

Morris Cottingham
Hibiscus Sq. Box 156. Providencials, Turks and Caicos Islands
809 94 62503.

Private Capital Management
Caribbean Place Leeward Hwy., Box 99 Providencials, Turks and Caicos Islands
Fax 809 94 13301.

Sabre Management Ltd.
Company Apts Bristol House, The Centre, Box 171, Providencials,
Turks and Caicos Islands
Fax 809 94 64850.

Star Corp Management Ltd.
HisbiscU.S. Sq. Pond St. Grand Turk, Turks and Caicos Islands

Logberge Corp Services Ltd.
Chancery Court Leeward Hwy., Providencials., Turks and Caicos Islands
Fax 809 94 4261.

Comerila Bank Cayman Branch
Box 513GT, British American Tower.
Roys Drive, George Town, Grand Cayman
Tel 345 945 4398

Comstock Int Bank Ltd.
Box 170 G.T., 4th Floor
Genesis Bldg. Grand Cayman

Fax 345 949 3451.

Deutche Morgan Greenfell Cayman Ltd.
Elizabethan Sq. Box 1984 G.T. Grand Cayman
Fax 345 949 8178.

Givens Hall Bank and Trust
Box 2097 GT, Genesis Bldg., Grand Cayman

I.B.J. Schroder Bank and Trust Co.
2nd Floor Harbour Centre, George Town
Fax 345 945 1295

Itau Bank Ltd.
Box 1379 G.T., Grand Cayman
Fax 345 975 4185

Lloyds Bank Int Cayman Ltd.
C.I.B.C. Finance Centre, Jennet St.
Box 857 G.T., Grand Cayman
Fax 345 949 0090

Morval Bank and Trust Cayman Ltd.
3rd Floor, Piccadilly Centre, Elgin Ave., George Town, Grand Cayman
Fax 345 949 9793

N.B.C. Cayman Ltd.
Calidonian House, Mary St., George Town
Box 31120SMB, Grand Cayman
Fax 345 949 4600

Royal Bank of Canada
Queens Court, West Bay Rd., Grand Cayman
Fax 345 949 9733
Telex C.P. 4244

Deutch Sudamerikanisch Bank
Anderson Sq. Bldg., Box 714 G.T., Grand Cayman
Fax 345 949 8899

Shepers Bank Ltd.
Jennett St., Box 513G, Grand Cayman
Tel 345 949 2158

Sul American Int. Bank
Box 31093 S.M.B., Grand Cayman
Fax 345 949 0866

Swiss Bank and Trust Corp.
Box 852 G.T., Grand Cayman
Fax 345 949 7308

Transocean Bank and Trust
Box 1959 G.T., Grand Cayman
Fax 345 949 7524

U.B.S. Int Trustees Ltd.
Box 2325 G.T., Grand Cayman
Fax 345 979 6907

United Mizrahi Bank Ltd.
C/O Box 1109GT, Grand Cayman
Fax 345 949 9639

Axxess Int.
Box C.B. 13663, Nassau, Bahamas
Fax 242 356 9559

Reportedly the above bank will furnish a Gold MasterCharge with a reasonable (under $10,000) secured deposit and doesn't demand too many references.

Bahia Bank Ltd.
Box N 7507, Nassau, Bahamas
Fax 242 356 6015

Bank of America Illinois
Box N 8334, Nassau, Bahamas
Tel 242 393 7411

Bank of Hawaii
Box N 4843, Bolam Hse, Nassau, Bahamas
Fax 242 322 8719

Citibank
Branches at;
Thompson Boulevard Fredrick St.
Family Islands
Toll Free 1-809 300 Citi

Citibank is a very well known offshore purveyor and offers a wide variety of services including Visa and MasterCard, ATM, checking and so on.

Euro Canadian Bank and Trust Co. Ltd.
Box N 3742
Fax 242 328 8994
Tel 242 328 8996

Fidelity Bank and Trust Int.
Box C.B. 12337., Frederic St., Nassau., Bahamas.
Fax 242 326 3000

You, Offshore and the Internet: A Source Guide

This is a list of resources on the internet for those who wish to utilize offshore banking, 2nd passports, or just keep abreast of current developments. Much is taken from Mr. Arnold Cornez, (used with his and the publisher's permission) as I have mentioned before BUY THIS BOOK, talk to the man, he's good.

It is now possible to roll out of your bunk bed at noon on your yacht *The Tax Haven* (formerly, *The Hedonist*), Panama registry, somewhere in the Caribbean, log on to a remote computer site in Abu Dhabi, Belize or Hong Kong and conduct your international business without leaving a scrap of physical evidence about the transaction. being a highly secured level of encryption (for example, PGP), readily available worldwide, your communications would be completely private. Using financial systems such as OAR, Digi-Cash, Cybercash, digital cash or money can also be moved privately, without any physical records linking the transaction back to you. And now the "smart" OS ATM cards are or will be available for moving cash external of the U.S. banking system.

Offshore Sites On The Internet

Privacy Publications And Web Sites

1. Full Disclosure Live. Privacy, surveillance and technology publishers. Glen L. Roberts, Publisher. Host for radio show on topics available on short-wave. See Web site for further details: http://pages.ripco.com:8080/~glr/glr.html

2. Electronic Privacy Information Center Home Page: http://www.epic.org/

3. Bacard's Privacy Page: http://www.well.com/U.S.er/abacard/

4. Cypherpunks 15th Archive by thread:
   http://www.hks.net/cpunks/cpunks-13/index.html#382

5. Scope International:
   http://www.britnet.co.uk/Scope/

6. The Offshore Entrepreneur:
   http://www.au.com/offshore

7. Asset Protection & Becoming Judgment Proof:
   http://www.catalog.com/corner/taxhaven

General Offshore Materials

1. The Global Group:
   http://www.dnai.com/offshore/offshore.html

2. Scope International:
   http://www.britnet.co.uk/Scope/

3. The Offshore Entrepreneur:
   http://www/au.com/offshore

4. Offshore Tax Haven, Trust and Banking Reference Page:
   http://www.cadvision.com/nolimits/offshore.html

5. Antigua, the Perfect Tax Haven:
   http://www.eub.com/eub2.htm

6. The Freebooter Newsletter:
   http://www.aztec.co.za/exinet/fb/index/htm

7. Why Costa Rica?
   http:/www.shore.net/~icorporate/netman/parad_2.htm

8. Burke's Offshore Tax Haven:
   http://www.inforamp.net:80/~nuyen/index.html

9. Aruba Travel Information:
   http://www.interknowledge.com/aruba/
   e-mail: atanj@ix.netcom.com

10. Currency and Currency-Exchange Rates:
    http://www.wiso.gwdg.de/ifbg/currency.html

11. Taxbomber's Home Page:
    http://www.geopages.com/WallStreet/2087/

13. A Guide to Living Abroad:
    http://www.livingabroad.com

14. Offshore Tax Help:
    http://www.rpifs.com/ostax

15. Koblas Currency Converter:
    http://www.ora.com/cgi-bin/ora/currency

16. Bloomberg Exchange Rates:
    http://www.bloomberg.com

17. Islands on the Net:
    http://www.law.vill.edu~mquarles/caribbean.html

Tax Information

1. TAXFAX World Wide Web site:
   http://www.pix.za/taxfax/ghaven-in.html

2. U.S. Tax Code Online:
   http://www.fourmilab.ch/U.S.tax/U.S.tax.html
   The complete Internal Revenue Code, 2.8 million words, 21 megabytes of data. Cross-references for the user throughout the tax code.

3. Tax Sites:
   http://www.best.com/~ftmexpat/html/taxsites.html
   Provides links to tax related sites, including U.S. federal and state tax forms, tax software, U.S. tax law and archives for newsgroups.

4. Villanova Tax Law Compendium:
   http://www.law.vill.edu/vill.tax.1.compen/

5. International Tax Resources:
   http://omer.cba.neu.edu/othersites/international.html

6. Irish Tax Site by the Institute of Chartered Accountants:
   http://www.icai.ie/

7. Internal Revenue Service:
   http://www.irs.U.S.treasury.gov
   Hint: Select shortcut to IRS tax forms to go directly to the IRS and instructions.

8. The IRS Tax Forms:
   http://www.U.S.treas.gov/treasury/bureaus/irs/taxforms.html

9. State Tax Forms:
   http://inept.scubed.com:8001/tax/state/state_index.html

10. Adobe Acrobat Reader (for reading IRS forms):
http://www.ustreas.gov/treasury/bureaus/irs/acroread.html

11. AM & G-Accountants and Consultants:
http://www.amgnet.com

12. More Tax Forms & Tax Code Information:
http://www.scubed.com/tax/tax.html

13. Tax Bullets:
http://www.arentfox.com/newslett/taxbul.htm

14. Tax Discussion Groups:
http://205.177.50.2/groups.htm

15. Recent Tax Developments:
http://www.halcyon.com/lesourd/recent.html

16. Tax Notes NewsWire:
http://205.177.50.2/news.htm

17. KPMG Tax Online_AU.S.tralia:
http://www.kpmg.com.au/tax.html

18. U.S. Income Tax Law–GPO Access:
http://ssdc.ucsd.edu/gpo/

19. Italian Taxation System: A Primer for Foreigners:
http://www.icenet.it/cosver/html/primer_uk.html

20. Tax Planning for Business and Individuals:
http://www.hooked.net/U.S.ers/mshbcpa/plan/index.html

21. Professor Doernberg's Tax Law Web Site:
http://www.law.emory.edu/~lawrld/

22. Offshore Tax Help:
http://www.rpifs.com/ostax

23. Internet Income Tax Information:
http://www2.best.com/ftmexpa/html/taxsites.html

24. Tax Resources:
http://www.biz.uiowa.edu/acct/tax.html

25. Tax News Groups on UseNet:
misc.taxes
misc.taxes.moderated

26. Offshore and International Taxation Page:
    http://www.law.vill.edu/~mquarles/int_tax.htm/

Asset Protection

1. Asset Protection and Becoming Judgment Proof:
   http://www.catalog.com/corner/taxhaven

2. Financial $olution On-Line:
   http://www.rpifs/ap

Offshore Banking And Credit Cards

1. Banks and Tax Havens:
   http://www.hks.net/cpunks/cpunks-5/0935.html

2. European Union Bank:
   http://www.eub.com/eub7.htm

3. Offshore Accounts and Credit Cards:
   http://www.cashmoney.com

4. Prosper International League Ltd. (PILL).
   http://www.flinet.com/~islandsun/belize1.html
   e-mail: lp-global@ix.entrepreneurs.net

5. The World Bank:
   http://www.worldbank.org/

6. The Excelsior Bank, Bridgetown, Barbados:
   http://www.village.com/excelsior/

7. Mark Twain Bank, St. Louis, Missouri, U.S.A.:
   http://www.marktwain.com

8. Offshore Banking and Financial Privacy Frequently Asked Questions:
   http://apollo.co.uk/a/Offshore/Privacy/fpn-faw.html

9. Offshore Banking:
   http://www.wiso.gwdg.de/ifbg/bank_off.html

10. International Money Fund:
    Gopher://imfaix3s.imf.org/
    Provides offshore banking information and currency exchange rates.

11. Federal Reserve Board statistical files from NY University School of Business:
    ftp://town.hall.org/other/fed

12. Offshore Visa Card:
    e-mail to ucs@bahamas.net.bs

E-cash Companies

1. Cybercash, Inc.:
   http://www.cybercash.com

2. Digicash BV:
   http://www.digicash.com

3. First Virtual Holding, Inc.:
   http://www.fv.com

4. Mark Twain Bank, St. Louis, Missouri, U.S.A.:
   http://www.marktwain.com
   Creates digital e-cash, a form of currency.

5. Netscape Communications Corp.:
   http://www.netscape.com

6. Offshore eAssets Reconciliation Limited:
   http://www.dnai.com/offshore/offshore/offshore.html
   e-mail: ucs@bahamas.net.bs

Global Business, General

1. Financial Resource Guide:
   http://www.libertynet.org/~beaU.S.ang/
   Provides information on currencies, stocks, exchanges, etc.

2. Doing Business in Mexico:
   http://daisy.uwaterloo.ca/~alopez-o/bU.S.faq.html

3. Pacific Rim Job Opportunities:
   http://www.Internet-is.com/tko/index.html

4. Malaysian Business Pages:
   http://www.beta.com.my/biz

5. U.S. Council for International Business:
   http://www.U.S.cid.org/

6. Canadian Business InfoWorld:
   http://www.csclub.uwaterloo.ca/u/nckman/index.html

7. World Currency Converter:
   http://www.dna.lth.se/cgi-bin/rates

8. World Stock and Commodity Exchanges:
http://www.lpac.ac.uk/ifr/

9. Offshore Insurance, Re-insurance, Captive Insurance:
http://www.webcom.com/~wrsl/

10. International Trade Administration:
http://www.ita.doc.gov

11. Library Map Collection, Perry-Castaneda:
http://www.lib.utexas.edu/Libs/PCL/Map collection

12. Jersey and Guernsey, offshore.net, The Offshore Finance Industries of:
http://www.offshore.net/home.htm

13. The World Fact Book from the CIA:
http://www.odci.gov/cia/publications/95fact/index.html

14. Travel Advisories from the State Department:
ftp://ftp/stolaf.edu/pub/travel-advisories/advisories

15. International Air Mail Service from the U.S. Post Office:
http://www.usps.gov/

16. Connected Traveler:
http://www.well.com/user/wldtravlr/

17. Export Today Magazine:
http://www.exporttoday.com

18. National Trade Databank:
http://www.sta-usa/BEN/Services/ntdbhome.html

19. Global Risk Management Network:
http://www.emap.com/grmn/

20. Links to Numerous Foreign Embassies:
http://www.llr.com/

21. CubaWeb, a business clearinghouse of information:
http://www.cubaweb.com/

Media

1. *The Wall Street Journal*:
http://www.adnet.wsj.com/

2. *The Economist*:

http://www.economist.com

3. *Fortune*:
http://www/pathfinder.com/@@N7PyjHCh0QAAQHoY/fortune.html

4. *Time* Magazine:
http:/www.pathfinder.com/@@wNe9a9B20QAAQHwY/time/magazine/magazine.html

5. The Bermuda Sun:
http://www.bermudasun.org/
This site, updated every Friday, contains full versions of all print stories, including business, investment, and legal listings. The *Sun* is beginning to accept advertising on its site, including job postings and page sponsorship.

6. Reuters Newsmedia:
http://beta.yahoo.com/headlines/current/bU.S.iness/summary.html

7. The Daily Record and SundayMail, Glasgow, Scottland:
http://www.record-mail.co.uk/rm/

8. Barron's Online
http://www.barrons.com

The Secret Life of Automobile License Plates

License Plates/Car Tags

Another form of personal ID is represented by the license plate on your vehicle. Not only can law enforcement, and in many states, anybody run down your name, address, type of car, previous owners, dealer who first sold the vehicle, other, more obvious triggers also exists.

The following is a compilation from several sources, but I would suggest you purchase The Official License Plate Book from Gould Publications, Inc. for a complete look at this phenomenon. (www.gouldlaw.com/licensetoc.html).

Also Available on CD-ROM.

License plates often have hidden meanings that can be recognized by law enforcement, serious collectors and motor vehicle authorities. This explains how states and providence's code their plates so you, like the authorities, will be able to look at a plate and tell such things as:

- In what county a vehicle is registered
- Occupation of the owner
- Special plates and what they mean
- Age, weight and vehicle use restrictions
- How to recognize a rental vehicle
- State, City, Federal Government, Diplomatic codes
- Indian tribes
- First initial of the owners last name or birth month

How to "read" a license plate:

- Expiration code: the registration expires the last day of the month

This book goes into great detail about which state uses what code.

- County code (state of Wyoming) the first number indicates which county in the state the vehicle is registered in
- On Wyoming plates when number exceeds 9999 numbering goes back to one, two or three numeric with a 2 alpha suffix
- Code-1, The first numeric on a Connecticut state owned vehicle plate is a department code. 1 is reserved for the Motor Vehicle Dept
- Color Code for Connecticut : for passenger cars are dark blue characters on a blue and white (graphic) background
- The numeric on the plate identify this individual vehicle

1. Look at the color combinations. Each section explains how jurisdictions use color combinations to distinguish classes of vehicle.
2. If you see a caption (a word embossed or screen – printed on a plate) you do not understand, look under the Distinctive Caption section and it will be explained. For example, JITNEY in Rhode Island is a caption for a repossesor plate.
3. CODES – Look at the combination of alpha and numeric characters (letters and numbers) and check the code section to see if there are any hidden meanings.
4. COLOR – Different combinations are used for classes of vehicles.
5. CAPTIONS – Words are embossed or screen-printed to give special information.
6. CODES – Series of letters and numbers (alpha, numeric characters) used in the plate numbering systems that are reserved for special identification.

The material in this book has been gathered from Motor Vehicle administrations of all 50 states, District of Columbia, 12 Canadian providence's and territories as well as contributions from members of Automobile License Plate Collectors Association (ALPCA). It is organized to explain how every jurisdiction (state or providence) uses these three methods to help authorities "read" a license plate and instantly tell if it is a valid registration, what county it comes from, its weight class, and/or use restrictions, the driver's occupation, and any other special information that may be available about the owner and his vehicle.

Buy it.

The next two pages are samples from the above book. I can't recommend it too highly.

MARYLAND

MOTORCYCLE

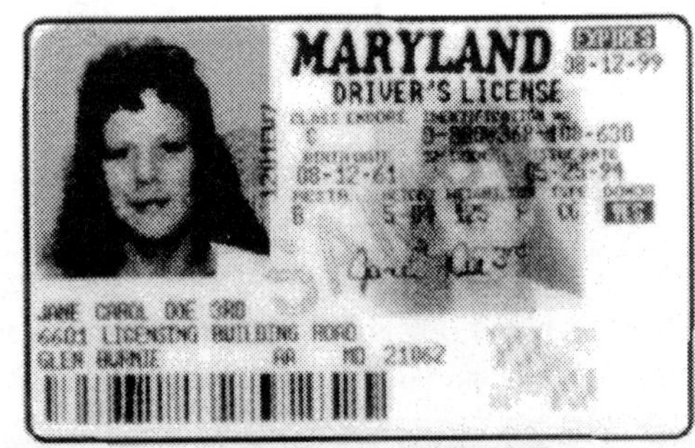

DRIVER'S LICENSE

POLICE PATCH

PASSENGER PLATES

PASSENGER BASE 2 PLATES 2 DECALS ON REAR

PERSONALIZED

HANDICAPPED

SAVE CHESAPEAKE BAY

STATE OWNED

LOCAL GOVT. OWNED

NATIONAL GUARD

FIREMEN'S ASSN.

DISABLED VETERAN

BALTIMORE BOWLING ASSN.

AMATEUR RADIO

DEALER

TRUCK and TRAILER PLATES

TRUCK OR TRAILER

APPORTIONED VEHICLE

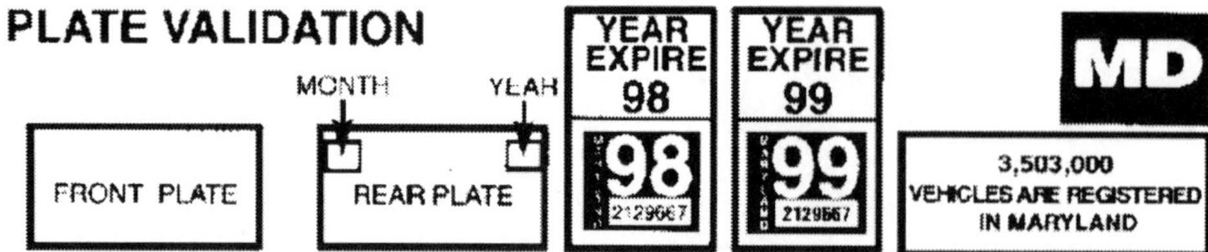

The "Old Line State" issues two fully-reflectorized license plates. Passenger and many other non-passenger types display the colorful state shield. A special plate to save the Chesapeake Bay is available for an additional $20 fee.

Distinctive captions:

FARM AREA - Vehicles permitted to operate on public road adjacent to a farm
FINANCE - Repossessed vehicle transporter plate
RECYCLER - Auto wreckers and scrap processors
TRANS - Transporter

Codes:

Maryland passenger cars are issued 3 alpha-3 numeric plates. The following alpha combinations are reserved for specific classes of vehicles:

Suffix **B** - Taxi, limousine
Suffix **C** - Ambulance, funeral vehicle
DV - Disabled veteran
D over **R** -Daily rental
Suffix **D** - Dump service
Suffix **F** - Truck tractors
F over **T** - Farm truck
H over **C** - Handicapped
I (capital i) - Buses for hire
Suffix **J** - Passenger vans (van pool)
L over **G** - Local government
Suffix **K** - Farm vehicle limited highway use
Suffix **L** - Historic Motor vehicle
Suffix **M** - Multi-purpose trucks, vans
Suffix **PSC** - Buses for hire
S over **G** - State government vehicle
TT - Tow truck

Maryland reserves the following prefixes for special groups: *** no caption appears at the bottom of these plates.**

AG Ali Ghan Shrine Temple
AL American Legion
BBO* Boumi Temple
BCF Balt.County firefighters
BJT Jerusalem Temple No 4
BNA* B'nai B'rith
BPD Balt. Pro Duckpin Assn.
BPW Md. Prof. bus. women
BSA Boy Scouts of America
BSQ Barbershop Quartet sing.
CAP Civil Air Patrol
CCC* Grace Bible Church
CDA Cath. Dau. of America
CGA Coast Guard Auxiliary
CGR Coast Guard Reserve
CMH Medal of Honor
DAV Disabled Amer.veteran
DCC St. Dem. Cntrl Comm.
DDS Dr. of Dental Surgery
EAA Exper. Aircraft Assn.
EEE Free State Square Club
ELK Elks Club
FOE Frat. Order of Eagles
FF MD. DC Firefighters
FPO Frat. Order of Police
FMA Prince Hall Gr.Lodge
FSU Frostburg U. alumni
GOP Republican Party
HC Hood College
HGA Hiram Grand Lodge
HIQ Mensa
HNA Holy Name Society
HPC Hawks Pleasure Club
JC Jaycees
JHU JohnsHopkins Alumni
JWV Jewish War Veterans
KAP Kappa Alpha Psi
KC Knights of Columbus
KOP Knights of Pythias
LHS Loyola H.S. alumni
LCO Lions Club International
M over**D** Maryland Democratic party
MP Maryland Press Club
MSA Maryland Soc. Account
MSP Md. St. Police Assn.
Suffix **NG** National Guard
ND Notre Dame Club
OPT Optimist Club
OSI Sons of Italy
PE Professional engineers
PSU Penn State Alumni
PSY Psychological Assn
PW Ex POW
QUE Omega Psi Phi Frat.
RI Rotary International
ROA Reserve Officers Assn.
RSC Ranger Social Club
RX Pharmacist Assn
SKI Baltimore Ski Club
SMC St Marys College alum.
TCL Tall Cedars
TJA Trial Judges Assn
TPA Telephone Pioneers
TSU Towson State Alumni
UAW Unit. Auto Workers 239
UM Univ. of Maryland Alum.
VFW Vet. of Foreign Wars
VPI Virginia Tech
WMC West Virginia Univ.
WVU West Va. Univ.
VB Vulcan Blazers
YG* Yedz Grotto

Maryland does not designate the county or weight of a vehicle on the plate.

Maryland Motor Vehicle Administration
6601 Ritchie Highway NE, Glen Burnie, MD 21062 Tel. 410-787-2983

License Tags – A Trick

License tags can also be a problem, there are few built-in security features in some state's formats.

Sometimes outrageous solutions will solve problems one didn't even visualize.

For instance: When I spent some time in Bolivia a cab driver I became quite close to offered to get a Bolivian license tag and registration for $200.

Okay, visualize this – first I should point out that one purchases the plates with eh car in Bolivia and there is NO RENEWAL date on the plate.

Basically it's good forever.

Now visualize the trauma of a parking maid, cop, highway patrolman, etc., attempting to find legal cause to tow or otherwise violate your car.

If you also happen to have a Bolivian drivers license and an IDP, it tends to be more of a hassle to hassle you than to "let you go with a warning."

Most ID's are only valid for a certain length of time, but months can be stretched into years with letters or stickers of extension.

Retrieving Public Records of Interest

If one has a need for a certain public record – anything from a marriage certificate to a person's DMV application, there are a number of ways of obtaining the information.

This list is in a vague order that stresses cost and then efficiency. The general rule is the more one is willing to pay, the less leg work involved.

But there are exceptions.

The first thing to realize is that location is the most important single factor in record retrieval. Where is the needed information stored?

Sometimes this information is very obvious; or can be solved with a single phone call. DMV info is usually at, where? The DMV.

A case in point is that, as of this writing, DMV records are not "publicly" available – but they are still available to "qualified" persons including private detectives. Many web-based sources will still obtain these records for a nominal fee.

Most states cannot provide instant record retrieval and there is usually a 1 day turn around time. DMV searches will let you check if a person has a license, their address, and phone number, as well as their criminal driving infractions.

California currently has a privacy law where a citizen can request that their home address be withheld from the records.

Marriage, court, criminal, bankruptcy, property and divorce, usually business licensee's can be found at the Hall Of Records, or whatever particular name the municipality in question may choose.

Some records are kept at a county record, some at state, a few at a national strata.

- Go to the Internet – as I've mentioned there are many free, or low priced sites that access 1,000+ local record depositories

- If the record is local, drive down to the city court or town hall and look it up yourself

- Call the agency in question and ask if they are on-line. Many court records are available directly from the court or through PACER, an on-line record agency

- Okay two big things here, maybe a bit out of order but stuff you should know; BRB Publications (www.brbpub.com) publishes a number of books on retrieving public records. One is entitled Public Record Providers

This book lists hundreds of people across the U.S. who will, for a small fee drive down to the local repository, single out your selection, copy it and forward on to you.

Next big secret is a book (and now also a disc) called The Guide To Background Investigations. This wonderful publication (T.I.S.I. 4110 S. 100TH East Ave., Tulsa, OK 74146) that is designed strictly to provide the means to obtain "background" screening records including most of the records we have discussed.

The book (almost 2,000 pages) is divided into four main sub-directories:

- State Records Directory
- The Locator Directory
- The Federal Records Directory
- The Educational Directory

The Guide is designed to eliminate many of the roadblocks to using public records.

The Guide is more than just a phone book, besides its many thousand entries users will be show exactly how to contact the correct office, find the necessary procedures, what fees are required and how to correctly access the data.

From UCC liens to college credits, from criminal conviction data to Canadian driving records, this book/disc shows exactly what is on file and how to obtain it.

Another mention should be given for Don Ray's (a great investigative reporter) books on locating public records. www.donray/donray.com.

- Information brokers. To make a long story short there are several types of info providers, each type dependent upon the records necessary. Straight and legit firms use information stored in databases

Not, quite so straight and not quite so legit firms will pretext for the required information.

- If you are going to use an on-line service that is not PACER or about to go through a pay-for-information source you might want to know how the procedures actually work

There are 3 general types of companies that provide information:

(1) SuperDatabases – A SuperDatabase is humongous company that keeps billions of records, but in 1 single specific area. TRW is an example of the aforementioned.

They are the largest collector/supplier of Credit Information in the entire world. There are 3 main companies that supply Credit information (as well as hundreds of minor league suppliers).

(2) Supermarkets – A supermarket is very much as the name implies, are big places, where you can get a variety of information. Supermarket companies usually have access to several SuperDatabases. This allows you to do a very wide variety of searches without having to pay the outrageous rates that the SuperDatabase companies usually charge. Most private investigators are hooked up with Supermarkets like Datafax.

Supermarkets, keep in mind, are NOT actual databases. Rather Supermarkets are just "gateways" to the SuperDatabase companies.

(3) 7-11's – 7-11's are basically similar to Supermarkets. You can look up a variety of BASIC information such as credit records, criminal histories, etc., for a very reasonable price. You don't have nearly as good a selection as to the kinds of information that you get with a supermarket, but the prices make it reasonable for a private individual to have an account with a 7-11 type system. In fact, a lot of 7-11 type systems, will let you do a "single-one-time-search." As opposed to the databases which bind you to a year long contract costing **$$$**.

- Newspapers may be searched at the local library (usually for many, many years of information by going to the local library and walking throughout the microfiche. Again, public record providers will do this for you in other areas

First, if one has access one can try Dialog, the world's largest public database or Nexis Lexis. BUT these records will only go back a set time, usually a few months to a few years, but some of the larger publications may hold 20+ years of information.

Besides, Dialog is REALLY expensive – especially if you don't know how to use it; one mistake and you're begging the pawn shop owner to take the house and the kids.

Wife's already gone.

You can get an expert to do this for you, which is still not cheap, but *cheaper* and much more efficient.

I suggest Lee Lapin's books How To Get Anything on Anybody series and especially The Whole Spy Catalog (www.intelligencehere.com) for the best resources.

PRIVICY 101

Think it's an exaggeration to think someone's always watching you? Here's a quick list of what's going on in your environment with regard to personal viewing.

Viewing of your person that is (please note I'm not including any electronic surveillance, police, or investigative agency or other "organized" efforts) easier than one might think...

Although the laws keep changing colors faster than a chameleon regarding the sale/sharing of information (no longer sell driver's license photo's, until court rules, no longer sell most DMV ID info without consent, although law subject to change, can still get credit header info, although law...).

With in-place technology available personal information daily statistics can now be correlated, including, but not limited to:

7:30 - a.m. - You exit the apartment parking lot where cameras, a card and perhaps a security guard record your movement.

7:45 - Pull onto a toll road, or bridge, where cameras, as well as a remote toll charging device takes down the time and auto tag – same happens when exiting the toll road.

7:48 - Automatic police radar Ka Band radar camera capture's personal and car photo speeding down freeway in order to make up time lost dealing with toll booth.

Ticket issued by mail to your address. Ticket is public record in many states.

7:49 - Caught in traffic jam. Local traffic camera records event, put it on-line in several cities.

8:01 - Use your cell phone to call the office to explain the delay. All information, including the exact GPS position, of your vehicle is recorded at the cell site.

8:32 - Arrive at the office parking lot where guard/card reader notes entry time. May have cameras to verify.

8 41 - Your card, or machine readable badge verifies one's arrival, as well as showing what other doors one may have passed through on the way to the office.

8:52 - Log on to your computer using fingerprint verification. The sysop records the time you log in.

9; 01 - Contact two colleges, leave an email for you boss and forward a joke to a friend. All times recorded. Sysop can read all messages legally and easily. Even worse, possibility someone has installed a "key stroke surveillance system" on your computer recording and passing on everything you enter.

9:33 - Phone call to your wife. Call legally monitored by the employer.

9:48 - Go to rest room, discuss asshole boss with co-worker at next urinal. Conversation legally recorded by employer.

10:15 – Use phone to order mistress flowers. Call recorded, credit card transaction entered, naming both parties, time, product addresses and expenses.

10:45 - Use a company car to visit a distributor. Check in/check out plus car may have automatic GPS recording system showing routes taken, speed and stops made.

12:01 p.m. - Utilize ATM for withdrawal. Time, transaction details, password and amounts recorded; machine automatically takes your photo and records it on CD-ROM.

12:10 - Purchase a gift for a friend. Store "club card " profiles the purchase for points and directed discounts. Sells information to a number of database and retail marketing agencies.

12:51 - See your physician due to small and personal health problem. All appointment information as well as any diagnosis will not only be disclosed to one's own insurance company, but forwarded to the central insurance database, filed by social security number and birth date.

Doctor legally obligated to disclose certain conditions to medical and/or law enforcement agencies.

1:10 - Pick up your prescription. Information (including address, drug, doctor and your phone number) will be cleared through one's insurance company, shared with various government agencies (especially for controlled drugs) and possibly with other pharmacies.

May also be disclosed to police agencies for purpose of tracking drug abuse.

1:32 - Return to work. All work related recordings apply.

1:47 - Call 800 phone number to confirm product shipment. You're number, and billing information immediately recorded and immediately available to recipient of call regardless of caller ID blocking.

1:58 - Check into several work related news servers and net groups. All connections recorded and available to general public via search engines such as Deja News.

2:02 - Check out three web sites. All images recorded in computers cache file for anyone to download. Note most word processors also create "temporary," or "work" files that may remain on both hard and floppy disc without notifying the user.

2:12 - Make (or receive) cellular phone call; date, time, both numbers as well as approximate geographical location available to legal agencies as well as from various information brokers.

2:22 - Receive pager message; once again all information available to/from above sources.

2:45 - Provide urine sample for employer's new drug testing program. Reveals use of targeted drugs, though not of impairment. If one has eaten bagel with poppy seeds may show up and be reported as opium related drug use.

3:30 - Meeting in a secure area. Pass through a security check, which scans your retina to confirm identity.

4:32 - Complete day's work on computer which has not only recorded your all file's contents, but possibly information about keyboard speed, error rate, and the lengths of pauses and absences.

5:15 - Leave the office. Act recorded by several computers, building entry system, security guard and parking lot.

6:30 - Buy groceries. Debit card records the purchase, while a loyalty card tracks selections for marketing and targeted discounts, trades this information with other databases.

6:48 - Pick up a video at Big Video. Store computer records your Social Security Number and viewing preferences. This allows the store to sell your viewing preferences to other companies for targeting mailings or more direct tracking procedures.

7:20 - Listen to phone messages; many machines, some voice mail easily hacked. Caller's phone numbers, recorded on your caller ID box (as will your be – unless blocked).

8:20 - Order product from online catalog. Company sends cookie or applet to your server tracking your preferences, sites vitiated, personal data and sells it to other interested parties. Supplier records your personal details and credit card number, sells the information to database marketers.

Ancillary note; when you send in warranty card from your purchase all details sold to several companies who will then sell all personal data you have filled into the little blanks to marketers, information brokers and private detectives.

8:30 - Subscribe to a new magazine. Magazines routinely sell their subscribers' lists to mass mailers as well as info brokers, credit agencies and PI's.

8:35 - Take call from a survey company. Such companies gather political views, social attitudes and personal views, though some surveys are actually marketing calls to collect personal data for future sales.

Could also be pretext call from ex'-wife's private detective, collection agency, etc.

8:45 - Political canvasser comes to your door. Political contributions of more than $100 (the amounts, and the party they're contributed to) are listed in public records.

9:32 - Your mother calls from a state which allows recording of phone conversations with no warning *even through your state doesn't*, records entire conversation about the sixties and what drugs you are doing now.

Mom has rolled over in order to work off a distribution bust. She now is working for the DEA.

Have a good day.

Don Ray's 104 Privacy Tips

Don Ray is one of the best investigative reporters/writers around. The following is a very accurate list of how best to stay private used with the author's permission.

1. Don't sue anyone.
2. Remote voice mail.
3. Consider not voting.
4. Don't enter contests.
5. Get married overseas.
6. Private post office box.
7. Postal Service P.O. box.
8. Don't get a radio license.
9. Don't get parking tickets.
10. Don't file for bankruptcy.
11. Get a confidential marriage.
12. Get on "No junk mail" lists.
13. Don't return warranty cards.
14. Don't have a messy divorce.

15. No more personalized plates.
16. Don't run for political office.
17. Non-published phone number.
18. Don't write letters to the editor.
19. Don't end up in U.S. Tax Court.
20. Use a door slot or locking mail box.
21. Don't forget to return library books.
22. Sign up now for Caller ID Blocking.
23. Check your credit report once a year.
24. Don't use "preferred customer" cards.
25. Go to traffic school if you get a ticket.
26. Get on "No soliciting phone calls" list.
27. Don't go to court to change your name.
28. No phone number on voter registration.
29. Don't complete customer survey forms.
30. Don't contribute to political campaigns.
31. Have parents' assets put in living trusts.
32. Don't get a concealed weapon's permit.
33. At college, have your address restricted.
34. Don't broadcast your CB radio call sign.
35. Don't fill out a forwarding address form.
36. Tear up the carbons on your charge records.
37. Don't own an airplane or boat in your name.
38. Use an out of state corporate filing company.
39. Don't get behind on your mortgage payment.

40. Have assessor's tax bill sent to someone else.
41. Don't dial 800 numbers from a secure phone.
42. Don't use your ATM card to purchase anything.
43. Don't pay someone to be in a Who's Who book.
44. Don't get into disputes with landlords or tenants.
45. Have pet licenses registered in your kids' names.
46. Don't do something so stupid that you'd get sued.
47. Don't show up the day they shoot school pictures.
48. Remember that building permits are public record.
49. Don't register your pattern at the department store.
50. Don't put identifying symbols/stickers on your car.
51. Put out your trash in front of someone else's house.
52. Request to be omitted from reverse/city directories.
53. Don't drop business cards in the "Free Lunch" bowl.
54. Have documents notarized in another state or county.
55. Use P.O. box for driver's license and car registration.
56. Give all your things away to your kids before you die.
57. Be creative with your occupation on voter registration.
58. Don't put "Student of the Month" stickers on your car.
59. Don't hire young baby sitters who live near your house.
60. Print post office street address on checks w/box number.
61. Don't put your Ham radio call sign on your license plates.
62. Consider not printing an obituary on deceased loved ones.
63. The most private form of business is a limited partnership.
64. Have a password put on your phone/utility/credit accounts.

65. Don't use personal property as collateral to borrow money.

66. Instruct magazines/organizations to not share your address.

67. Don't incorporate in California (or your state of residence).

68. Obliterate your name that's been written on your gas meter.

69. Don't have garage sales at your house if a permit is required.

70. Don't give out credit card numbers over the phone or modem.

71. Don't apply for citizenship in the area where you want to live.

72. Use money orders and your P.O. box when you use mail order.

73. Don't say anything on a cellular/cordless phone that's sensitive.

74. Don't say your phone credit card aloud when others are around.

75. Don't ignore the calls of bill collectors or government agencies.

76. Instruct family members on limiting information they volunteer.

77. Don't place classified ads displaying your secure phone numbe.

78. If you kill yourself, address your suicide note to someone specific.

79. Don't sign guest registers at museums, national parks, caverns, etc.

80. Don't give out your Social Security number without protesting first.

81. Settle or win all lawsuits quickly to eliminate outstanding judgments.

82. Remember how easy it is for people to listen in on baby monitor radios.

83. Imagine everything you type as e-mail being put on highway billboards.

84. Put your real estate into a family trust – but one not named after your family.

85. Don't get behind on alimony/child support payments and then leave the state.

86. If you must give the bank your mother's maiden name, give some other name.

87. Don't file fictitious name statements – use your real name (Don Ray Plumbing).

88. Read every contract or application and look for waivers of your right to privacy.

89.Use just your zip code and P.O. Box number for return address (Box 91503-4375).

90. Don't announce your phone number on your outgoing answering machine message.

91. Don't rent videos from stores that require personal information – use cash deposits.

92. Don't put your name on the outside of your apartment mail box – put it on the inside.

93. Use short version of your name when you can (Bill Jenkins – not Wm. J. Jenkins, Jr.).

94. Use a notary public who personally knows you and doesn't need your driver's license.

95. Don't let sales clerks write down your drivers license number on credit card purchases.

96. Get a copy of everything Privacy Rights Clearinghouse puts out (on the internet).

97. Don't write checks at Radio Shack or other stores that computerize your address and phone number.

98. Don't permanently stick company, school or apartment complex parking stickers on you car.

99. If you plan on moving into another house you're buying, have a straw party buy and hold it for you.

100. Don't be a best man or maiden of honor. If you do, scribble your address on the marriage certificate.

101. Don't bank where they allow phone-in computer access using Social Security numbers as passwords.

102. Make sure you have a current copy of Don Ray's A Public Records Primer and Investigator's Handbook.

103. Have your main phone line installed in a nearby friend's home and use call forwarding to your secret number.

104. Get a copy of Don Ray's Checking Out Lawyers to learn more about public records.

Suggested Reading

Anything from Paladin Press on Privacy or Identification.
Paladin Press
POB 1307
Boulder, CO 80306
www.paladin-press.com
email service@paladin-press.com
fax 303-442-8741

Loompanics Unlimited
POB 1197
Port Townsend, WA 98369

Anything on ID, especially by John Q. Newman.

Eden Press 11623 Slater "E'
POB 8410
Fountain Valley, CA 92728
www.edenpress.com

Pretty much anything, Barry Reid was the first...

Index